DWARFING GIANTS

DAVID OF BETHLEHEM

AND

GOLIATH OF GATH

By

TERRY ATKINSON

Spiritual lessons from the battle between David and Goliath.
A reference book on how to deal with trials and temptations.

New Living Publishers
164 Radcliffe New Road, Whitefield, Manchester M45 7TU England
www.newlivingpublishers.co.uk

Copyright © Terry Atkinson 2004

The right of Terry Atkinson to be identified as author of this work has been asserted by him in accordance with the Copyright Design and Patents Act 1988

First published 2004

British Library Cataloguing in Publication Data

A catalogue record for this book is available from the British Library

ISBN 1 899721 05 3

Cover design, Typeset, Printed and Produced for:
New Living Publishers, 164 Radcliffe New Road, Whitefield
Manchester M45 7TU England

by

Agape Press (UK) Limited
www.agapepress.co.uk

dWARFING GIANTS

DAVID OF BETHLEHEM
AND
GOLIATH OF GATH

By

TERRY ATKINSON

Dedication

This book is dedicated to all those engaged in
Spiritual Warfare
who are feeling the heat of the battle,
yet have the certain knowledge
that they too, will
Dwarf Giants.

CONTENTS

Introduction

Everything you need to know about *Dwarfing Giants* is found in 1 Samuel 17:1-58. It has become a real arsenal throughout the years. Those defeated and oppressed have re-read this story afresh, and it has constantly breathed new life into fainting spirits. Every inspirational Psalm commences in this valley. The battle between David of Bethlehem and Goliath of Gath sets imaginations racing. We love the story. It appears sweeter every time we read or hear it, because we love the small and the weak to triumph over the mighty. Through this combat we realise the small can beat the tall, the small ant can bring the elephant crashing down. In this story the foolish and weak triumph over that which is well organised and encased in brass. Every action, word, thought or deed witnessed is a commentary on *Dwarfing Giants*. Seen in this fray is the part you play in life, as part of your *Spiritual Warfare* as you fight the 'good fight of faith'. You are fighting against the world, the flesh and the devil.

In Genesis chapter 2, we have recorded the Fall of Man with all its implications. In the battle between David and Goliath, Israel and the Philistines, we have in rich colour, mostly red from the giant's severed head, the war between the Church and the World. When we read what took place between these two men, it is as if we are reading a diary on warfare, kept intact by this young shepherd of Israel. There is advice for the ordinary, on how to be a conqueror in the daily round of life. What is recorded gives us a more intimate view of all that took place.

In David's struggle with Goliath, we see the struggle between darkness and light, the Christian fighting with temptations both great and small. As Israel's youth faces Gath's adult, the history of the war of the flesh against the Holy Spirit is being tabulated. The method of warfare is unusual, as the militaries are not those used by fighting men. How to fight and win is being re-written in a valley.

In the valley of Elah where the fight takes place, you are able to see yourself warring against fleshly lusts and dark temptations, and, as David did, receive a throne, crown and kingdom at the end of the struggle. This story is your story! In it, there are so many beautiful suggestions, as many as there are gleams in the eyes of young lovers. Those eyes are the eyes of David, who loves his God with all his strength, mind and power.

The battle brought a little unknown lad into prominence. He came from a tent with a few loaves of bread and cheese to take to his brothers, yet in his battle with the giant he received weaponry for future warfare in experience, a suit of armour and a sword. He surrendered things of time and sense for trust in the living Lord. This was some exchange! Bread and cheese taken to the battle front for his brothers exchanged for a suit of armour, a shield and a sword! The bread and cheese would soon be eaten, but the influence of those who conquer lasts forever in the hearts of future generations. The hills around the valley became sure and everlasting witnesses of what took place that day.

We come to many situations and as we do we need a promise from the Word of God the size of a pebble. There is a stream in the Bible containing many pebbles. We have something far greater than Goliath's armour; we have the shield of faith, the whole armour of God provided in Ephesians chapter 6. Jesus took all the weapons of your warfare from Satan when He defeated him on the Cross at Calvary. There was a throne to be occupied at the end of the battle. John 14:1-3 speaks of our palace and throne. We are going through the valley so that we can serve the King. David might have overcome in the valley but he didn't stay in that valley, mountaintops and a crown awaited him. For the Christian, there are seven crowns, the Crown of Life, the Crown of Righteousness, the Crown of Faithfulness are but three of all those promised when you overcome temptation even as Jesse's son overcame Goliath.

The songs that were heard at the end of the battle remind us of Heaven where they sing the Song of Moses and the Lamb. The song you can sing is not that sung by the fair daughters of Israel in every village, town and city, but in your heart, for that is where the evil has been overcome. The best songs are those describing a struggle. When you get to Heaven, you will have a song of your own. As we fight to win it is rather like trying to produce music from cymbals. That is not easy producing music from brass. In every trial of life, you learn to handle the gold (good times), the silver and the brass with equal measure, and in doing so they become equal treasure.

The wind blew, the storm raged, blowing and howling. The hen-shed was blown over, dismantled and tossing the birds inside around as balls of feathers. The cockerel, which the day before had stood so proud and had rallied the day with his call, had been sent flying among the broken boards as a shuttlecock. Struggling to break free, squawking and struggling with feathers flying, and his pride lost along with his feathers, he appeared from between the broken boards. His broken feathers, seeming to gleam with new colours in the sunshine. All mixing together as the wind blew. Appearing as a rainbow after a storm he scrambled upwards without his usual strut. Climbing to the top of a broken piece, he sent out his usual cock-a doodle-do! Previously his customary call lacked depth, it was just a voice. After the storm, there was a depth in that call. It had gone from being a mere tin whistle to being a trumpet of silver, penetrating woodland glade and forest alike. It sounded clearer and travelled further. The suffering had deepened his famous dawn call. Suffering will always add something to us, just as it added to the shepherd boy David, turning him first into a man, and then into the greatest king that Israel has ever known.

Don't despise your circumstances they are God's way with your soul. In *Dwarfing Giants* you will find all these principles at work, until the son of Israel is turned into a son of God, and until you, as a son of Adam, become resplendent as a son of the living God.

Chapter

1

Spiritual Warfare

Dwarfing Giants is not something you can organise among a number of people- to march around a city, or go into a needy area; even to ascend hills around a town to bind Satan is only part of the truth. Much of *Dwarfing Giants* takes place during every day living for Jesus Christ. Sometimes it is in the lonely, and not in the spectacular. When Israel went marching around Jericho, they didn't just have an idea or a thought, it was a God-given plan. There is an immeasurable expanse between quoting a promise and one given to you by the Lord, Who keeps all His promises. To be successful, you require the whole army of truth as revealed in the Scriptures, the whole truth and nothing but the truth.

A part of *Dwarfing Giants* is found fully illustrated in Hebrews chapter 11. Everyone mentioned in that chapter were engaged in what we call *Spiritual Warfare*. Ordinary people who became champions of their day in many different ways as they *Dwarfed Giants*. There was no set pattern of attack. The thing they all had in common was their faith. Whatever they attacked and completed, most of it happened where they were. As King David did they also took from their circumstances, and prevailed where they were, in homes, caves, valleys, cities. In commerce, as in the quiet parts of life, they defeated giants. In public and in private places their *Dwarfing Giants* is proclaimed and they illustrate principles for us to follow. Notice the weaponry they used; it was 'by faith'.[1]

Scripture illustrates Spiritual Warfare

Sarah receiving strength to conceive when she was old is an illustration of *Dwarfing Giants*. The using of carpenter's tools by Noah, cutting down the first tree to build that sturdy ark was *Spiritual Warfare*. He made a declaration as he did what God had told him to do. As an old man, Jacob leaned on his staff to worship God. Here is the *warfare* of worship seen in an old man. When Jacob's grandchildren were blessed through his prayers, Jacob leaped over time barriers, and into the future, and he used *Spiritual Warfare* to accomplish it. Moses, refusing this world's glory entered into battle. The opening of the Red Sea, as the falling down of the walls of Jericho like confetti in the wind were all part of a public and private *Spiritual Warfare*. Abraham, going out in obedience, not knowing where he was, yet he arrived, is of the same essence in the conflict. The offering of Abraham's son on an altar, his name was Isaac, and the lifting of the gleaming knife blade,[2] was part of *Dwarfing Giants*. Joshua declares *Spiritual Warfare* when he says, 'As for me and my house, we will serve the Lord.'[3] All these faced giants in different shapes and sizes.

When Paul, while in shipwreck in the Acts of the Apostles, said 'I believe God,'[4] pronounced a declaration of war against all that was opposing him. It is not enough to accept what seems be the 'flavour of the month'. It is refusing to accept what your eyes see, ears hear, and your touch tells you. It is to surrender and say 'yes' to the claims of Christ when entering into the Battle of the Ages that makes a loser into a winner. *Spiritual Warfare* isn't up in the skies, engaging in the nebulas. If it is in the Heavenly realm or the Heavenlies, then, according to Ephesians 2:6, we are 'seated in Heavenly places in Christ Jesus.' The battlefield is here and now right where we are. We must not fear that which is 'formed' against us. In the stench of defeat it is the smell of victory that counts. We don't have to go to the place where others fought their greatest battles. Each conflict is one of the human heart flowing through the life. Where Satan operates is where we love God. Satan comes with pretence wrapped up in all the works of the flesh, to warm his hands on your zeal. While he is there he seeks to turn the majestic thing into that which is minute as a midge. He gives to us the coldness of his own heart, seen sometimes in tradition and repetition. The conflict is where we are, in our own home on our own doorstep. It is wherever we walk with Jesus Christ. It can be on the Emmaus Road or the Jericho Road; it can be conducted on Mount Sinai or the Mount of Transfiguration. It is wherever and whenever the Kingdom of God is established and enlarged. The gospels are the gospel of *Spiritual Warfare*.

The Lord is with you in every battle

Satan is described as 'The Prince of the Powers of the Air'.[5] The air which you breath, and which is all around you. This is where the battle rages. It isn't only to be sent overseas or into another nation, it is here and now. You need to see the God of the here and now in operation as Jehovah Shama-the 'Lord is here'. The opening of your Bible, and the weakest prayer uttered is a trumpet blast of your intention to fight and be part of the *warfare*. Your praise is the fluttering of a flag, telling of another world and realm that you belong to. Each victory is an enlargement of God in your spirit. That weak finger pointing to the Cross believing that Jesus died is more eloquent than a thousand orators with their silver tongues seeking to inspire the soldiers of Rome. This *Spiritual Warfare* is not the building of an empire it is eternity on earth, letting His will be 'done on earth as it is in Heaven.'[6] It is the setting free of the purposes of God in your life. It is like yeast going right through the dough, until the Bread of Life appears in you. That is Kingdom power and authority. The prayer of Jesus is answered as you take your stand for right. 'Let your kingdom come on earth as it is in heaven.' These words of prayer and witness, along with a righteous walk are signals of what you intend to do. They declare that you are going to be a winner. When the going is difficult, the secret is by His power, to be dynamic. It is not something you feel but something you are. It is being 'fully persuaded' of God's ability to operate in any situation. That small phrase 'fully persuaded' is the same phrase that is used when Paul writes to young Timothy 'Make 'full proof' of your ministry,' 2 Timothy 4:5. It is used in Luke 1:1 of 'things which are 'most surely believed' among us.' The picture is that of the juror, who, having heard and seen all the evidence then makes a decision whether the accused is innocent or guilty. As the evidences of the miracles of Christ and the power of God are presented before you then you are 'fully persuaded' as to the reality and authenticity of them.

The nature of your Spiritual Warfare

The secret and the success of this *Spiritual Warfare* are found between you, the world, the flesh and the devil. The flesh will ever be with you as part of your human body. It has cravings which make a coward of your conscience. There are more calls from the flesh than from a crowd at a football match! These are not 'cat calls' they are flesh calls. The world is ever around you to seek to overcome. It is there like some great ocean. Things work well when it is a servant but what a tyrant when it is the master. The Devil comes and goes, he cannot be everywhere at once, but God is 'here and now' all the time.[7]

The Devil comes to stop you advancing, and he has many troops to call to his aid. These troops are made up of many 'divisions'. They take the form of fear, doubts, discouragement and unbelief. These are his puppets and he pulls the strings. To counter every attack and to bring you into the experience of repulsing those attacks, you have the Holy Spirit within and around you.[8] As you confront these forms of evil and opposition, whether in a group or alone, it becomes *Spiritual Warfare*, leading to spiritual welfare. The moment you resist anything that would resist you, you have made your stand. Extra weapons are yours, because one New Testament word for 'power,' 2 Corinthians 10:4, means a 'weapon'. These weapons are varied and multiplied. When you command so many it is impossible to count your munitions. Men and women have been engaged in *Spiritual Warfare* alone. Some in small families, others in boats and on long journeys. When no one would believe, they have persevered. In 'persevering' they have been very strict with themselves and in their devotion to God.[9] Wherever faith is, there is *Spiritual Warfare*. This battle discovers the very 'substance' of your faith. In Hebrews 11:1, faith is the 'title deeds', 'substance' and 'evidence in writing' of things hoped for. It proves just what belongs to you. Most families can trace any riches and relatives back to a Family Tree. All you have come from faith and from the Will and Testament of Jesus Christ. In the American Civil War, as in the Wars of the British Empire, certain battles were named after what happened and where they were fought. Can today be called 'Joy Hill'? 'Victory Valley'? 'The Prairie of Light'? Can any be called 'The Place of Triumph'? To say 'no' to any temptation is *Spiritual Warfare*, and it can bring you into your inheritance, as it brought Jesse's son into his.

Be powerful enough to overcome

You have decided to take your stand and make your mark where it matters. That is good, and glory will follow. Whenever we walk God's path in victory that path leads into the heart of God. There is no easy way through to the other side. To chase the enemy you must first learn to run! Not to run away or run in front but to run behind them. To limit any temptation by killing it, you must learn the art of destroying. Drown it in the blood of Jesus Christ! To destroy, you must become destructive. The Kingdom of God is taken by force. Be a 'Gurkha', meaning the 'bravest of the brave'. There is that which must be fought for and taken. To give in is to yield to the Devil. That is not warfare, it is weakness. That is why the Apostle Paul tells young Timothy to 'War a good warfare.'[10] There will be injuries received that can be healed by the grace of God. There are marks that you will receive that can't be seen in the flesh. Deep indentations in the spirit that will become part of you. Some are wounded in spirit. Much of Christ's healing power will be displayed here. When you are sore wounded, feeling as if you are in a hospital, God fills that hospital, and fills your pained heart with many doctors of healing. Medals for achievement will be mounted where it hurts the most. The full bottle of His medicine can be taken and used. God loves to see the saint with an empty wineskin. The soul and spirit becomes marked forever- marking you out as a champion for God. I don't want to arrive in the presence of God with an unused testimony or a talent wrapped in some piece of cloth, or with my spir- it as it was on the day of my birth, unchallenged and never moulded. The life given, stained with so many of life's exploits are so eloquent. It reveals that each battle is a testimony of killing a Goliath. The cloth discarded and the talent fully used is the best testimony, to reveal as a medal, received for grace. Greatness will be discovered and allo- cated to you according to how you used what was given. Never giving a blast on the silver trumpet that is recognised and is responded to, just making an 'uncertain' sound will leave you uncertain! Having that as if it was still packaged was no way for David to win. To still be rest- ing on his earthly father's arm or his mother's breast would not have brought victory. Even eating bread and cheese, and drinking a little wine for consolation with his brothers would not have defeated the giant.

Life can be clustered with love

If you never enter into temptation the 'many' colours of grace (mani- fold) will not enter into the grey areas of your life, and produce rain- bow qualities. All the hues of a new life have to be dispensed through your life. Life can be a battle, but it is in the battle that blessings can be received in achievement. Wherever Kings of old conquered, they enlarged their maps of the world by adding to them those areas of conquest. Having overcome one thing we are able to overcome many things, and by overcoming 'many things' we can overcome 'all things'. The word 'overcome' can describe one combatant getting another to yield, as in a wrestling match. It can suggest what happened when a city was captured. The whole area was ploughed into a field; sometimes stones were thrown into the field. On other occasions, it was sown with seed. It was complete. Luke 6:40 speaks of the servant being 'perfected' and if he is, then he will be as his Master. The word 'perfect' means 'fully trained', and describes the colt being taken through a training programme until it can be ridden, and worked in the field without rebellion. It is called 'being broken in'. It was not the 'breaking' of the beast's spirit that was the intention of the training, but the harnessing of it, to a plough or a yoke. The natural power of the animal must be taken and used for another purpose.

The conflict might commence with a small stone,[11] as it did with King David, but that stone was the first step to the throne of Israel. The resurrection life of Jesus Christ commenced with the rolling of a stone away from the tomb.[12] Most great trees commence as a small seed. The greatest architecture in the world began as a thought, a sketch or a thumbnail drawing! What began as a thought, and was simply lead in a pencil or something on a computer screen was taken and applied. The sling with its leather thongs that the shepherd boy used for conquest might not seem to be much, yet it gave the stone its ability to strike. With God's help the small things in your life can be used to master the large. That leather was to be turned into the silk of Israel and as the story was repeated the facts were woven into the fabric of society in all manner of garments, because a shepherd boy was faithful to God. That leather thong became the essence of speech as the story was retold to the children of Israel. Small things do matter. 'Big Ben' in London, England keeps to time, because small coins are placed on a balancing weight attached to the pendulum of the clock.

The Lord Who takes you in will lead you through

The experiences of conflict are brought about when we fight against the enemy of our souls. To believe God is to put your self on a 'collision course' against the enemy. If God is helping by governing your life, all will be well. You will travel at His pace in His race. Hence the opening verse of Psalm 23:1, Japanese Version 'The Lord is my Pacesetter'. He will gently bring you to a halt, to feed and to fill you. The Lord will do this to challenge things as they are set against you as an unmoveable object, to meet with an irresistible force. When this happens, it is Jesus who stops and comes alongside to help you in your time of need. His 'moment of help' fits into your 'hour of need'. These enemies, and there is a whole army of them, gather together to over-come us. David only had to face one at this moment but they can come in ones or twos, and many more. Many Philistines had to be met with later. This challenge to crush you into non-existence can happen at anytime and in any place, and that is why God is everywhere. To the atheistic spirit that says 'God is nowhere', we reply 'God is 'now here!' You can't throw the life of God into oblivion. Wherever the power of God can come, there grace can prevail. That is where the conflict, the Conflict of the Ages commences for you. The conflict for you might begin around the next corner, or be at the heart of the next decision you make. Conflict is always there as an opportunity, because it is in the conflict that we win the battle and learn *The Secrets of Spiritual Warfare*. Men of war learn their skills in the war. They learn to submit to their leaders, but never to surrender to an enemy. The measure of their submission to leaders is the measure of their conquest over oth-ers. How much you are prepared to submit will measure how great you become as you overcome the enemy. When you surrender to a friend you gain a friend. When you submit to an enemy that enemy becomes the enmity within your soul. Whatever you surrender to brings all that it is into your heart. The ability to war and win is not found in any textbook. It is when the heart becomes the place of learn-ing. Just as the Old Testament prophets had particular places to teach enduring lessons, so we have experiences that become great teach-ers. Elijah at the brook called Cherith received new lessons. At Zarephath there are some more lessons to be taught. On Mount Carmel, there are still more lessons to be received, until finally there is the Juniper Tree. The battle is only won when the lesson is learned, and then only can I pass on to another the measure of God's grace in my own life. The word 'war' will never disappear from 'warfare'. It means how did you 'fare' in the 'war'?

Spiritual Warfare is evidenced in David and Goliath

There is one story in the Bible that totally illustrates every *spiritual conflict*. The Dwarfing of Giants is found in 1 Samuel 17, along with many other references that are made to it. It is the story of David and Goliath. It is amazing that in such a small portion of the history of Israel you find the map for every Christian and the stratagem for every battle. There are far more weapons to be found in this story than in a sling, stone, sword or a Goliath's armour. God's armoury is in the heart of the believer. The skin of the lion and the bear would keep the young shepherd warm as he wrapped them around his cold form. As he felt the warmth, fond memories would expand with the heat. If these skins were placed as part of the roof or the wall of the tent, it would be like watching a film as he gazed upon them and memory performed its perfect work. There are spiritual weapons, lessons and applications here. The valley they met in is like an arsenal for the believer. If you think like David and follow the plan he lays out for you, then you will be declared winner by a head![13] If you follow in the footsteps of Goliath there will be nothing 'giant' about you. The armoury will be lost. If you think as Goliath thought then your honour will be trodden into the dust. While Israel were being challenged and defeated they were referred to as 'the followers of Saul.'[14] Saul will always suggest human endeavour, pride and natural ability. He was 'head and shoulders' above others which is why he became the human choice and the pleasing voice. If you crown that natural gift you will serve the same! The only thing Saul had at the end of his life was found in a crippled son called Mephibosheth who went and hid himself in Lodebar, meaning 'the place of non-commitment', the placed of 'no communication'.[15] That is not victory, it is shame. It took a son of Jesse to bring Israel under the name of the Lord of Hosts.[16] He could lead or carry sheep across a stream and into a fold, even bringing them 'under the rod' to count them. David had a heart of compassion when dealing with sheep and men, and that compassion was used when he dealt with Mephibosheth. The nation of Israel moved from following Saul into a new realm with the Lord. If you follow Saul with his fleshly pride and desires you will not only run, you will be chased and chastened! If you follow the Lord, going on to know the Lord, then you will slay giants and dragons. You will eat them up as the oxen eat grass!

Be victorious in spectacular fashion

When as a young lad, unknown and unnoticed by men, but chosen by God, David killed this challenger; he did it in spectacular fashion! The Philistines went from being an army to becoming a tumult. The Israeli army went from being scared rabbits to chasing foxes with the scent of a kill. Israel transferred their allegiance from following an earthy king to following God. God leads on when men are defeated. If you follow natural inclinations and dictates the end result will be abject failure. History and spirituality will rise up and condemn you. Goliath leaves nothing for us to remember him by. His epitaph is short but not sweet. King David leaves a whole dynasty with its throne, and the many psalms written through inspiration. He is the man that commenced building for God with a stone from a stream. His life reads like the history of a nation. Battles didn't make Bethlehem's son great, but the winning of them, learning lessons from them and the defeating of the enemy did. Through the shepherd boy's mistakes, he learned, as you must, that you must be teachable in order to learn. He learned fifty ways how not to attack a Philistine, and ten ways how the sword shouldn't be held in battle. To David, there was only one correct way, and that was God's.

Someone looking on taking notes as the battle develops and David triumphs writes the story of David and Goliath. As Doctor Luke, the attendant of the apostle Paul wrote the 'Acts of the Apostles', so the writer of the happenings in the valley of Elah describes the conflict from close quarters. The story of the battle and the life of David are dealt with from every angle. Defeating Goliath was neither the beginning of the battle or the end of it. It was only part of a conflict to come, but it meant going to school, the School of Jehovah for the young prince in waiting. It is as if the Person writing the story is in every place at one time. He is in the camp of the Philistines. He is with David watching the sheep, seeing him mature in faithfulness, witnessing him mature and begin his warfare, as he took bread and cheese to his brothers.[17] If the future king of Israel could carry bread and cheese, he can lift stones, a sling and the head of the giant. If you want to determine character, watch how a person does a small job while nobody is watching! The small thing had to be lifted before the great thing could be attempted! The Writer had insight into both representatives of their nation. One moment He is with Goliath making notes, and then He is with David. The writer is obviously God, who sees 'all things', knows 'all things', and can conquer 'all things'. He has knowledge of the shepherd boy, and He has insight into Goliath and his big brothers. The Penman writes with the inspiration of the Holy Ghost Who knows all things. He not only sees the conflict you enter, but enters into it as the Comforter, the Paraclete, meaning 'to make strong or brave'.[18] Only God sees you complete. He alone adds all the bits and pieces together. God alone can see you from every angle, and still love you as much as ever. He appreciates you from every aspect of love. When you think, what you think, where you go and what you do, He is Jehovah Shamah; 'the Lord is there'. Jesus, in Luke 24:16,31 appeared to His disciples in another 'form'. He is there in many ways. From broken bread and small fish He produces a miracle. From your 'bits and pieces' He patterns something intrinsic and beautiful.

Take one step at a time through your conflict

Dwarfing Giants takes you step by step throughout 1 Samuel 17 and, applying every happening to your life, you soon realise that you can overcome. It is not a doctrine or a message to the chosen few, but to all. While in the valley you can take what is necessary for your well-being. You do not take it as a crutch to lean upon and feel pitiful about yourself. It must be taken as legs to run with, wings to fly with. Take a fresh breath and go into the battle. As you breathe in, you breathe in the Holy Ghost. The valley must be travelled to the other side and up the mountain that might be as large and difficult as any giant encased in brass. Each step, each move forward is a battle to be won. The next step only appears as you complete the previous one. Here is the real 'Pilgrim's Progress'! We can follow in the footsteps of David's greater Son, Jesus Christ. Follow Jesus like eyes following the direction of a sound. Those who walk in the Spirit of David can defeat every Goliath.

God will always prepare you before He leads you into any temptation. The 'fiery trial' will only come when you are baptised in fire. The Spirit of God 'led' and 'drove' Jesus, like a ship with wind in its sails, into the wilderness to be tempted.[19] There is always a purpose in every temptation. We can't see it because we get so taken up with the temptation itself. What was meant to take you through the valley sees you going deeper into a recess. It was meant to help you through, not take you further under. The God that leads you in will bring you through. As you enter into any trial you will find that God walks in it with you. Others can see the Form of another with you. When you cannot see His footsteps look for His fingerprints! When the vital evidence of fingerprints is missing then feel His warm breath filling you again with love to help you to conquer. If these things are missing then see Him smiling in every flower, singing in every bird, and speaking in every gurgling stream. When the footprints are absent He is probably carrying you, as He carried Israel, as a father carries his son. He is with you in the midst of the fire, but He is also on the other side seeking to pull you through. He doesn't always quench the 'fiery dart' of the enemy. He leaves them for you to put out. Will you 'put up' with it or 'put it out?' God doesn't stop the temptation, that it falls at your feet. You have to wrestle with it until it surrenders, then you give it to Jesus as a trophy.

God is where you want Him to be

It was like this for the son of Jesse. There was no visible presence of God with him. God was in the stream, the sling and the stone. One of the 'unwritten sayings of Jesus' says 'Lift the stone, and I am there. Cleave the wood, and I am there.' Providence is not seen as the armour bearer. Yet we witness the fullness of God at work in a victory proclaimed from the lips of every Israeli, and we hear it tremblingly coming from the lips of every Philistine soldier. One means triumph, while the other suggests tragedy! The victory, the silver trumpets of Israel declare that God was with David. While the mute instruments of the Philistines are more eloquent through their lack of sound than any instruments laid aside or being polished, their quietness says it all. Born to rail and shout they are as dumb as a cloud, speech and song has been divorced from their lips.

After the event it is so easy to understand, but it is trust while passing through the valley that is required. A few shoved the young boy into battle by patting him on the back, assuring him that he would win. All were waiting on the other side of the conflict to offer their congratulations. There are always more witnessing the giving of prizes than you meet along the track as you move swiftly but lonely along. We tell missionaries that we are behind them. Sadly, it is sometimes 10,000 miles behind them! Only Jehovah was at his side, but that was sufficient. They were as a 'one man band'; ready to offer their congratulations with all manner of plaudits and musical sounds. Some of the sounds were 'sounding brass', they didn't believe Jesse's son could win. They never thought they would see him again. After the event they knew David could do it!

Spiritual conflict mellows you

It is so much sweeter than what is happening around us which is forming us into what we shall be, which mellows us. The clay may not be much to look at when it is handed to the potter. Wait just a short time and you will see the wonders of the Hand that can shape and cause to shine. What was just a dark blob radiates with colours that have been glazed onto it. As we come through any battle, we are sowing seeds of trust in friends, and doubting enemies. More enemies are defeated by what you do than by any thing else. No place must be given to doubt and fear. The word 'doubt' in the New Testament sometimes means 'to be pulled two ways'. God will bring you through, as He brought David through, because God is on the side of right and triumph. It is not enough to reveal what God can do but it is enough to let God do it. Some things on one side are just scribble which we cannot understand. If a Hand appears and forms that scribble into words then we can read and become knowledgeable regarding our own situation. Love makes all things possible, because according to 1 Corinthians 13:7 it 'bears all things.' The love of God for you and your love for Him make all things legible and acceptable. God didn't want to write His love in the sand of the valley, but in the heart of this young giant-killer.

You must see the Divine Hand behind the entire thing happening to David. As you read the story of David and Goliath, the Hand of God is seen at work time and time again. David's weapon is God. David's prophetic inspiration and army is God. His future is not only 'in' God, it 'is' God. Everything is recorded, every jot and tittle for our learning and admonition. The Hand that created the world is creating your world. That which is within, without 'form and void'[20] must be shaped. The Carpenter of Nazareth must take pieces of driftwood and turn them into furniture fit for a palace. It must be pieced into destiny if it has been broken by hurt. It is from the Hand of God that the victory over Goliath comes. It comes from that Hand, just as miracles came from the Hands of Jesus. Each part of the story is pieced together as a puzzle. Some things are puzzling to us, but not to God. He never sees your life in part; He sees it as a whole. It is never in 'fragmentary portions', a little here and a little there. Even as David thought he was choosing five stones, the Hand of God was making a greater choice. Jesse's son was choosing a stone, yet God was choosing a man. Nature had formed the pebble, while Divine nature created the man. As the shepherd boy was choosing the stone and crossing the stream, God was crafting a man, who would be after His own heart. David was picking up stones, while God was changing a man into a servant and at the same time was arranging the throne for this future king. The thing that overcomes must be taken and used.

Greater in He that is within you

There are two elements presented in this *warfare*, there is light and darkness. The Lord's people are here. The Powers of Darkness are involved. The honour of God is behind shield and banner. David, as his name suggests 'lover', 'zeal', 'devotion'- to God is in this battle. He is a 'love token' of God and of grace. The love of God is at the heart of any battle. From that love comes David's ability to obey God. When God takes hold of David to help him, it is that love that He takes hold of. The heart-strings of the Sweet Psalmist of Israel are tugged. The battle between the champion of the Philistines and the shepherd boy of Israel is light against darkness. It has a basis in David's love for God, and God's love for David. David's love throws a stone, but God's love topples a giant. In zeal you can send a stone from a sling that goes nowhere. It is the Almighty Who makes it strike the target. Goliath represents human endeavour, the flesh with all its strength. This story teaches that love will always overcome the flesh, no matter how strong, big or fierce that flesh is. Goliath of Gath can mean 'an exile', one banished by God. Goliath, fierce and tall is an illustration of human thinking and the carnal nature that rises up to challenge God, and it will not surrender. No man shall glory in His presence. Little David in his surrender to God went far higher, while Goliath in his great stature simply fell down. One died, the other arose from the dead. The very one who was head and shoulders above others, King Saul, failed for the same reasons? Gesenius in his Hebrew- Chaldee Lexicon to the Old Testament says the name 'Goliath' comes from a root word meaning 'to take away the veil', 'to make a thing bald'. Taking the hair, and lifting it back to reveal the naked ear.[21] It suggests that uncovered, to see it as it really is. All that is against Israel is exposed in the man from Gath. What happens when David fights with Goliath? One is exposed while the other is exalted. Goliath's name suggests what is going to happen to him. He is about to be 'defrocked'. That which covered in darkness is darkness. This is the naked flesh. We may only 'see through a glass darkly', but when God steps in we see face to face, and we know as God knows. In all that pomp and show, within the armour of brass, there is but a man. Move David to one side, and you don't have a man at all, you have God.

Have a clear understanding of your enemy

We need to know the enemy as we operate in *Spiritual Warfare* we need to see things as they really are. Envy and zeal are closely associated but we must know the difference. Death and having left your first love can be interpreted as faithfulness, because you are always there in the same place, doing the same thing. Self-righteousness can be mistaken for righteousness. Variance is sometimes mixed up with choice. Emulation and copying Christ can appear to be the same. Honour and pride can seem to be the same. Longsuffering and weakness can appear on the same page. Jealousy is zeal that is placed in the wrong action. Being a leader and wanting to be seen is not the same thing. All these things are involved in *Spiritual Warfare*. To recognise the difference is to defeat the enemy. The battle commences when the flesh lusts against the Spirit, as if two cymbals were being clashed together for effect. If controlled by the Master Musician, they become part of the music of the spheres and can move you to tears.

The whole purpose of the secrets of *Spiritual Warfare* is to 'take the skin off things', so we really see them as they are. Goliath was only a pile of flesh that the birds could come and feed on. He was like something encased in a tin can. When a stone and a sling opened the armour which the giant wore and which surrounded him there was found to be a sardine inside the tin! Did David take his thoughts from this battle, and place them in Psalm 23:5?[22] 'You prepare a table before me in the presence of my enemies.' This awful giant, this temptation became a table for birds and dogs. God always takes the 'front' away. The hypocrisy must go. The false face must disappear. The defeating of all that fleshly and devilish is *Spiritual Warfare*. King Herod represents Satan. His name in the New Testament suggests 'the glory of the flesh'. Worms came and ate him up![23] The Spirit of God always works against the opposition until all you have is a body without a head. No eyes to see, and no ears to hear, no mouth to speak. No ability to overcome, or to think out a plan of attack. The opposing enemy can be found lying at your feet without movement. In fact the head could move only as David's hand purposed when it was chopped off. The only way we can accomplish our victory is by being an Ezekiel, ' the man who God strengthens'.

Notes: -

1. 'By faith' used 20 times in Hebrews 11.
2. Genesis 22.
3. Joshua 24:15.
4. Acts 27:25.
5. Ephesians 2:2.
6. Matthew 6:10
7. Job 1:6,7. Matthew 4:3,11.
8. John 14:16,17.
9. See the 'root' meaning of 'perseverance'.
10. 1 Timothy 1:18.
11. 1 Samuel 17:40.
12. Mark 16:3,4.
13. 1 Samuel 17:54.
14. 1 Samuel 17:8.
15. 2 Samuel 4:4; 9:4,5.
16. 1 Samuel 17:45.
17. 1 Samuel 17:17.
18. John 14:16,17; 16:7.
19. Matthew 4:1.
20. Genesis 1:2.
21. *Gesenius Hebrew - Chaldee Lexicon to the Old Testament.* Published by Baker Book House.
22. See author's book *Paths of Righteousness in Psalm 23.*
23. Acts 12:23.

Chapter

2

THE STRIPLING

David became known by many different names. He appears as a servant, then a warrior, later, he is called 'The Sweet Psalmist of Israel.'[1] He is also called 'The Light of Israel.'[2] Saul refers to him as a 'stripling' in 1 Samuel 17:56. What people call you may be indicative of your character, whether it is a good name or not. What they see in you is what they call you all the days of your life. We all know what people mean when they refer to somebody as 'Judas' or a 'Jonah'. A 'nickname' will stick longer than mud. In the mind of Saul the fact that David had done such a great thing didn't allow the shepherd boy to become a man. There are those around you who would keep you immature and prevent from being recognised. Saul could never accept that some of the 'giant stature' had entered into this Israeli youth. There was potential here that was not recognised. You require the eyes of Jehovah to see as He does. The very stones David took from the stream were now not only being used to kill an opponent, they were being built into his own life and future. Promises, as stones from God, are not given just to overcome another; they are given for you, as well.

David was called a 'youth' and a 'young man' and a 'stripling'. From this word 'stripling', we have a branch or a tender shoot that would grow in grace into a tree that would provide shelter. There is great potential for growth in the term 'stripling'. It is conflict that develops us into something more than a thought or a word, through to a deed. The thought becomes a word, the word becomes a deed, and the deed becomes an action into victory. David was more than a mere man would make him. Where the Almighty takes you, making you, He makes you into the best.

This battle is the hammer, the sword, the chisel and the machine used to shape the raw twig into something more. It can become a shepherd's staff or a sceptre to rule a kingdom. There is no recognition of achievement in what Saul said when he refers to David as a 'stripling'. Saul saw the young shepherd boy just as he was before he met with

Goliath. The fleshly mind will give you no recognition in *Spiritual Warfare*. Any achievement will be taken from you. Medals will be plucked from the chest and thrown into the dust. You are not the person that your friends see. You are not the person that your family sees. You are not the person those at work or on the street see. You are the person God sees, knows, hears, understands, and seeks to mould, bringing into victory, to stand with the achievers of all ages. Become gold in the Kingdom of God, not wood, hay or stubble, soil or clay.

Battles make you more than what you are

In the term 'stripling' there is room for growth and fruit. The bridal wreath is taken from the customs of the Romans and Greeks who used it to indicate triumph. From a small seed a flower appears and others are added to it, to be arranged into a wreath. It is the battle with Goliath and those around you that make you into something more than you are. Great vessels require much making. If you are creating just a small wooden vessel from a piece of wood, then it will not take long, yet even for this to be shaped there must be the first cut and the blow struck. When God makes His kings and priests, He has to commence somewhere. Most of us do not commence our 'training for reigning' facing a giant. The Eternal in His mercy leads us first to the shallow and not the deep, to the shadow and not the substance. The young David had to learn to cross streams before he attempted to climb mountains. The Eternal does not lead us into that which we are not able to bear. The model and the mould are brought together. Into the mould God pours mercy and grace so that the model might be real and effective in what is produced. David grew taller than the giant he brought to the ground. As he sings a psalm and writes words to the music of the harp, he sings 'Your gentleness has made me great,' Psalm 18:35. To be 'great' is not to be as tall as a giant it is to be obedient like a servant, as an image reflecting a son. In Genesis 21:20 the word 'great' describes Ishmael and Isaac who both became great. Isaac went on growing until he grew great. The crown of greatness is maturity.

In *Dwarfing Giants* you always become more than the things you overcome. You become taller than the ladder you climb, higher than the mountain you scale. Having been the average, you can become the achiever. In the asking of the Lord, and taking from God the small can become great. Your receiving must become as large as your asking (praying). The El-shaddai becomes the all 'out poured one' to you. The little can become large. The sparse can become much. Goliath would have crushed the bones of David into dust, but God spoiled his plans. Trials and disappointments will always reduce us to nothing. There are things larger than any Goliath that God wants to get into the heart of David. That heart has to be enlarged first and then God can let new and inspiring things enter through a battle. It was a battle that the Bethlehemite could not win unless God was 'at' his side, and 'on' his side, even as in our battles in life. There are temptations which if you don't overcome them will shut the door to the future. They will not only shut it; they will bolt and lock it! As they did with the Lord Jesus Christ when He died and was buried, they will roll such a great stone over you, leaving you buried in your emotions and remorse forever. The power of God shuts the door of the past, opens the door to the present, and takes you into the future. The 'stripling' became the mote or the plank in the eye of the giant that Jesus spoke of in the New Testament.[3] There was no one to cast it out. The zeal and the boldness of the shepherd boy overcame Goliath. Such an unusual plan was used, but in God it worked. It wasn't the same as Israel marching around Jericho. It had to be different from anything that had happened before. Therefore it could not be copied from someone else. The young lad from Bethlehem became a true pioneer for God. The Eternal defeated the giant with a 'stick' as seen in the word 'stripling'. Thousands copied what he accomplished, later. No one else 'seized the day' as this young man.

The stripling can grow to full potential

When David is described as a 'stripling' he has developed from a sibling into a son, into a servant, and finally 'stripling'. He is like the One who came later called the Branch.[4] The Root out of a dry ground grew into the Rose of Sharon.[5] The word 'stripling' is 'youth' with all its qualities to be developed in conflict. It describes the starting of a journey. There would never be a time when David stopped growing, as long as he listened to the inner voice of God. David might look immature, immature and under-developed as a branch that has never borne fruit, yet he became the maturity of God in this situation. He was the wisdom of God and the power of Israel's God. David became like Psalm 23, in green pastures of tender grass, and sweet flowing waters.[6] God doesn't paint pictures of landscapes, He grows trees and unfolds green hills from His bosom. It was right here that the Almighty grew a man instead of a tree, and a soldier in place of a sheep. The Eternal does not sculptor things in brass but He does produce men of quality. The artistry of the Almighty is in the creation around us, and in the heart within us. Saul is like a person looking at 'fine art work', but unable to see, understand or appreciate all the finer details shown by the artistry of the artist. The dull piece of clay that is seen in David is still dull and un-wrought. The man who is going to lead is told and taught to follow.

In the term 'youth' you have all the zeal, vision and potential of your first love for Jesus Christ. 'Stripling' means 'a lad', one with a youthful disposition. A raw convert, one who is a conscript but can be trained to succeed. It can mean 'one who is hidden', just like someone in the shadows waiting for the full sunshine, and then stepping into that beaming light breaking forth as a shining metal spearhead. From the shadow of Goliath, Israel's future king steps as a ray of hope, as one back from the dead. Out of some great *spiritual conflict* a new, fuller, deeper, lovelier person emerges, someone who has been in the dark waiting for the light of day. As the son of Gath fell, that light appeared! Held in reserve that which was holding back is suddenly severed, released, as if catapulted through the air to land where it meets with its destiny. The young Israelite was reserved for such a conflict as this. He would only become the king when he overcame the giant. As the stone used by the sling to defeat the giant had spent time in the dark, unrecognised, in the stream as in the scrip, in the sling and in the hand, so it was the same pattern for David.

There is such a contrast between good and evil

There is such a great contrast in this conflict between David and Goliath. Goliath means to have 'the veil removed', while 'stripling' suggests that the veil be kept in place until the proper time. It is Jesus who tore the veil into two pieces, to reveal all the heart of God, which men had hidden for so long in religion. One part of the veil was the evidence given to men, whilst the other part was given to God, proving to both that Jesus had conquered. God would not let David be king of the realm until he had been fully trained. The training ground is the battleground where you are. You were made for this, just as much as a ship is made for the water it enters or the aeroplane the air to fly. One temptation overcome is not the full training programme. For David, and for you it goes on throughout life. Your future is in the present. Take your conquest forward into your future. The secret of overcoming Goliath is for the stripling to grow, as he overcomes the problem. From this small piece of wood called 'stripling' many shapes will be carved with care. The shepherd boy became larger than the stone he threw and the giant that fell. The 'stripling' is required to grow until it is large enough to be formed into planks to be made into ships or to become the shaft that holds a battering ram. As this little twig grows it can reach over the wall and touch other things that it would never influence if it remained just a stick. The stick must be the friend of a sparrow. It might beat a dog or be used to draw pictures in the sand, pictures of a battle, but it would never rule a nation. We measure things by a stick, and the 'stripling was the measure used by God and the measure of Goliath.

The servant's heart is revealed in conflict

One of the secrets of this young Bethlehemite's success was that he was willing to be a servant. As a 'stripling' he could be bent by the wind yet not break. This makes him and you vulnerable, because others will place all sort of things upon you, some of which God never intended to be part of your service. Men will manipulate, while God will magnify. Victory and recognition came because Jesse's son was willing to become God's servant, disguised as a stick. This service was the first but not the last. In that service he went through every room in the house until he reached the throne. He served in tents, in the field, then in a home, until that home became a king's palace. In 1 Samuel 17, the term 'servant' is used four times.[7] This future king was a 'servant, he was a 'son' and he is described as a 'stripling'. He became a soldier because of the conflict. He became a servant because of the service. He was a stripling because of God's work of grace in his young heart. The greatest work and most glorious achievement was not in defeating Goliath of Gath, it was in the submission of David to God. The twig can only become the branch as it surrenders to the trunk. It must learn to bear the weight of both leaf and bird, before it can be a perch and security for a man. The shepherd boy had a Goliath of faith and obedience inside him. There was within him devotion and faith just waiting to get out. There had to be obedience to all the inner qualities of his own heart. He had to be true to truth.

The word 'servant', used in 1 Samuel 17, is from a root word meaning 'work'. A great temptation must be treated as work that the servant must prosecute. Goliath was a field to be ploughed, harrowed and seed sown into it. The future king had to work it in, work it out and work it through. He had to do his best as a 'stripling', before he could move into a greater work. If your talents are few, and could be counted on one finger, make them count! Count your gifts by the hand of God and not the hand of a man. Whatever you are, let it suggest a good one! Be your best and do your best where you are, then there will be other opportunities. Mark, the Philistines were already sharpening their swords for the next encounter, even after Goliath was dead.

Battling and *warfare* is hard work. Service can be the discipline of ploughing the field. The word 'service' describes a field being ploughed, or the building of a house. At the end of the attempt there is achievement and ascension. The 'twig' is turned into a sword, as David draws the giant's sword from its sheath. The first step up for David was when he lifted his foot, and placed it on the head of the dead giant. Growth appeared in David's disposition all the time. It is the word used for 'servant', describing 'work' that is found in the Ten Commandments, 'Six days shall you 'work'.'[8] In the 'six days' of creation, God touched the sun, moon and the stars. He touched every realm with His power. It is in service that the stripling grows in usefulness. There is more than one branch of thought and desire when loving God. The future king becomes the willing servant of Saul. It was his servant-hood that defeated both lion and bear, and it would deal with Goliath.

Whether servant or 'stripling' it has to be taken and used, and in the using of it, there is the overcoming of every Goliath. The servant's heart will surmount all the obstacles even if they are as large as a field. If only we can see and understand *Dwarfing Giants* as being part of our service. It is something that God trusts you with and He expects you to do well. The giant must not tread on you; you must crush the giant under your feet. They knew the 'stripling' had been a success, when they glimpsed the light as it flashed from the giant's own sword when it was drawn. Goliath's head was chopped off with his own weapon. Blessed be those who turn temptation into triumph! The promise of God to Israel was that wherever they trod, they would conquer. Here it was in the valley of Elah.[9] The next time it might be at the top of mount Sinai. Victory must be victorious in every realm. The shepherd might gain a great victory in the open field, but he has to gain victories in his own home, the palace, and in his own heart.

Your victories are in the things that are defeated

All the weapons Goliath owned became David's. He chopped off the giant's head with the giant's own sword. Little did Goliath realise when that sword was made that it was being designed for his own death. In Goliath's defeat there was a whole armoury. Here is the Ephesians 6 of the New Testament with all its armour of the Roman soldier. It is the 'whole armour of God.' Even words become weapons. What was said this day struck terror into the heart of every Philistine. In every temptation, there is another weapon for you. Your blunted dedication, though having lost its cutting edge, can be re-shaped and re-sharpened. A new point for penetration can be yours as you fight the good fight with all your might. Fight with 'might' but fight for the 'right'. God is waiting for you to learn, with David how to overcome giants and be successful in *conflict of a spiritual nature*. There has to be maturity, the 'stripling' must become both soldier and servant. The 'stripling' is young and tender and can be twisted and turned into many shapes.

It reminds me of the great oak trees that I have seen intertwined. I asked myself how could these two great trees be twisted together like that? The answer was that as young trees someone took them while they were supple enough and twisted them together so they now appeared as lovers in each other's arms. All that is Goliath was taken and used. As the giant fell, David, the new son of Jesse, stepped from underneath the fallen body. It was as if he had stepped into the shade to change his uniform and come forth as one fully trained for war. In the past when anyone was entering into a covenant or commencing a work for God it was said, 'Take the shoes from off your feet, for the ground you are standing on is holy ground.' This wasn't taking the shoes off your feet it was taking the head off a giant! This 'stripling' was as glorious as the rod held in the hand of Moses when the Red Sea was parted. This giant was of Red Sea proportions!

The 'stripling' with the power of God became a spear and sword for war. He went into the battle expecting, excited but he came out with experience, which is the greatest teacher of Nature. The only way out for the shepherd boy was through as he faced the machine of a man revealed in the giant standing in his way. Behind the giant was a throne. Exaltation will only come through endeavour. *Dwarfing Giants* is the training ground for spirituality. It is where we learn to trust in God. David believed God before the battle, during the battle, through the battle and after the battle. The metal and the medals were found here. Many believed that God could overcome Goliath, this young boy proved it. It is not what is written on paper or in books, it is what is in the heart that achieves. This wasn't a battle on a stage, put on as some performance from history. First David fought with a lion, then a bear, then his brothers, and now a giant. He overcame all of them with just a few weapons, but with a large trust in his Master.

Desire for God brings renewed strength

The 'stripling' as it reaches for the light grows. It depends totally on the roots of the tree, as the young man of Israel depended on his Lord. The stripling is adorned with buds, leaves, blossom, and then fruit as it grows. As Jesse's son reached for God, he struck Goliath such a blow that he never recovered from it. Branches and roots can crack rocks, walls and tear down fences that get in their way! Tie a piece of string or wire to a strong growing 'stripling' and watch its power demonstrated before your eyes. Faith, operating in God, can overcome all things and reach a place where it looks down upon its surroundings. David had decided not to listen to the taunts of the enemy. The word 'stripling' can suggest 'hiding the ear', as if not to listen, because the ear is veiled. David's ears are closed to the taunts of the giant. The Master knows, He only has to whisper and the future leader of Israel will respond. Be deaf to defeat but listen when victory is mentioned. Don't listen to what is suggested. Be so hidden in God, as the ear under the hair of the Israelite child. Live as the echo of the Voice.

'Stripling' is anything that is hidden, but as the battle commences all the hidden rarities are revealed. The Lord says, 'Hear no evil, speak no evil, and think no evil.' If you ignore these words, then you become a partaker of that evil if you yield to it. There can be qualities in all of us, waiting for such a challenge as this. Sometimes power is not given to us for the power and ability we already have is released. The 'stripling' grows into a branch, sturdy, sure, restful and true. Think of the cricket bat coming from the willow tree, it commences as small as a stripling but it matures. The nature of the wood is so yielding. In that maturity, the cricket bat in the hands of a trained man can knock the cricket ball all over the field, 'making' many runs, and bringing great success. In that cricket bat is the 'sweet smell of success.' The secret of its success is its ability to bend rather than break under the strain. When the son of Israel faced the son of Gath, it was as if the bark was peeled off the small stick to reveal the sap and the inner core. His true nature was revealed.

One lady had a walnut tree that never produced walnuts. She took out the spade one day and beat the tree with it. The next summer, beautiful walnuts appeared on that tree. We are encouraged by the things we suffer the misunderstandings and pain, to bear fruit. What had been a stick or just a stripling was found to have fruit after it had gone through a severe test! Some trees require much pruning. When you are grafting one tree to another or one kind of rose to another stem, there is some cutting before there can be any fruit bearing or flowering. One person used to sing to the stems where flowers had not appeared! I don't know if it was the range of the voice, but flowers appeared after a few days! There was a song not a sigh in David's heart. His only tears were those of deep and profound joy. Storms always do their work whether in the garden or in the open field. We need battles such as this one between David and Goliath to bring the best out in us. It brought the worst to the fore in Goliath, which represents natural ability, but it brought the best out in David, representing spirituality. What is entered into keeps the mind sharp and the sights correct ready for the next time. War and combat will test both blade and bearer.

Every temptation will test your resolve and loyalty

The 'stripling', a small stick with the bark peeled off can become the shepherd's staff. It must become the king's sceptre! It can form the handle of the sword that knights. Others can lean upon it, once the knife has done its work in the hands of the craftsman. It might be crafted into a bow, to send an arrow to it's target. There is in the 'stripling' that which is still growing, developing into something new. Every spiritual act will test your willingness. It will stretch you into that challenge at your feet, so that you tower above it as David stood over the giant. What has been but a straw must be made into something more enduring. It is facing up to that which surrounds you, making you into more than a match for every circumstance. The small can be made tall. As God attracts you as light attracts plants, as you reach for Him you will grow, and your potential is limitless. The 'stripling' was not broken, bent a little, yes. He might have been bruised. He was not banished or battered but bettered.

Timothy was only a 'stripling', (Novice: one newly planted) maybe nineteen years of age when his spiritual father, Paul, formerly called Saul of Tarsus, wrote to him. Timothy was in charge of a church, and needed to grow in grace and the knowledge of our Lord and Saviour, Jesus Christ. 'Let no man 'despise' your youth,' Paul wrote. He seems to have had a weak stomach.[10] He is exhorted to 'stir up the gift', because he seems in danger of letting his zeal for Christ grow cold. Through it all, he developed into a fine man of God.[11] Titus was of the same bulldog breed. He was left to ordain Elders in every city.[12] These young men were surrounded by temptations, yet they wouldn't give in. It is not the beatings we take or the bruises we show it is the person that such happenings make us. Remembering the battle and hardship in detail is not the important factor are we still battling through! Long after the hurt has healed we need to be standing on our feet, still aiming higher for God. 'Next time I can do better,' so says my spirit to my soul. Those who aim high, strike high. Attempt the impossible, and see it happen. Believe it, and let God do it! That is working together 'for' Good, and 'with' Good.

The battle is light against darkness

There are two elements presented in this warfare, is light and darkness. The Lord's people are here. The Powers of Darkness are involved. The honour of God is behind shield and banner. The zeal of the sheep-keeper is described as a pot on a roaring fire, bubbling forth having heat placed under it.[13] He is a 'love token' of God and of grace. The love of God is right at the heart of any battle. From that love comes the shepherd's ability to obey God. When God takes hold of David, to help him, it is that love that He takes hold of. There is something in all of us that needs to be stretched until it cannot be measured. The purpose of God is never to minimise or destroy ability; it is to make that which is useful, useable. The core lesson is one of producing capability, even when men cannot recognise it. The 'stripling' had the victory; he had accomplished it long before others accepted it. The heart-strings of the Sweet Psalmist of Israel are taken and tugged as he faces Goliath. David needs to know that God is in more than sheep or sheet music, more than hills and a sunset. God is in all things. You can't put all there is of God into a shout or a battle cry. Although, the second word used for 'shout' as Israel marched around Jericho is 'a great shout', in Joshua 6:5,10,11,16. It is as if God had stepped into the final shout. That is why the young man from Bethlehem used the name of the Lord, when he says 'I come against you in the name of the Lord of Hosts, i.e. 'the battling God'. The 'stripling' has no power of its own until it is given to the hand of God. That Name was not used to describe running into it as some tower, but to run with it, as one carrying a torch, to overcome an enemy. The battle between the champion of the Philistines and the shepherd boy of Israel is light versus darkness. It has a basis in the love of God for David. Goliath represents human endeavour, the stride, the wrestle, human force, flesh with all its strength. This story teaches that love will always overcome the flesh, no matter how strong, big or fierce that flesh is. Goliath of Gath is the full description of the elephant-sized man. 'Gath' is the place of the 'crushed grape'. The proverb states: ''Sour grapes', said the fox, when he couldn't reach them.' David came, he saw, and he conquered. The giant is sent back, even as the Devil was into his history. A stone is placed into Goliath as if to emphasise the fact. The adversary is dead and buried with a stone epitaph laid over his body. In the giant it is human thinking standing to challenge God when it will not surrender. Goliath lived to fight David had to fight to live. The very one who was head and shoulders above others, King Saul, failed for the same reasons as this Philistine giant. Light, just a small flash of it will displace a whole room of darkness. We need to know, as we operate in *Spiritual Warfare*, about things as they really are. Both David and Goliath would be known as they were known; God was going to reveal all.

Spiritual Warfare exposes the enemy

Conflict produces character, and the charter for future conflict. You, dear reader, can take all your weapons from this battle. You can read the story, look, listen and think, then go away and say 'I, too, am a soldier!' The son of Jesse came out a 'stripling', yet he was something and someone more than that. He wore a crown he had taken in battle. It wasn't visible to the naked eye, yet it was tangible to those who understood. He came out, with much more, he now knew the Almighty could topple challenges in every realm, for God must reign everywhere or nowhere. The discovery had been made; the best way to become part of God and His power is to surrender to Him as the rivers surrender to the sea. He might have known Majesty in the sheep pastures before or the God who excited him to write psalms and poetic verses. In the battle, as in *Dwarfing Giants*, you discover, not another God you realise that your Leader can give you the victory. The Lord becomes the Lord for all occasions. There is more to God than you thought! There are attributes, to be arranged for you. There is the part of Elohim we need to discover and enter into in order to gain the victory again and again. He could rescue more than sheep. He rescued a king and a nation with a small pebble.

David saw what was underneath this Goliath; he saw what was readily concealed, needing to be revealed. There was nothing covering David as he went into battle. He had no armour of thick leather. Sincerity needs no covering. David is one with God even as a smile is a part of joy and mirth. That which is sincere, without wax does not require covering, because there is nothing to cover. What the shepherd lad was at the beginning, he was all the way through. The triumph didn't give him any false ideas, only true ideals.

The ideals in the sheep-keeper were discovered in the young shepherd boy, and were as important as any mountain in Israel or any battle fought and remembered. It went from one corner to the other in the valley. It was far more substantial and longer lasting than an echo or the bleat of a sheep. Goliath wore his armour on the outside while David, in God, wore his armour on the inside. Strength enters into you as you feed on the Bread of Life. Jesus Christ is our 'Hovis', from the Latin, meaning 'the strength of man'. There is sunshine for the shadows and, when rainy days and dark clouds gather, as we pass through the valley there is the Bread of Life. You may enter this battle as a 'stripling', but you will leave it as 'sterling'.

Striplings, servants, soldiers and saints have battles to fight

The 'stripling' must become a servant, and then a soldier. Servants make gallant soldiers, because they use their weapons, as any servant would use household goods. What is around them, the servant uses to serve with, so the soldier uses that which is given to fight with. Each must learn to fight and win God's way. The person called Goliath was like a machine, a corn and bone-grinding machine. While David, in Goliath's mind was the mite. He was less than a 'stripling'. Goliath describes him as a stick coming against a dog. A 'dead' stick. The results of what the conqueror accomplished was 'might over matter.' The only way out was through the valley. Somewhere over the horizon in the distance was a throne. This big man stood in the way of David and the future throne. He appeared as a black blob, blotting out the light. The servant of Saul wanted to see the sunshine beyond the giant, and the only way for that to happen was to lay the giant down. As Goliath fell, it was as if from the particles of soil that flew up into the air another man stepped forward to be the model of faith for all future believers facing opposition. In the particles of the valley the true gem was found. The life and victory of El filled the space that the large man had occupied. God would offer a daily challenge in the future through the lips and deeds of this young man.

Saul only saw things with his mind. He never reached out and touched things with his heart. This is why, even after the triumphant battle he still refers to God's champion as a 'stripling'. The King of Israel saw everything in the natural and physical. David still looked the same, he sounded the same, and he measured in man's measurements the same. He even wore the same shepherd's garment, but he had grown by the measure of a giant. Not outwardly, but inwardly David had grown by giant proportions. He now had two heads, as he carried Goliath's in his hand. He now had a sword that could be called his own. The 'strip.' has become the full garment. The child has grown into a man. One so small and seemingly incapable has fought a man's battle, a king's battle, a nation's battle and God's battle! The battle birthed the man of God. This history can live in your spirituality. Israel's son came out as a strong staff able to defeat an enemy. He had never killed a giant before. David came out with more, that which natural eyes could not discern. Having placed his hand in God's small bag, he took what he found and used it with all his might. The shepherd boy had learned another lesson in his training to become a king. He might have known the Majesty of God enabling him to write poetic verses and psalms, but now he is part of the God of power, Who defeats giants with a small stone. Just as Jehovah had defeated Jericho with a shout something so insignificant, so now a stone was used. His God was bigger than bear or giant.

In the battle, as you *Dwarf Giants*, there is the discovery not of another God, but that this Elohim can give you victory in every situation. What had been in the desert and pastures unknown and unseen by others was now witnessed by the whole nation. That private in the servant and saint became public in the 'stripling', and the soldier. It is one thing to fight in private but another thing to repeat the same in public. Using a pebble he rescued a king and a nation. Behind before and beneath it all was the Almighty, proving His Everlasting Arms reach into the valley of Elah. He was his God and more than ten thousand soldiers, and a thousand armies. David had been turned into an ambassador, and here he had received his letters of recognition. The evidence of his calling was as sure as the dead giant at his feet.

Notes: -

1. 2 Samuel 23:1.
2. 2 Samuel 21:17.
3. Matthew 7:3-5.
4. Zechariah 3:8; 6:12.
5. Isaiah 53:2.
6. See author's book, *Paths of Righteousness in Psalm 23*.
7. 1 Samuel 17:32,34,36,58.
8. Exodus 20:9.
9. 1 Samuel 17:2.
10. 1 Timothy 5:23.
11. 2 Timothy 1:6.
12. Titus 1:5.
13. See *Dr. James Strong Concordance to the Old and New Testament*. Published by Baker Book House.

Chapter

3

The Discouragement on the Battlefield

There will always be those who fire the fiery dart at us when they think we are in the wrong. There will always be something in human nature that is ready to fire those darts. It is human nature that readily provides weapons of evil to destroy. Nobody and nothing hurts humanity like humans. The fiery darts can be, sometimes launched from the tongue with venom, and they are more like missiles than arrows. The false accusation, along with the discouragement did not come from outside the family or from one of the Philistines; it came from within David's own family. When we come together and hear everything clearly, it is in that close proximity we can easily tread on one another. The hottest waters which burn the most are those that come out of the pots in the home. Hurting does not come from the springs or the geysers in the mountains, but right where we are deep down in the valley with Israel's young champion.

We can be discouraged when we are rejected

The rest of Jesse's family didn't mind having a deliverer, so long as it wasn't the youngest in the family yet he would be accepted from any other source. If Jesse's youngest delivered Israel it would be an insult, pride would be pricked. Those closest to you sometimes hurt you the most. David's brother Eliab could have done more damage to this deliverer in training than many Goliaths or a pride of lions. Hurtful words have to travel but a small distance before maximum hurt is achieved. They rarely miss the target.

Courage can be developed through relationship

Nothing breaks the spirit like words on fire with anger and jealousy. David had to be very careful that a spark from that anger didn't burn a hole in his soul. The wounds of the wicked are deep and sore. Eliab spoke with kindled anger, and David could have taken a spark or a burning brand from this fire, and let a fire burn in his own heart. There was no room in his heart for bitterness, only bigness. He could have tried to justify himself but he did not. The future warrior could have said the same words to his brother. If he had done this, it would have made him a partaker of his brother's evil. He would have swallowed some of the hatred of his brother. Mud thrown at others leaves a deposit sticking on our own fingers.

There is an armoury we require to deal with things launched at us in accusation. It is not that which is found in what a member of this family said. It was not in his brotherly relationship or in a house in Israel. The armoury to fight in *Dwarfing Giants* comes from within through a relationship with God. It is allowing the Hand that holds and guides you to work it all out for you. If there is to be any pointing or poking the finger, let it belong to the Hand of God. Unpleasantness can be redesigned! The armour is the ability to control your own spirit when under attack by surrendering it to God. That is better than many arrows, bows or shields. This weaponry comes birthed in your walk with God. It is in allowing the Hand that holds you to control you. It is of little use making Jesus Christ King of kings if he is not King of your humanity. This man who would be the future king had shield and armour within. The discouragement tested Bethlehem's best. How would he react? What we have within is always greater than outside influences. That is why John the apostle of love said, 'Greater is He that is within you, than he that is in the world.'[1] The person who was in full flow, using his ministry of discouragement, was seeking to take others where he came from in his spirituality. Eliab used words as stones against David.

Words are cheap and they can be painful

Each stone had mud clinging to it. He had neither a cause against David or evidence to prove what he was saying, 1 Samuel 17:28. Words are cheap, but pain is painful. Two brothers brought up in the same home with the same influence, yet as different as milk and water. They are almost a representation of Cain and Abel. Brothers in name and birth only, part of the same family but not of the same nature. They are different from Cain and Abel, because what was said didn't result in murder instead a man was made into a national leader![2] It only takes a small thing to discourage and that is when courage has had its heart torn out. Never go as low as a snake when dealing with a snake.

When accused, it is so easy to let all your weapons fall to the ground. The opposite happened to this young deliverer. After this event he went to the brook for the stones.[3] What was meant as a slap, he took as a handshake and congratulation. If you are criticised by those unwilling to attempt what you seek to do, in doing the will of God, be sure that there will be many to discourage. Maybe this is why the Bible says 'David encouraged himself in the Lord his God.'[4] Things said to you can leave you bleeding and dying on the Christian Road. The battle facing the shepherd that might have discouraged him became as fresh water to revive his soul. While others, (and his brother Eliab was one of them) were working out fifty ways how they couldn't defeat the giant, the shepherd boy was telling them one way they could and would conquer, and that was God. David was planning a way to defeat giants, and many would copy his action. The sweetest and most serene words in the argument were from the youngest in the family. Eliab's years had not been as a schoolteacher to him to teach him better.

Jesse's youngest looked at the battle, and he spread words of faith and deliverance. How different the young lad's words were to Goliath than those spoken to him by his brother! He did not become a reflection of a hurting spirit. If ever he was tempted to turn to one side he had only to look to God and that upward look took him towards his destiny. By perseverance the snail came into Noah's ark. By constant perseverance and the flapping of wings the ravens fed Elijah. It takes a large battle and a giant to be defeated to keep some of us on course working towards our destiny. If you get lost in the work before you there will be little time to discuss the foibles of others. David met with the Goliath in his own brother. If you can control one you can subdue any! You either control that which is coming from your brother, or it will control you. Subdue it or be subdued! There was a giant being subdued in a brother. The boy shepherd was able to control this giant, and that control became training for the other giants. If you can control the giants in those around you, then the giant in the valley, who seems to be so large will be squeezed and be displaced by you. We meet with giants in the 'Valley of Shadows', where shadows become more than the substance. When accusation is accepted as a fact the unreal becomes the real. David did none of these things.

The plans for your life can be broken

Through words, plans and dreams can be smashed just as Moses dashed the tablets of stone on which the Ten Commandments were written to the ground as he descended the mountain.[5] I like those plans of God which are as the 'burning bush'. It burns but it is not consumed.[6] God is in the middle of it, talking to you. When your plans are in the palm of His hand others will not easily remove them. None shall pluck them from His hand. If those plans are broken into a million pieces they will be fixed by God to form a new shape in your destiny.

God was in this battle, calling the boy into it for deliverance. That same Lord was established in a family feud first. He was in the battle with Goliath before the young shepherd boy arrived. God did not take David into the battle. God called him into it, because God was in it already. God came into it from every side. Remember this, if you deliver yourself, become victorious, so may you deliver many more people. Many will walk in your light. You will influence others for good or evil. In John 21:3, when Peter said, 'I am going fishing,' the others said, 'We are coming with you.' Later, in Acts 2, Peter influenced the new Church in an entirely different way. He had received the Holy Spirit. The rabbit has become the weasel. Rather than being chased he was chasing others. In the midst of shipwreck and a hopeless situation, the servant of God the man called Paul the apostle said, 'I believe God.'

Be a physician and not a nurse to your wounds

There would be no Appeal if the finger were only pointed at us. Sometimes it is not pointed in condemnation, but comes and is poked deep into the wound, and then acid is added making it far worse in our moment of torment and suffering. Don't become a nurse to your wounds. The best physician and medicine is to do battle with something greater than a brother, something that simply doesn't affect a family but affects a nation. There is such a thing as adding insult to injury. Some are not happy unless they are discouraging others. They seem to feed on discouragement until they become fat. Discouragement, the lack of courage, becomes as natural as the air they breathe. When some are hurt and afraid they are like the hedgehog, they roll up into a ball of spikes, ready to penetrate and injure. Insult and injury take many prisoners. David took both in his large stride and heart. David never treated his hurt as a medal to be displayed, every occasion becoming a parade ground.

Goliath would have added to what Eliab had already said, but by this time David was listening to God. He was one heart and voice with God. The spirit of adventure and victory had entered into him. There were five voices he might have listened to. The voice of Eliab his brother, the voice of reason telling him it couldn't be achieved. This must not become the teaching of the day. The voice of Saul who had all the authority to kill or make alive, and which must not be acceded to. Ears, mouth and words must not be united. The voice of the army of Israel suggesting many things. The voice of Goliath as he referred to the coming king as a dog and who must be challenged in combat. He listened to none. He listened only to what Jehovah had to say and believed it, and then proved it by the battle he entered into.

Taunting can be a 'form' of discouragement

What Eliab said to the future king began as a mere taunt but then it grew into something very different. How would David deal with it? His mind was not on what was spoken so as to dishearten him but the *Spiritual Warfare* before him. He focused his mind on bigger things rather than on small insults. If you would fly then make eagles your companions not robins or sparrows. You only grow as tall as your own maturity. The young Bethlehemite grew taller than a giant before entering into the fray. David stood on the head of this giant from Gath and touched Infinity. 'Jesus endured the cross, as seeing Him who is invisible.'[7] The Invisible made him invincible. Don't make 'little people' your object in life. Go for something big, and it will enlarge you. Aim for a star and you might hit a hilltop. Aim for the sky, and you might just hit the moon. What we aim for we become. If you stretch for that which is taller and beyond you, there is an enlargement as you stretch.

True spirituality is discovered in our attitudes

Dwarfing of Giants is discovered in our attitude of heart towards hurt and those who hurt us. It is having the ability to go on and to go through, whatever is said or done against us. A grudge will birth a bad attitude. That which is nursed whatever it is, will grow into something larger than Goliath. If you are responsible for it, you must deal with it. Don't totally reject it, but use it. God helped King David to overcome the giant because he was not responsible for any grudge. Remember, the word 'grudge' suggests the 'grunting of a pig'. It can suggest the 'growling of a dog'. It can then develop into 'cynicism', suggesting the 'snarling of a dog'. The best way to stop an argument developing is to kill the speech as it is being birthed by not listening.

The army of Israel at this time was a reflection of the heart of their king, Saul. Fearful, running when shadows took the place of substance, defeated, and in need of leadership. When Goliath of Gath challenged them morning and evening the ground shook as he bellowed out his challenge, and the hearts of the soldiers of Israel quaked along with the earth they were standing on. All that Goliath sought to do to a nation, Eliab sought to do to an individual. David, as an immature child might have done but he did not tell his dad Jesse, he informed his Heavenly Father. The correct attitude in David was to let God do the fighting. When God fights for us we always win. The finger on His Hand becomes the finishing tape. He holds it up, declaring you to be a winner. Any firm convictions were shaken when Goliath challenged. David challenged by his brother kept his. The largest quake at this time was when the body of the giant hit the floor as if thrown from a height, and of a very heavy weight. Goliath made such a great indentation in the earth's surface as he fell, mortally wounded. Yet it was nothing in comparison to when David defeated Eliab, for in that victory there was the pattern part of a plan of longsuffering, faith and love in the young man's heart. God said, 'Take this pattern and see what I can do with your enemies.' The only thing left of Goliath would be an imprint in the dust of the valley, which a blowing wind would cover eventually. The spirit of the shepherd remained the same, not to get taken up with his own hurt feelings. What was in him remained forever because it is called character, and is part of the heart of God.

When you are hurt go to God

The way the man from Bethlehem accepts what was said, recorded in 1 Samuel 17:28, and turns it for his own good is part of *Dwarfing Giants*. He might have been like the ostrich and buried his head in the sand, but maybe there was no sand in this place, only hard rocks. He could only hide in God. He had the firm conviction that he had nowhere else to go. He didn't mind where he went so long as it was forward to the mouth of the valley. His hurts and pains were washed away in the battle before him. Most soldiers go into battle encouraged by the presence or a few words from their leader. The shepherd of Israel went into battle after being torn by his brother's tongue.

It is so easy to throw sticks at those who throw them at us. Being called a dog by the giant, it was reasonable to expect that David would bring the stick back to his brother. But no, he reserved all his strength for Goliath. If the stone and sling brought Gath's man to the floor, David required strength to lift the sword, and remove the head. The temptation is to tie dirty rags to the stick before we throw back the accusation. I must not return with that as a skull and cross-bone, declaring my piracy, and right to self-determination. The magnanimity of the shepherd boy was the same in defeat as in victory.

The royal nature is being developed in David. The taunt of his brother was, 'Why did you come from the other place? Keep your place, and know your place, it is one of inferiority to me.' Eliab wanted to keep David in his place that is why he asked him why he had left his place. He wanted David to occupy the place of the sheep dog. This was the erroneous theology that once a boy always a boy, once a shepherd always a shepherd. Where he had been placed, there he should always stay. That is the essence of what was said, 'whom have you left those 'few sheep' with? Have you let them be scattered while you are playing at war? I know your pride and the naughtiness of your heart, for you have come down just to see the battle.' It was for entertainment that Eliab thought David had come, to see the scenery. What David's brother didn't realise is that God had been training him for this moment, for the 'fullness of time' had come. There are five accusations, making up four fingers and a thumb on one hand. When David took the stones from the stream, he took five, one for each accusation. Pained but not panicked. Hurt but not helpless.

When we are rejected we hurt others

Remember there was a certain amount of anger in his brother Eliab. All this might just have been because Eliab was the first brother that Samuel looked upon when he was sent by God to anoint another king in place of Saul.[8] Had Eliab remembered this? Was he going to use all the means he could to dissuade the youngest son of Jesse? Remember, in their minds, the oldest in a family always came first in the birthright and never the younger one. Eliab, whose name suggests strength, appears as the weak link. If we are weak we minister that weakness to others. Eliab emptied the contents of his stony sorry heart. David didn't hurt others, he killed a giant and defeated the real enemy. If we are hurt, we hurt others in the same way. Out of Eliab's weakness and not strength he tried to make the heart of the man of God melt. If only he could reduce him make David think he was ordinary, then he would never go into battle. The brother, with no brotherly similarity wanted to make David far less than God had brought him to. If you can be made to think that you are ordinary you will never win. The only chance of recognition or glory for the young shepherd was to do battle with giants. How we receive an accusation, whether it is true or not, will depend on how we exhibit our acquittal. The temptation was to squabble with his brother, but this was resisted. As he refused to be drawn into argument, by conquering one thing, he conquered another.

False motives, pride, naughtiness of heart were all attributed to sincere (without wax) David. What would all this do for the future deliverer? There appeared to be an axe head being swung at his head, to remove it. There are lots of people who swing the axe like Elijah, but they don't have Elijah's power or God.[9] If you constantly 'put down' others, you will be 'put down' to the depths you intended to send them to. You will be 'put down' and trodden underfoot of men. It could have turned the sweet sour, and the stones to be used on the giants could have been used on his brothers. Do not spend time with lesser objects when the real target is before you. The brother could have been given the same treatment as the lion and the bear, but David chose to treat him like a lamb. He won the argument and battle by example, not retaliating to his brother's taunt. You will not be offended if there is no offense in you.

Your talent will be wasted if you harbour resentment

Time and talent would have been wasted if there had been any resentment in the accused. You can be accused without any evidence. There would have been no growth in God for this young man if he had met this attack on his character with a like 'tit for tat' response. In

Dwarfing Giants part of the battle is attitude to others. You being a winner makes something of losers. You make winners out of losers in *Dwarfing Giants*. Talents can be buried in more than earth; they can be hidden under malice and anger.

There wasn't an enlargement of a 'bad attitude' in the son of Jesse. He didn't go to meet with Goliath thinking of all the counter influence in his soul. There are things that are said which would blunt the weapons of your warfare. If you trust in God, weapons or talents are not so important. Leave that sort of thing, discouraging words and the like, with the man who revels in them, and drinks them daily. You have been called to better things greater goals are yours. There are no short cuts to Heaven, only to hell! David is marked out as being holy in this conversation with his brother. His only answer was in the battle before him. Always conquer by example, not clever arguments or answers. What you say might correspond with the ear and the mind, but not the heart. The brother Eliab would dishonour David. He wanted to push him back into his place. He would only ever be good enough to feed a few sheep. There are those who will never understand you or your walk with God. They always interpret your faith as presumption. The reason for this is because as David was a giant ahead of Eliab, so are you as you resist. When we grow in the Almighty we grow so big that these small flies neither bite us or hurt. You can outgrow the impeachment. The Bethlehemite lost none of his sincerity. It was a weapon helping him to overcome, granting him great confidence, bringing within his grasp sweet success.

Some excel at discouraging others

The brother of David might have been very good at criticising and being negative, but when it came to the ministry required to send a brother into battle, he was weighed in the balances and found wanting. Eliab could not destroy the giant by destroying others. The giant remained. He put more into criticising his family member than he ever produced in faith or used to fell a resident of Gath. Your negative criticism can keep the giant on his feet. Eliab had no ministry at all, only misery. It is easy to pluck a duck, but who can grow a feather? What he was, he said. It was an overflow from his heart. There are those who, like artists, love to draw and paint storms. They are very good depicting ships in storms, sinking and drifting towards the rocks, and so are some people with their negative attitude. There is no healing in harsh words. If you use abrasive paper, you will 'rub up' people the 'wrong way'. Eliab was very good at running away from challenging giants, but David was excellent at running to them, and killing them. In the past, I have given them a piece of my mind, but it has been the worse piece. Always let it be the 'peace' of your mind you give. Others have been told what I think, but as with this story in 1 Samuel 17, they are not bettered by what I said, they rather grow worse.

There is the possibility of probing a wound with a rusty instrument. Those words are rusty instruments. If you do speak all your heart, the Bible says you are a fool.[10] You may tell a scarecrow that there are deficiencies in it, but it will still scare the birds away even after you have shouted at it. What came out of Eliab's mouth was the water of the Dead Sea. There was enough said to drown any man. No lifeboats sail these waters! It is every man for himself. There was no hand out-stretched to help David back. It was not refreshing, as a fountain, but was as brackish water. I have told people what I thought of them, but only after many years of serving God have I realised that if it is done, with the spirit of Eliab, as this was done, I have lost my ability to help them. In speaking roughly to them my influence over their lives has been lost. Wouldn't it have been nice if Eliab had offered to lend his sling or a few stones? It wasn't the older brother who had formed the character of the younger it was the Eternal. Many men would seek to smash with their tongues what God has built. Jehovah had been working in David's life for a long time.

Hurtful words must be forgotten and forgiven

The future king was not prepared to ride into battle with these words. Not one word would be used as a whip or a spur, but as a rein to limit. The King's colours he wore going into battle were God's. He came out with them intact. Negativity would not be his attendant. The doors between what the ears hear, the mind understands and the heart receives were closed. The destructive criticisms would have been worse than the armour of Saul to this young giant- killer. With these in the back of his mind there would be no going forward into conquest. David's mind might have been on what his older brother had said, rather than what God had promised. If that had been so he would have been 'pulled two ways', and that is the New Testament meaning of doubt. In Luke chapter 15, we have the same family arguments between the Prodigal Son and the Elder brother. The brother cannot accept that returning the son has been changed.

The enemy always knows the best moment to attack, just when you are preparing to overcome a temptation or defeat a giant in the valley you are passing through. When you are spiritually standing on one leg, they push you from behind. Unable to swim you find yourself in deep waters. John Bunyan in 'Pilgrim's Progress' depicts this giant as Giant Despair. We all meet him in the valley. The words uttered were meant to bowl him over but because of his heart attitude, they spurred him on. The utterance wasn't to take him forward but back, they were meant to make him inward instead of outward, to take him down and not up. He could not allow himself to think of anything else for the next three days and night. David did not allow the words to become ropes or chains of bondage. He would not enter a prison, and he would take no prisoners in the words spoken.

Keep true to your vision

David kept true to his vision of defeating a giant. When he was discouraged he realised that boldness is courage with its boots on. He went on telling others that the giant could be defeated. What he said could be done, and he believed it before he attempted it. He let the harsh words run as water off the proverbial duck's back. Many thought God could use them to overcome this huge giant of flesh, some even said it, but only the young shepherd was prepared to do it. The 'action man' must become the 'man of action'. He was prepared to do it alone and become an example for the whole nation. These harsh words spoken by a member of his family became hurdles that must be leaped over. During a horse race one racehorse refused to jump the hurdle, and then stood there eating the very thing it should have jumped over. When the son of Jesse fought with Goliath of Gath, angels had aching feet as they stood on their toes, craning their necks to see the man of God in action!

Self-pity is a giant we must all defeat

The would-be giant-killer did not make a prison of self-pity through the rebuke he received. If he had, he would have faced Goliath looking through prison bars from a condemned cell. He proved his strength by being better and bigger than his brother. David saved his strongest words and most sure aim for Goliath. He aimed for a new thing, something that nobody else had been prepared to do. Self-pity would have made him smaller. Eliab might be good with words, but he was very poor with stones and killing giants. His heart had received no healing ministry. Self-pity closes every door of opportunity. The sun that shone that day had never shone in his heart. There were dark corners of misery within. Those who would rule as kings must learn to be king of their own spirits first. That is why in the New Testament it speaks of 'reigning as kings in this life.'[11] The kingdom within must be ruled well before it can rule others. Words must be used as trained soldiers, not as a rabble, ready to lynch the innocent.

What an awful description of the character of the shepherd boy is given by his brother. Who needs an enemy when you have not only brothers, but also friends who say things to discourage you? It would have been more acceptable if archers had shot the Bethlehemite. The indictment reads like a man on a charge in a courthouse. He is accused of pride. The word pride describes a toad that has inflated itself or the feathers of the peacock, put there for display but not real. It is that attitude of heart that says I am better than anybody else. The words of Eliab became an empty echo as David appeared carrying the head of the defeated foe. Pride is why Satan fell. It is the very opposite to the glory of God. It was the very armour the boy refused to go into battle with. Once a thing is said, it is easy to say other things that follow. The giant-killer must remain humble and never be accused of being 'big headed', because if that was true, the crown awaiting him would not fit not his head, and the throne meant for him would be far too small for him to occupy. Accusation is multiplied until, like the broken splinters of a smashed ornament, they cannot be numbered. Once corruption is established the flies soon follow, and then the grubs. Every situation you enter will offer you a garment of self-pity, putting it over your shoulders as you pass through. Self-pity obliterates the King's colours. Self-pity defeated no giants, but having a high regard for God's love and mercy will conquer all. Self-pity leads to a pitiful self.

Others may never recognise your true worth

Eliab had seen the 'naughtiness' of the warrior's heart or so he thought. 'Naughtiness' is a fig that has gone beyond its ripeness, and is out of reach of usefulness, not even useful enough to adorn the ground as part of a heap of rubbish. Flies lay their eggs in it as it splits open, and it develops all manner of evil. At the slightest touch it falls from the tree to the ground. Eliab is declaring that this young brother will bring nothing to fruition. All he does will fall as an untimely fig. Did they expect this to happen to David? The man of God's choice is being called 'a good for nothing,' yet he has kept sheep faithfully, and carried provisions to the battlefront. There was no desire to be at the forefront, because when Samuel called he was with the sheep in the field. According to the assassinator of his character, he is good for nothing, but in the Lord he is good for everything that is called giant. There is much better stuff in all of us than the evil thought by many. David appears to have had the same reputation as Joseph the dreamer. The man who was described as having the heart of God is first accused of having a 'naughty' heart. A naughty heart is a heart that is not for the real thing, nor is it willing to see anything through to the end. Naughty can sometimes become haughty. It is a heart that simply mimes in mimicry and has no commitment. He is accused of coming to see the battle in order to be entertained, watching others do the fighting, and listening to Goliath shouting. The fact that David had come to win the battle was never anticipated. David did, which is why he gathered other stones, to be used after this affront. That this boy should be the real deliverer was never thought of or mentioned. It was as far away from the mind of Eliab as east is from the west! There always will be those who keep shoving you to the bottom of the ladder once you begin to ascend it. They have trodden on your fingers as they have marched on, regardless of the pain they have caused. When some speak, we have to overcome what is said. This is part of the conflict. They, when criticising are emptying the contents of their heart hoping that you will enlist and become part of the soldiers in their army. These words spoken out of their hearts are just chaff. Let the wind of the Holy Spirit blow the chaff away.

Success will mark you out for criticism

There will be times when you have done nothing wrong. The fact that you are a winner and are not willing to follow others in their despair will mark you out for criticism and discouragement. As a leader, you will be independent of men, but totally reliant on God. Leadership can mark you out for loneliness. Don't grapple with lesser things that people say about you when you can meet with greater things that will make you truly great. William Booth, the founder of the 'Salvation

Army' used to refer to people like Eliab as 'small beer'. All who engage in negative criticism see but one aspect of your life, while God sees all, hears all, and knows all. If you overcome the giant in your valley, you will overcome both Eliab and Goliath, Eliab appears to be more at one with Goliath than with his brother David. You, in your trial of conflict, will only ever become the same measure and power as those things you overcome. Defeat a giant and be a giant! The wrong was not in Israel's future king, but in the heart of the one uttering the words. Sometimes what is said about you is ample cover for the state of the heart of another. What was said with anger would win no victories. The lad from Bethlehem would not carry this into battle with him because it would mark him out as a loser before he even began. Jesus had such words whispered to Him in the temptation in the wilderness. If the sheep-keeper had allowed this discouragement into his own heart the defeat would have come from there and not through any giant of the Philistines. Eliab would have done with David what the brothers did with Joseph. His words would have surrounded him like a pit. He would have been sold into slavery, along with the whole nation of Israel. The man accused kept his spirit straight and true. He would not, and must not be deflected from what God had purposed for him. 'Mud will stick', but only if there is something for it to stick to. There was no offense in this young man so the accusation went right through him, and returned to the person who had said it. Let what is said about you bounce back as a rubber ball to where it came from. We can be of such a disposition as this 'Sweet Psalmist of Israel', that whatever is spoken as a bad word can be turned into a beautiful song. We can hear what is said as the silver tongue of an orator, and that which was spoken against us can work for us. The word spoken in hatred by Jesse's oldest son was meant to break the bone, but instead it made the man. David could now set out to prove that these things were not so. He was not an onlooker, and he would not leave the battle to others. He wouldn't just be a part of it, he would become the main protagonist.

There is only one way to settle a matter. Go and do the very opposite of what you have been accused of. We must not allow others to give definitions of what we are and such be believed. While they are cursing, you start praising! We are God's people entering into *Dwarfing Giants* with God at our right, left, behind, and to the front. Understand that Jehovah is more than words of hurt. As the words which are spoken split your soul wide open, it is only that grace might be poured in. It might be to let more revelation of God flood your heart. God uses words, good and bad, as missionaries, to reach and teach the way of Christ. It might be that defeat needs chasing out and victory allowed in. This showed the largeness of David's heart, the words disappeared as arrows flying beyond their target, never to be remembered again, developing the future king's favourite pastime of forgetfulness. The only accusing finger for Eliab was the upturned finger of Goliath of Gath, pointing, as he lay at the mercy of God's shepherd-soldier.

Notes: -

1. 1 John 4:4.
2. 1 John 3:15.
3. 1 Samuel 17:40.
4. 1 Samuel 30:6.
5. Exodus 32:19.
6. Exodus 3:2.
7. Hebrews 12:2.
8. 1 Samuel 16:6-10.
9. 1 Kings 18:40.
10. Proverbs 29:11
11. Romans 5:17.

Chapter

4

The Defeating of the Lion and the Bear

King David, the son of Jesse from Bethlehem, and formerly a shepherd had a great history of achievements in God. These mentioned are for his qualification. 'Your servant slew a lion and a bear' wasn't just history; it was part of his spirituality, and the kingdom within his own heart. What had happened to him in conflict with no one watching, had probably happened while he was watching sheep? This became part of his diary of achievements and ranked alongside other greater battles. The defeating of both the lion and the bear is mentioned three times in 1 Samuel 17: 34-37, and didn't happen by chance, nor were they created in order for him to pass an idle hour. The conflict with these animals was a matter of life or death. The circumstances surrounding you are the pit that you fight in. Your character can be as a lion's cage requiring a lion-tamer. These were free roaming beasts of the wild hillsides on which he looked after gentle sheep. We need the rough with the smooth, the lion with the gentle lamb, the bear with the sheep bearing. These things balance us. It wasn't enough for David to count lions and bears he had to defeat them. It is not enough to recognise a temptation or its source, it has to be defeated and that defeat will lead you on to greater things. If you can cross a brook or a stream when you come to it, you will be made ready to sail seas. You can never sail any sea without the 'tang' of the salt in your face, a strong wind blowing with water like whips lashing your cheeks it is part of your training for seamanship.

Prove your worth as a warrior

When any sheep were attacked, it was part of the shepherd's role to rescue them. Any shepherd who did not have scars or marks telling of his escapades was not worth to be called a shepherd. Those who carried no battle scars were called hireling, being hired for a day. The right to carry the shepherd's rod and staff had to be earned. Some of these rods were marked with notches, denoting battles entered into and won. The rod of David had many marks, declaring his victories.

Yours are in the cross of Jesus Christ. When any wild beast attacked the sheep, it was also attacking and sometimes tearing away the honour of the shepherd. There was a difference between the shepherd and the hireling. The hireling would flee from the beast, while the shepherd would chase it away and slay it. The word shepherd not only suggests being a leader, feeder and guider, but also a defender.

The same applies to the Christian engaged in *Dwarfing Giants*. It is a matter of pride and joy and great consolation when we defeat the enemy of our souls. Your heart is the sheepfold, and all the sheep in it are the good things God has done for you, your many answers to prayer. It isn't a matter of where and when or what is attacked, but what we rescue and have at the end. Everything that happens to us should 'better' us, not simply bruise or batter, leaving us bleeding and dying on the Jericho Road. When passing through a dark tunnel, I don't want just the end of the tunnel I want the light that is at the other end!

The weapons you require can be taken from the battle

Within the 'hug' of the bear or the 'claw' of the lion, there is part of God's ability in designing a life. We look to the carver of wood to design a beautiful object, or to the mechanic's spanner to rectify. The very marks on the wheel nut tell you that the spanner has been applied, and within that grip of the spanner all is well, the wheel will not roll off the vehicle. What tools are to the workman, so resisting a temptation can be for you. Tools are usually kept in a dark bag. Each enticement is to allow us to take hold of the weapons of our warfare. Within each trial there is something waiting to be set free, not to destroy you but to come alongside, making you into a better person for God. The New Testament calls it being 'fully furnished', 2 Timothy 3:17. Suggesting a house full of furniture all arranged in its own place and serving in the best possible way. It suggests things being where they should be. The term 'thoroughly furnished' is bringing before us the figure of the new sword coming from the artificer. It has a handle the blade has been burnished, polished and sharpened. It is a complete weapon. The real wisdom of what happens to us is to see God in it and to accept what comes 'in' it and 'out' of it. The whole of nature, including your nature, declares His handiwork (Greek, poetry).

Each battle requires a new anointing and a new approach

We are not told if David used a sling on these occasions when he was battling with the two beasts, but we are told that God delivered him. He gives all the glory to his Master and Friend. He took the bear by the beard and rescued a lamb from between its teeth.[2] A battle, whether with a lion, a bear or a giant requires a new anointing and a new approach. The shepherd boy saw Goliath in the same context as these marauding beasts. The old oil on the stone, or on another stone would not do to face Goliath and overcome him. It had to be a new stone taken from fresh water that helped the shepherd boy defeat Goliath. It was never accomplished by digging into the memories of the past; it was accomplished by believing God. Trust became the main thrust in this battle. Very few raise their families or make fortunes on 'Lover's Lane', for love must expand far beyond that, and must be practical. It is much more than a 'lane', it has turns and twists; there are bends and hills with deep valleys. Love is love when it overcomes all things, such as a lion and a bear, but it can 'bear all things', being as gentle as a lamb when handling anything of a lamb nature. True love for God is seen and explained in the battle of the beasts, as in the children's story 'The Beauty and the Beast'. There is a beauty in every heart that is kissed by Jesus Christ that can out-run and out-manoeuvre anything in the world. Its skill is in His will that leads to *Dwarfing Giants*.

There are degrees of temptation

There are a many gradations of temptations. This was a lion and a bear. Not together to form a chain, but the Devil knows no rules, and he sometimes sends them as a pack of wolves. The nearer you move to the Lord, so the temptations multiply. You cannot move from one temptation to the next until the first is overcome. There is an 'A' to 'Z' even in temptation. God will only allow you to face another enemy, and overcome it, when you have defeated the one that you are presently wrestling with. Learn that His nip is greater than your grip. We master one at a time, just as David learned to walk through a puddle, then to cross a stream. Bread has to be eaten one slice at a time, including crusts. We move from one experience to another even as we teach our children to build with bricks one at a time, learning the alphabet before they learn to spell the word.

A minister preached the same message in the morning as in the evening. When asked why, he replied, 'I have done this because you have not done what I suggested this morning. If you had carried out the instructions from the Word of God, I would have brought a different challenge to you.' David had to take the challenge of the lion and use it to prepare himself to meet the bear.

Temptations are multiplied

There is no 'single' temptation that is why Jesus depicted them as birds in Matthew 13:4. One follows the other as penguins going into the sea from an ice float. Sometimes they are seen in the figure of chaff being winnowed from the corn by the means of a large shovel, creating a wind to blow the chaff away. Satan operated through many 'pigs' in Gadara. Peter describes these 'fiery trails' as 'manifold', with 'many folds'.[3] There are as 'many folds' in grace as there are in temptations. Thinking you have gained the victory, but then something else comes from it. You thought that defeated was dead! Wait a moment! Goliath has four brothers that need to be overcome before the conflict is finalised. In the morning light, after a dark night of struggle, new forms of temptation appear. Job met with them in his family, friends, then his house fell down during a stormy wind, and the Sabeans came and did their destroying work. You cannot climb mountains before you get over the small stone on the ground before you. Temptations are like steps in stairs each one leads you higher, until you reach the heart of God, or, as in this youth's life, the throne of Israel. The steps leading to the highest office, whether it is to be King, President of America or the Prime Minister of England are the highest steps in the world.

Temptations are not easy to handle

There is a certain roughness in the bear needing to enter into you, to help you deal with those things that seem to have no handles for you to take hold of in order to defeat them. Both bear and lion have explosive qualities. You require meekness when dealing with the roughness of tooth and claw. The energies are within them to arise and attack to win. Let these energies become yours! There are many corners on some temptations, that is why they cut and pierce. In Greek mythology, when one head was chopped off the beast another two heads rose up in its place. We all have to be schooled to meet a bear like a bear, but if we have never met with one, how are we going to defeat it? The very trial is meant to furnish you with more than red ribbons. They are character building. According to this happening in David's life, trials are always there to remind and encourage us. If you overcome both the lion and the bear, two white mice will not chase you. Let the achievements of life come because of the anchors of life. Let them go further and deeper than just being placed in your diary. Let them be placed 'into the heart of you'. The Almighty who created the lion and the bear, also created the rough and the smooth. That which is coarse can be turned into silk by spinning and weaving as you fight your way through to victory.

Past temptations can help you with the present

Past temptations provide the power to help you in the present. Do not go around in circles. Repetition is a good teacher but a poor inspirer. If you have done it once, you can do it again and again. The person who has climbed Mount Everest smiles at a molehill. If you have been to the sun, you can handle a small spark. The resurrection of Jesus Christ from the dead was not the first occasion or the last that God raised someone from the dead. It had been done many times before. The footprints leading to the lion and the bear are there for you to walk in and conquer. Enough room has been left in each print for you. The place of attack might be different but the enemy still remains the same. The conditions may alter but the enemy does not. What came in Goliath was in both these animals. The place may be different, the size of the temptation may be different, but God is still the same! It might be in the night or in a valley, but the areas of strain and pressure will ever be as common as sheep being attacked by wild beasts. 2 Samuel 17:10, we have a remarkable description of David by one of his friends, Hushai the Archite, the man who was a pioneer and leader. As Absalom rebels, this friend of the King, Hushai refers to David, as some one 'Whose heart is like the heart of a lion.' Something of that lion's heart had entered into David. He had been enabled and strengthened by what he had passed through. Allurement may be like the lion but when it is overcome, there is honey in the carcass. It was there in Judges 14:8,9 for Samson. Wherever we go, we must go with open hands and heart, with open ears and eyes, to hear, to see, and take from that which is around us that will help in the future. Our defence is attack. In going forward we take the ground held by others. The soft heart readily receives impressions. That which is formed in wood has to be carved! Let a lion spring into you! We have heard the saying 'Saving for a rainy day.' That which is happening to you, take and save it for the future. If you only take something small from it, like an umbrella, it will still help in the day of rain! The knowledge of your temptation will become wisdom when dealing with future things. There are seeds to be found in every field, seeds that can be planted as the heart is softened. Whatever happens, don't become a sketch, become a masterpiece!

Use each temptation formed against you

To come through a temptation and overcome is better than a quiver full of arrows. That which is overcome is the quiver of arrows as from each encounter you take another weapon, another arrow which can be used in future attacks. You do not stand defenceless again. Once you have been there and faced that it is like having been trained to use an armoury. These achievements give you a loaded gun. You are not as green as grass when some of the black or the brown of bear or lion has entered into your soul. Let that spirit of yours become the lion's den. If you have a 'lion heart' within you, there need be no fear of lions attacking you. Be as King Richard of England described as, 'Richard, the Lionheart' because of his bravery. If that 'bear nature' has been birthed within there will be no fear of bears attacking you. If they do, you have something of their nature to help deal with them. You have no need to fear attack, just loose the lion within and watch it work for you. The Bible is a lion, loose it and let it go! 'Christ in you, the hope of glory,' is the Lion of the Tribe of Judah. We are all part of whatever we have met, and whatever has happened to us. That need not make us negative, but positive, as it made the man destined to be king. He has done it before, and he can do it again. David knew that the power enabling him to dis-harm and disfigure both lion and bear could deal with anything whatever its size. He could have said to the mountain, 'Be cast into the sea!'[4] Sometimes God expects us to climb the mountain and kill the bear and the lion upon it. It was not David using the same sling, stone or shoes that granted him the victory. It was the Elohim of all creation. Overcoming a temptation, in God is another creative act God has performed through you. In the hands of God you become a mighty threshing instrument when *Dwarfing Giants*.

There are teachings in temptations

There is a teaching session in every temptation. David, in *Spiritual Warfare* had a lion for a Principle of the college, and a bear as a lecturer. Here, the history of Israel was being taught. The writing tablet was not of clay, but an impression made in wax. There was no paper on which to write just the gentle, pliable heart of a shepherd boy, and the heart of God was touched, because he was 'a man after God's own heart.'[5] When you are learning or have learned a foreign language, you don't really know that language, until you begin to think in it. It is not enough to hear, repeat or quote it, it is only sufficient when you begin to think in it. The learning of the secrets of *Spiritual Warfare* is the same. These lessons, with this young man from Bethlehem are learned only when they are as much a part of us as skin was to the lion or its paw, and the hug which is part of the bear. It must become more than the wearing a lion skin or bearskin, taking what others have slain. It must enter our spirits. When it does we overcome evil spirits.

Everything that happened to David was part of his journey from Bethlehem to Jerusalem. We are on the same journey, walking the same pathway, meeting the same opposition. We need to understand the nature of these wild beasts. The apostle Paul saw men as wild beasts.[6] In Acts 8:3, when Paul is describing himself making 'havoc' of the church, he uses a metaphor of the wild boar. It runs through the undergrowth, snatching to the right and to the left, tearing and uprooting every tender plant. Many an acorn that would develop into an oak is crushed the moment it falls to the ground. The ground which was meant to nurture it into something greater is the means of its death. Things can crush us, when in fact we should use them to help us grow, and mature. These dire moments can be just like that.

The temptations that assailed the Bethlehemite were of a wild nature. Temptations do not normally come to us on a sunny day or a calm sea. In our *Spiritual Warfare* they come to us as they came to Job, from every quarter.[7] The moment we are swept off our feet, we land in His arms. They are arms that span the centuries. When David needed stronger arms and feet greater vision and new strength, he looked to God. He saw the enemy in the shadow of God. Jehovah became his measure for all things, and his music through it all.

Deal with all temptations with the same power

It was a lion and a bear that was overcome. It was not a 'fox' that spoiled the vine[8], but something that was far greater in essence and measure. That 'fox', or some small influence, robbing you of your spiritual fruit must be dealt with or the vine will be spoiled. Animals are given as illustrations of enemies in our battles. The New Testament speaks of 'dogs', that we must beware of.[9] King Herod is likened to a fox in Luke 13:32. Some are spoken of as swine, Matthew 7:6. Others are described as eagles feeding on a carcase, Matthew 24:28. Satan is figured as a lion, 2 Timothy 4:17,I Peter 5:8. 'Thy servant slew a lion.' It was only one lion, not a Pride. It is enough for David to meet and defeat one at a time. Later on, it wouldn't be the whole family from Gath that David would face, it was just Goliath.

'Lion' is referring to its beastly nature, not it's golden mane. It is not the roar of the lion that we need to fear; we need to be watchful about its deadly activity, yet we must not fear any part of it. The Lion of the Tribe of Judah will prevail over every lion. We know that our adversary the Devil 'goes around like a lion' the future king fought with. Some end the quote there, forgetting that it says 'seeking whom he may devour.' He fully completes his mission when it says 'whom he may devour.' [10] This is one of the secrets of *Dwarfing Giants*, to make such an impact that we 'devour' that which would 'devour' us. We need to be the chaser, not the chased. Be the cook, and not that which is on the menu, in the pot or in the mouth!

Use temptations, and see them work for you

The lion was the emblem of St. Jerome. The story is told that a lion entered the room, and all the early disciples fled. Jerome stood firmly as the lion lifted up one of its paws. He saw a thorn sticking out of it, and he withdrew the foreign-body. The lion stayed with him, and would wander around with him. Jerome illustrates that you can overcome a lion, not only with aggression, but also with kindness, removing the thorn-offending thing from the argument. 'Androclus and the Lion' illustrates the same principle. While running away as a slave, taking refuge in a lion's den, which was a cave, he removed a thorn from a lion's paw. Later, Androclus was in the amphitheatre a lion was loosed to destroy him. It came and licked his hands and feet. It was the same lion that he had conquered by removing the thorn! Both these stories illustrate what happened to King David. He took something from the encounter that was going to help him in future battles. Once you have looked upon the face of a lion and felt its hot breath on your cheeks you do not fear the face of men. Hercules, the Grecian hero, was given twelve things of great danger to accomplish by the Argive king. Some of these feats involved killing wild beasts. He had to slay the Nemean lion. He had to slay the Arcadian stag. The Cretan bull had to be taken captive. Then he had to bring up the three-headed dog from hell called Cerberos. When he had accomplished these and other tasks, he would become immortal.

In Heraldry, there are lions in every pose possible. Some are emblazoned on shields couched, ready to spring into attack, others are rampant. Sometimes it is a 'full faced' lion as on the English Standard, while at other times it is even a lion looking back, speaking of being circumspect. We must meet Satan in all these guises and disguises, overcoming him, whatever stance he takes. We are only 'more than conquerors' when we have been successful in every department of trial.

Three times David makes known the fact that God had delivered him from the lion. The word 'lion' suggests to pierce and to pluck. It illustrates an aggressive nature. It is the epiphany of lawlessness. There is that which every disagreement would take, to reduce you to make you less of a person than what you are. This is why in Matthew 4:6, during the temptation of Christ the Devil commanded Jesus to 'throw himself down'. You can do just that through speech or your estimation of yourself. God wants to make you the best, turning an unknown shepherd boy into a king. The Devil wants to do the opposite, which he did through King Saul, a man head and shoulders above other men born to be king. Defeat turned him into a beggar and removed him, leaving him without a history. God wants to make you count; the Adversary wants to discount you!

Every temptation seeks to weaken

There is the element in the name 'lion' of immense cruelty, terror and fierceness. Dr. Strong, along with Gesenius[11] says the word 'lion' comes from a root word that describes its plucking action when it tears the meat, like plucking grapes from the vine. The lion as it attacks, kills, and eats the victim. That which is taken in battle adds strength to the lion and aids it in the future. Let us learn from brute creation! What the lion does is a description of cattle as they tear grass to eat it. Jesus said, 'The thief comes only to destroy and kill, but I come that you might have life.'[12] There is only one winner in this battle, and I must take the side of the winner. The Elohim[13] that brought David through has also taken many millions through the battles of life. He will take you through to the other side. Don't stay with the small things such as the lion or the bear; go for the Goliath's. In defeating him, you defeat many lions. When Satan appeared to Martin Luther the reformer, he came disguised, pretending to be Jesus Christ so that the saint could not recognise him. He came as so many do, pretending to be helpful. Martin Luther, in order to discover who he really was said to him, 'Show me the scars in your hands!' The figure disappeared. He had no battle scars in his hands.

The temptations may differ but their nature is the same

David had to overcome the bear. The attack of the bear is totally different from the attack of the lion. In a sense, the hug of the bear is love gone to the extreme. Some things we suffer seem to want to hug you. They simply, as a bear, want to get closer to you to kill what you are. Certain trials are meant to squeeze you into their mould, squeezing the spiritual life out of you, leaving you bleeding and dying. God wants to enlarge the eternal life within. It happens when all barriers are removed. This hug is a type of lawlessness. What should be a soft embrace becomes a crushing blow of defeat. What should have been a pat on the back in encouragement is the very push that would send you over the edge. The handshake crushes and hurts instead of congratulating. The bear hug demands and domineers until all life is taken from us. The bear illustrates the pressures and forces of life when we seem to 'come up against a brick wall'. Walking on all fours, the bear is reduced in size but raised to its full height it would block out the light and hide the very path you have been called to walk. To a bear, you are honey and attractive. Temptations will come to you as bees to a honeycomb. These torments must be overcome. We are the servants of the Lord, not the servants of things. I serve God, I love God, and out of that, service to others abounds. I must not get it wrong thinking that by serving others I serve God. It is service to God first and last, with others in between. Serving and loving God can never be an 'off-spin' of serving others. I must love the Lord my God first, then my neigh-bour. The water must not come before the cup. One will be served in the other. My 'neighbour', that Jesus spoke of lovingly, must not become my God or a replacement for God.[14]

Be 'meek' to conquer the bear. Its name suggests that which is uncouth, ragged, shaggy, sword blade blunted and not sharpened as the 'steely' temptation. It represents the rough side of those who are in the warfare. It is always important, when using firearms, that the gun barrel should be spotlessly clean. When we fight back, it must be a fight in holiness. This is not so when dealing with a rough, uncouth bear with its claws and feet like great sputniks travelling towards you at speed. You will meet with many like this, and in the arena of grace you must overcome them. The bear isn't called 'grizzly' because it is easy and smooth. Dealing with one is like handling the edge of a bro-ken bottle or broken glass, shattered into a thousand needles. It read-ily became the national emblem of Russia at the height of the Com-munist rule in many countries. The bear is a dominating spirit, rearing up to crush you. Fight it! Break it! Reduce it to the size of a fat mouse! Then trap it!

No temptation is greater than the power within you

The power of the Holy Spirit within you is greater than any realm around you. Each trial overcome is a display of the completeness of the power of God. The word 'bear' can suggest 'quiet strength'. The bear is always waiting like an extinct volcano, ready to return to a vol-canic eruption. We require devotion which turns rock into ash. We have to penetrate that confidence, and disturb the quietness with a storm. The quietness and strength there as that which is un-assailed, not bothered by any kind of force arranged against it until you come along. It might be complacency that we have to overcome in *Dwarfing Giants*. The word 'bear' comes from a root Hebrew word meaning 'to creep', describing the ambling movement of the bear. This root word describes 'slander',[15] the slow moving of the tongue in speech. That which moves along slowly as a stream or sea of mud that has to be checked. There is a great temptation to talk about others instead of talking to others. There maybe a suggestion of an indolent spirit in the word bear. Its strength is in the knowledge of its power. It can wait qui-etly for the right moment. That which is so slow to obey God, and do the will of God is of the bear nature. Some Old Testament creatures such as the tortoise were considered unclean, because they were so slow. These spirits, attitudes and emotions must be overcome before we have our greatest victory. Talk to the Master of both lion and bear.

It wasn't lion and bear together, or even the bear and the lion. God allows every attack. It is first one for David, then another. What the lion fails to do in tearing our work to shreds so that it looks as if it has been chewed into small pieces, the bear will destroy, if we let it. We must use Jesus, as the Door, and close that Door to every marauding beast. The only way out was over the dead body of the bear. To run for escape invited further attack and sure death. Whatever method of success the king used, we must use the same, as we find ourselves in private battles, leading to public victory. The future king was well trained as he counted sheep and stars. He spent many hours practising with the sling and the stone, yet he must depend on God more than on the sling. God will take his private practise and own it publicly. You will be no greater in public than you are in private. If you are a cloth that all wipe their hands on in the kitchen, then out in the world or in the palace, you will never be the silk that clothes the king at his coronation. You are an investment, invested with the power of God, Acts 1:8.

Learn to use your capacity to conquer temptations

'By my God,' so says this same young man in Psalm 18:29. That is his charter and secret of success. The same word 'slew', used by David to describe the slaying of the lion and the bear in 1 Samuel 17:35,36 is used of the shepherd boy slaying the giant in verses 51,51. One had been practise for the other. Your servant 'slew', meaning to 'strike severely'. It means to strike with a stone, a rod or an arrow. There was the certain pleasure of being 'on target'. Defeating the bear is bringing the attack to a premature end, drawing a line in the sand, and saying 'no further!' It means at that place the enemy dies and falls where you have said 'no!' What a full stop God produced as the giant thundered to the ground! The future king put all he had into this service of killing the wild beast. He could be a tender-hearted shepherd to sheep, yet he was a hunter and a warrior to wild beasts. He never surrendered all his capabilities to one beast or one attack. The nature of wild things must be stopped from getting into us. We must not take on the nature of the wolf, we must see the nature of Jesus being constantly developed in the life. We have been called to be sheep among wolves, not wolves among sheep. The wild horse and elephant nature, charging when enraged must not displace the dove and the lamb nature. In destroying the lion and the bear, David kept his own heart, which was after God's own heart, intact. By limiting evil we let love loose. In the limiting of one, the other is released.

Notes: -

1. Romans 1:20. Psalm 19:1.
2. 1 Samuel 17:34,35.
3. 1 Peter 1:6.
4. Matthew 17:20.
5. 1 Samuel 13:14.
6. 1 Corinthians 15:32.
7. See author's book *In Sickness and in Health*.
8. Song of Solomon 2:15.
9. Philippians 3:2.
10. 1 Peter 5:8.
11. *Strong and Gesenius Concordance to the Old Testament*.
12. John 10:10.
13. An Old Testament name for God, describing his creative abilities and power. Found in Genesis 1:1.
14. Mark 12:31.
15. *Strong and Gesenius Analytical Concordance*.

Chapter

5

The Proving of Your Armour

There will be many offers for us to pretend to be what we are not, just as David was offered Saul's armour that he had not 'proved'. Twice in 1 Samuel 17:39 the word 'proved' is used. When the word 'proved' is used it suggests the 'assaying' of metal. It has to be tried in the fire until all the clay and earth are removed. Then the scum is removed from the surface of the pot into which the raw material has been placed. To be put to the test makes our armour personal to us. Sometimes we believe doctrines we have never learned. We accept what anybody offers to us as the foundation for our faith. The Scriptures tell us to 'prove all things.'[1] Become as the Bereans who searched the Scriptures daily, Acts 17:10,11. David would not use what he had not proved. We have to examine everything because some things in life are not what they seem to be. As we examine spiritual issues so they become part of us. God is 'working together for your good'[2] in every trial in order that we might stand complete in Christ with an experience that we can call our own. I don't want anybody else to write my testimony. I must not take another's validation of grace, and make it my own. I need to accept the old proverb: 'To understand another, I must walk in their shoes for at least three days,' but then I need to continue walking in my own shoes, in order to have my own relationship with God. There is the temptation to wear the skins of the lion and the bear that have never been killed by me. My testimony may be that which is on my gravestone, written and placed there by another hand, but it is not good enough for me while I am alive. The unreal must not become the real. You can obtain second-rate armour at any jumble sale, but what you require is first-hand enabling from Jesus. That second-rate is readily available at any scrap-yard or on display in some museum. God can grant you that which you need to overcome every giant in every valley! It is a matter of using what God has already given. Proverbs 24:34....'as an armed man.' The margin for 'armed man' is 'a man of the shield'. It is something he has been taught to handle skillfully.

We feel the need to be accepted

The reason we try to use other people's lives and not our own as an example is because we want to be accepted. We, then, become the imitation, the plastic or the synthetic of the real. Others have achieved and we want to take what is theirs and use it as if it were our own. We must be able to register our own patent, thus claiming that which is our own. It is a poor thing if all we have of recognition is what we bought in an auction, as they auctioned the history of a famous person. The future King of Israel would not do that. 'When in Rome do as Romans do' is only a reality if we want to be accepted in Rome. There is a doctrine of identification that brings us recognition, which we accept readily. That is why we refer to people 'jumping on the band wagon.' They are trying to use another person's success attempting to make it personal to them. If it is not homebred, then it is not acceptable. That is why shepherds have to cover a rejected lamb whose mother has died, with the skin of a dead lamb in order to get the mother of that dead lamb to accept it. If that fails, then a spray is used, until the other sheep accepts the lamb. Most creatures will reject that which is brought to them for adoption. When we pretend to be what we are not, that can and does degenerate into hypocrisy. That word 'hypocrisy' means we are 'play acting', wearing a mask to cover up what we really are. We become as those who go to the theatre and are part of a 'fancy dress show'. King David wanted to be as real as the stone, and as real as the sling.

David would not be a person of 'two faces'. He would not even accept the offer to use another man's armour. That which is worn by another person is 'old hat'. Can I not believe the Almighty to create something just for me? Salvation is as individual as the sun or moon, and so are my happenings with the Eternal. Who wants to wear those sweaty pieces of armour taken from another's battles? Your dealings with God are measured to suit you, to fit in with your personality. David had to believe God for something new, a new plan that nobody had ever conceived before, so outlandish that, if God was not in it, it would look ridiculous. That which has already been marked and stained with the blood of another found upon Saul's armour, is something you have no memory of to assist you. It is like fighting with a tradition rather than the truth.

The plan of God is for the individual

That which is used by you and is what you are is what God has made you. That is what helps you to conquer all things. Let a chair be a chair, let a table be a table, but you be the distinctive you. What God has given to you use to its full potential. It was designed with you in mind. It might only be a pebble from a stream but if it has been proven, then it has served its purpose. Even the pebble had to be 'proved' by being in the water. Fancy having swirling waters around you, and you can't swim! If that is so, then you require a hand to come and lift you into service. Experience doesn't come all at once. We receive an ounce each time we do battle. If the experience serves its purpose then it is excellent. The very word 'perfection' describes all the parts fully working together. It describes fruit commencing as a small growth on a branch passing through all the seasons and reaching maturity. You, fully clad in God's armour gives you the ability to be successful. When the Eternal gave you His heart by His Spirit, there was something in it just for you.

Using that designed for another makes you feel inadequate

In 1 Samuel 17:38,39, Saul not only offered his armour to David, also he placed it on him. Some people, and in particular minister's wives, have roles thrust upon them, roles that they were never called to fulfil. There are many that fulfil the proverb: 'Some are born great, some are made great, but some have greatness thrust upon them.' Clad in this metal tin, the shepherd boy felt awkward. He had not worn it before or 'proved' it. He might have only seen it on another man. A destiny not decided by God was being placed upon him. More than that, it was being thrust upon him, as if there was no other armour but this. God has as many ways do deal with us as sparrows in a hedge. The son of Jesse was being asked to walk in another man's footsteps. If he had done so he would always have operated in the shadow of another. We can never win our *Spiritual Warfare* by simply quoting a promise, we must believe it. That famous line or saying is all right but did the Author give it to you? When we are not familiar with things, we not only misquote them, we misapply them. Another's endurance will cause you to stumble and fall. A line from a book or a chorus will not throw the giant to the floor. The plan of God even if it is only pebble-shaped will do it. You cannot be the echo of another's voice. Don't even be the musical note, be the musical instrument! Better still be the Master of Music! There has to be substance to a saint. Those only found in stained glass windows will cut you if you break them! Their lead falls out!

Many times in the Bible, people, individuals, armies and nations overcame through worship. If you are going to be a winner in *Spiritual Warfare* let the worship be from your heart, not just a chorus singing session. Don't borrow the brass or the strings from the instruments, if you do your worship will be as brass or a piece of string. My heart's cry, as David's was, is for reality in all things. I want armour and music in my soul, not just in a metal mouth organ!

The best achievements are still in you

The best music in not in the instrument or the notes on the page, it is in you. 'Sing unto the Lord a new song,'[3] means God has answered prayer, and given you something to sing about. There is that which is bubbling forth because of what God has done for you. The battle before David could not be organised by men. That was Saul's way of doing things but it was not God's. After dealing with a lion and a bear there was still enough grace left to deal with a giant and Saul. The defeat of both, through God, came because the spirit of youthful endeavour. If the Lord is with you, victory and the ability to *Dwarf Giants* will be in you.

When we hear, see and know what others have done, then we need to be provoked to love and good works. We can never do exactly what they did or do. What others have accomplished let that be the spark. You are the flame. If they present to you the song, then be the music. They might give you a thought, but you do the deed. Many have seen God move, and then tried to copy only to discover that it doesn't work where they are. The arrow was constructed for the bow; the pebble was at home in the sling. You would never think of trying to squeeze a mountain into a sling! Yet we do that when we pretend.

God will grant you armour for warfare

Saul offered his armour to the shepherd, but it was too large for him. It was too much too soon. The echoes of Saul's commands were still in it. Saul's armour was meant for Saul. What others have might be too big or too wide for you. God knows the size of your heart. He narrows experience down to your size. The tiny crumb is handled well by the ant. Leave the large things to the elephants! The sparrow can't tear flesh like the eagle. God created the worm for the small bird. We can't all be the same. Some can handle one sort of armour while others can handle battle dress of a different sort. We cannot all be leaders; most of us must be followers. If you become leaders, nobody will be led! In following, and being led, we need never surrender what God has done for us. You bring your own defence into battle with you. There is nothing quite like a familiar, friendly weapon to a soldier. Your miracle moments in God are meant for you and not for another. If you keep your life with God green, then nothing around you will turn to dust, to be blown away by a wind. What you have can be shared as with the miracle of loaves and fishes, but you must eat the first part of the loaf. 'Every tub must stand on its own bottom.' When you have accomplished, there is a shine about it, a familiar ring. If it is bent, broken, or even blood stained, at least it bears your name and the testimony of grace as to what has happened in your life.

One king of Israel died when he dressed in the garments of another, 1 Kings 22:30-35. The archers mistook him for someone else and in the battle, instead of a conquest, they had a crisis. It is so important to prove God in everything before you take it and use it. In the New Testament, the sons of Sceva[4] tried to use the name of Jesus Christ without knowing Him as Lord. They wanted to control demon powers, and the result was they were injured, as the demon possessed men leaped upon them.

Every tree must bear its own fruit. If it does, that fruit will be sweet to the taste. Remember the fruit is the glory of the tree. If another's gifts are mimicked, then we are heading for disaster. We become mere puppets or a ventriloquist's dummy when we become the mouthpiece of another. We must draw water from our own cisterns.

We copy the real thing because it attracts

There are those who have tried to preach and witness in imitation of others. They appear as the shadow of the other person as their mannerisms are copied. We must have our own character, and not be a clone. To copy a person is a 'form of flattery', but it is only a 'form' and not the substance. To copy Christ is the glory of the Christian character. When what you take and use is your own, gained because of what has happened to you, then you will be a winner in *Dwarfing Giants*. David was not a miniature Saul. Some creatures of the wild catch others by mimicry, but we attract no bees to our honey unless we have visited the flowers.

The experiences you pass through enable you to know how to handle any situation. Many times all we have is the blade of the weapon to be used. God has to provide us with the handle. We are so impatient we cannot wait long enough for the Designer to complete the work. The danger is when we take a weapon from someone else, and begin to use it. We end in 'Failure Field', living in 'Remorse Row'. Wait God's time, in God's truth, and you, as the man of Gadara in Luke 8:26-37, will be found clothed and in your right mind.

There is natural armour we can wear

It seems as if these weapons of war were suddenly thrust upon David. The temptation not to be yourself can come in the heat of the moment, especially when you are thrust before a great crowd. Not everything that is offered comes from God. These weapons came from a man of natural thoughts. The imagination is a great weapon provider. That is why the Serpent beguiled Adam and Eve, attacking their minds.[5] It was through natural ability David was offered the weapons of a king. If Saul couldn't defeat Goliath using this armour, how could David accomplish it? He would have been using the same weapons. Thousands in history have lost their spirituality by pretending to be something contrary their calling and proven ability. Even if they are the weapons of a king, manufactured in the royal mint, they have to be refused. God will not grant you a victory because somebody else has suggested that you would do well. If you travel as a missionary, or into some other area of work for the God of Israel, what others have said of you will have no effect. Only that provided which is provided by God will bring you through. Observe the contrast between what Saul 'offered' and what the Lord 'gave' to David. As a final gesture Saul offered to David his own armour thinking, 'He might as well die in his armour.' There was no faith, here! The heart of Saul was as empty as the armour. He was but a shell of a man. It is not enough to wear any armour. It is not enough to have every part covered by another person's achievements. The medals pinned on you show that which has been won by you. I don't want a dead man's medals. You must be as a little lad with a stone and a sling, if that is what God has called you to be. David is just David! Being yourself you exercise your greatest and longest lasting influence.

There is a great trial for every son following a father into the pulpit. You ask any minister's son! These young men and women have to prove their own armour. There is no greatness in generation ancestry!

We put off the natural that we might put on the spiritual

The man going into battle was rewarded with success when he threw away the armour he had not proven. Men's methods held no melody for David's heart or harp. In throwing to one-side what was offered he made a place for that which had been given by God. To be himself did not make him more vulnerable; it made him more virtuous. These things the shepherd boy was asked to carry into battle would have made him into an easy target for Goliath. Trying to be somebody else always will. He would stand as lead, unable to dodge any blows. To use only natural ability will set you up as a target that cannot be missed. Natural ability can both hold you back and weigh you down.

If he wore that armour the future psalmist of Israel would think Saul's thoughts, thoughts of rebellion and not submission. When we seek to obtain metal for our armoury we must take it from those things happenings to us, then we shall have a target in the giant that we cannot miss. David would have been better carrying the bread and cheese he had brought for his brothers' lunch than going into battle with that which was not proven. At least, with the bread and cheese, he could feed a friend! With this armour he could not defeat an enemy. Thank God he has more than bread and cheese for us to carry! Wearing the Master's armour commenced here. It concluded with a giant in the dust.

Spiritual abilities must be developed

David had not 'proven' the armour, meaning he had not 'won his spurs'. When a man was knighted, he was given his spurs because he had proven himself in the field of battle. To receive 'spurs' he must have a number of scars or captured weapons to prove his worth. Cities and towns had been taken, in the battle and the man was developing into something more useful. It was here that peasants became princes. Riding into battle as a farm labourer because of development, a peasant came out an Earl, given lands as part of the pleasure of his king towards him. In Scotland when as a guest you had eaten all that you could and there were no provisions left the lady of the house would 'dish up the spurs'. She would bring in the spurs, suggesting it was time to ride into battle. May this book bring the spurs to you, and challenge you to be yourself! Every time we have something to overcome, as we challenge it, we enter into further maturity. The true enhancement of character was not found within the walls of the armour that David was given. He didn't count it a great privilege to act like a king. He had to be a king by ruling in his own life.

When we pretend to be what we are not we need far more scheming ability than if we listen to God. An ounce of experience is worth more than a pound of talk and suggestion. In the armour that Saul offered there would be no easy tread. The light of the day would be shut out as this small son of Jesse went forward into battle. We are blind to some things when we are immature. He would have made a clumsy spectacle, as 'he assayed to go.' The son of Jesse couldn't run into the battle as he did when he relied on God. In that which he 'put on' he could only stumble and fall. Fighting a crisis in your own strength will make you clumsy, cramping your style. To 'put on' what God provided, he had to 'put off' what Saul suggested. In the New Testament we are advised to 'put off' the old, and to 'put on' the new. God has something new for your life. It must have its source in you, and be resourced by God.

The real armour is God's ability

The real armour was actually in David. There was no need for extras to be worn. In defeating Goliath you have a display of the youth's heart for God. Take care of your heart, be the best that God has made you, and leave the rest to the Lord. In battle, Goliath was hidden in his armour, while David came with no armour cladding. He would be seen, and known as he was known. One was encased in steel, while the other was an open book. One had no encounter with God, while David had a rich faith that was about to be revealed in his achievement. The natural armour he put on would cause the giant to fall.

When they gathered on the hills of Canaan, had David used Saul's armour then this testimony would have been 'I won this battle against the giant using another's testimony, another's sermon, and experience.' Paper roses are awful when compared with the real flower. Who wants to be as a cardboard cut out! We have all taken up an instrument at some time and pretended to play great musical pieces! In my mind I have conducted great symphonies. These are not real, they are simply pretence. It was an exercise but not an endeavour. Many of our choice moments can be thoughts without deeds.

Receiving another's suggestions, makes you feel your own wisdom is not good enough. Wearing another's battle dress makes you inferior. The borrower becomes the servant of the lender. When Israel entered the Promised Land there were those who complained that they hadn't been given enough land. The advice of Joshua was, 'You are surrounded by land, go and take more for yourself!' The heart needs enlarging to such a capacity that we don't need what has happened to others in order to fight. The heart can be so full of what God has done that there is little room for falseness! A borrowed sword or weapon must be given back to its owner. You can never claim that the victory was accomplished simply by you. The only sword required is the Sword of His Mouth, which goes forth with two sharp edges. Whatever weapons you use, axe, sword, gun, radar or missile, they must be part of the arsenal of the heart. Everything you accomplish must be through an act of faith and not the works of the flesh. All your endeavours must be acts of assurance from your salvation. What lodges in the heart by the Spirit of God is weapon enough to defeat an army of aliens. It might only appear as a stone in a sling, but it is mighty in the Lord to the pulling down of strongholds.

The real armour is within

The weaponry and the armour Saul gave to the young man were all outward, a helmet of brass and a coat of mail. The real weapons of our warfare are within, what we are and what we have accomplished in God. It is that which is hidden as the stone in the sling, or hidden in the stream, the hand and the bag. The stone was hidden until the precise moment when it would do its finest work then be lost forever in the head of a dead giant. Promises, however small, as this stone was, are there to be used. Faith was in the heart of the boy, there before, during, and after the battle. There is that which we can put on, but note, it had to be taken off. The real victory for the lad from Bethlehem-Judah was within his own heart. If you reign here, you reign everywhere. If you are not an over-comer here, you will not overcome anywhere. We all need that which moth and rust cannot corrupt and no thief can break through and steal.[6] The ornaments of faith are in the heart. It was using that which couldn't be taken off and put on that brought the victory shout. It made the trumpets of Israel blare. They heard a sound they hadn't heard for a long time. The cobwebs were removed from the mouth of the trumpet. It was the sound of the special trumpet only used when there had been a great victory. It was this trumpet that sounded the first note, as the women danced and sang about David's conquest.

The armour distinguishes between winners and losers

We don't want plastic when we can have the real. It isn't metal that wins in the battle for truth; it is men, human men. The men whose hearts God has touched and turned into flaming torches. Remember, the torch that lit all the torches along the Apian Way as the soldiers held their 'Triumph', leading into the city of Rome was kindled from a fire on the battlefield. They kept one torch burning. They wanted to return, their return being lit by the light of former victories. If this conquest were greater than any former achievement, the lights they carried would displace the lights along the Apian Way. When the first Olympiad was held the man bearing the torch lit it on the battlefield. These torches were lit from burning villages, carts and fences and wanting to carry the victory further, they lit other torches. It is not the packaging but the content that counts. We may fool friends and even those very near to us but there comes a moment in the real battles of life that we need substantial things. There is a walk and a wisdom that comes from the mind and not the heart. There is that which is in the outward form that needs to be put off. The old man and the old nature need putting on one side. We need to put on Jesus Christ. He is made unto us wisdom, righteousness and redemption.[7] These are the thoughts of a soldier who has fought as the apostle Paul fought. 'Put on the whole armour of God,' and stand. Cover and camouflage is all right but when the real firepower and challenge come, we had better be ready. Having no armour for the battle means that at the valedictory, God receives the garland of achievement.

There are times when we can not run. If we have run before the enemy, we can't run any further. The armour put on for the occasion will not stop the onslaughts of the enemy. The weight of the very thing we use, because it is not ours and we are not used to it, will hold us back. David had to learn to keep sheep and then carry bread and cheese before he could face giants. We will watch how people handle the bread and the cheese, before we determine how they will fare in *Dwarfing Giants*. There are principles learned while keeping sheep, when no one was watching, waiting to be used by the young man. The sheep-keeper will become the giant-killer.

Armour must be great enough for all situations

David had proved God in some situations but not in all. As he faced Goliath, here was a different battle. He couldn't meet it using what he was not or did not possess. You only possess what possesses you! He had to become a shepherd boy again for the occasion. Having little, wearing no armour, the Arm of God could and did protect him. 'Prove me now,' God says.[8] 'Prove me', as you would test metal. 'Go with me through every sort of heat, and see if I don't remain the same. If you are melted, it will be into another mould that I have provided. You will be melted into Me. The fire will not burn Me out.' In getting to know God you will find that all the power over the enemy is yours. What the quiver is to the arrow God will become to you. Just as that arm carried the shield of brass, God will hold you. His might and character will never bend under the strain. 'My Sword, the Word of God will never be blunt. The helmet as hope shall never grow dim. The breastplate of faith will not allow penetration. The very shoes you wear as the gospel will become a foundation for standing and will keep you all the days of your life. What I am I will always be.' This God of David's did not go down with the setting sun or go home when needed.

The Philistines, when they saw their 'champion' was dead fled. God never runs away. The Lord stays as eternal as His nature. You are part of this God. 'Go on to know the Lord.' Discover Him in prayer and praise. Make new discoveries by making every day a new mountain to climb. Be as Christopher Columbus, whose first name means 'light bearer'. Discover new worlds in God. Use what you discover to circulate the world of the spiritual.

The armour must be proved

David had not 'proved' the armour. To the shepherd, it was an unknown thing. Armour, even someone else's armour was from another world. He had his trust in the Master of the Skies. David could count sheep better than wear pretend armour. God was a known Person, and he would continue to follow God. 'Proved' means it didn't belong to him. He would not borrow for his battles. He would only take from God that which was as fresh as a flowing stream. A new battle demanded using old weapons in a new sphere. When it says 'He put his staff in his hand',[9] he had laid aside the armour offered. David was going to be his natural self. He treated this encounter with the giant as if Israel were the sheep, God was the Chief Shepherd and, working under God's direction, the great bear called Goliath would be buried as it sought to attack those sheep. Leave the trials the torments, doubts and fears in the valley.

For David it was back to original principles and first love. He took the past into the future. There is nothing like being natural for overcoming great temptations. All his triumphs had been with the staff in his hand and he would continue fighting in the same way. The armour can be the wisdom of this world. I have witnessed people who didn't know a lot of theology hold at bay those who were steeped in it. It was just like Jesus talking to the Doctors of Law in Luke's Gospel. Simplicity is a great weapon. I was once invited to play golf. Never having played before, I just whacked the ball as hard as I could. To the chagrin of my companion it disappeared down the hole! Jesse's son was continuing to do what he had been trained to do. Saul's sword must not replace the staff in his hand. You can lean on a staff, but to lean on a sword is suicide!

The son of Jesse had not 'proved' the weapons. It suggests the unfurling of a banner for all to see its colours. This is what happened in battle. The flag was unfurled for all to see. When they couldn't see their leader they simply followed the flag. Even if they couldn't hear the trumpet sound the charge they followed the unfurled flag. Through the flag being unfurled came recognition of each warring army. Each part of the pattern on the flag means something. The word 'proved' is the word translated 'tempt' in Genesis 22:1. It means to have discovered it to be true in every circumstance. Fully surrendered as a sacrifice on the altar, with every part fitting onto that altar. Decoration, and that which is put on is alright if you don't have to fight. That which is used in conflict must be personal to you. If you have proven that it works then you will use it with confidence. Some weapons fit neatly into your soul and spirit. They are like old shoes, familiar friends. These weapons that the 'Sweet Psalmist of Israel' required were not born in him, he had to be trained to use them. He had not been trained in armoury. It is wonderful to see that the challenger of the giant returns to his weapons, the stone and the sling. He had turned aside from worldly advice, even though it came from a king. It needed the future king to take and use his own weapons. If he had used Saul's weapons then the next time a battle took place, it would have been Saul wearing what David had conquered with. Old traditions, and the armour of past history are not as good as a stone dripping with water freshly baptised and ready to be used.

The most powerful weapon is your experience

There must be an ability developed to call upon the Name of the Lord. The largest and most powerful weapon anyone carries is enrichment in God. It is vital to you. Your testimonies of grace will overcome many giants. The armour and weapons must be proved. When we speak of 'proving' a thing, we are thinking of 'adventuring the foot' onto the ground for it to bear all your weight in running, jumping, dancing, skipping, and taking you backwards and forwards all the days of your life. That is 'proving' your foot. Use what you have, and don't try anything that is artificial. Don't use a peg or a wooden stump! Use what nature has provided you with and all will be well. If the horse runs well and can take you from one place to another it has been proven on that journey to be what you wanted it to be. The word 'conversation'[10] used in the New Testament suggests a full journey. Going to the market place, and travelling all the way back. It is the full circle of explanation. The full potential must be released that is in you when you take armour from others and hide behind it, there will not be full development. As you pass through the hard knocks of life, the hammer blows fix into you essentials that will never alter. You will be changed as a person, but truth remains the same. When David entered into battle he was inexperienced, but when he came out he was enabled. Your incapacity is poured into His capacity when you surrender your own ability.

Fully armoured you were destined to defeat giants

You were destined to defeat giants. Not to hear of another's conquests only, but to enter into your own. When Israel came through the River Jordan they all came into the Promised Land. You may commence your conquests stepping over stones, then onto kerbs, even going on to leaping garden gates until you leap over a wall by the help of your God. Use it or lose it! That God given ability must develop further. Wearing the armour of Saul will not develop you or David any further. The person who should be sowing seeds and gathering in the harvest will only be left clutching straws, unless he uses what he has. The testimony of the man who sows is in an empty bag when all the seed has been thrown into the field, as the testimony of triumph of Israel's son was in an empty sling.

There are things that we cannot 'prove' by smell, taste or touch. They can only become successful in use. What they are and what they represent is only seen as they are taken and used. It is as if you are using a mirror, you know it reveals your form by taking it and looking into it. David proved that the Greatest doesn't win by using second-hand armour. God never wins when you are handed something in pity. Taking from others when there are better things in you can be a 'handout' and a 'put-down'. It proves others cannot fight your battles for you. Old doctrines, no matter how good, unless they are found vested in God will not win in today's world. Victory or failure is a matter of choice. There is a world of difference between defeat and the defeated. The defeated giant became less than other men. The only largeness Goliath retained was in the size of the hole his dead body filled!

Spiritual Warfare will only be fought successfully by allowing God to put something into you. It is God making you into a full rounded person. It is to be made more of a man or a woman. It is the stretching of your personality to its full height. Let all His work of grace activate your heart so that if you enter great crisis it is overcome by the work of God in you, and not the armour you are offered. Saul's armour is for Saul, while God is for David. The shepherd lad encased in metal will not win. The shepherd's son enfolded in grace and faith will always win. With other people's weapons you will not go far. In God's provision the other side of the valley is reached and the body of the giant becomes but a stepping-stone.

Notes: -

1. I Thessalonians 5:21.
2. Romans 8:28.
3. Psalm 33:3.
4. Acts 19:14.
5. 2 Corinthians 11:3.
6. Matthew 6:19,20.
7. 1 Corinthians 1:30.
8. Malachi 3:10.
9. 1 Samuel 17:40.
10. Hebrews 13:7.
11. 2 Samuel 22:30.

Chapter

6

The Faint-Hearted

The words of encouragement spoken by Israel's youthful representative in 1 Samuel 17:32, 'Let no man's heart fail because of him,' were not the words of the proud or boastful. They were the utterances of a man's convictions. He was a leader in the making, not exulting in a past achievement, but in a present challenge. He was 'counting his chickens before the eggs hatched'. These were not the words of one returning from a great battle, these words were spoken before entering into the conflict. Others had faded and fainted away, as a leaf turning from green to brown, because of the daily challenge. The shepherd wanted to change that challenge through conflict into conquest. It is easy to say something good after an event, but we have been called to know and to say even before we enter into a dark valley. If you can speak in an assuring manner before facing the enemy at a distance you can do the same when you come face to face at close quarters. If you enter into any experience with confidence then the greatest giant in you has been overcome already. Then, you are ready for the next temptation. If the troops are well prepared and trained, then what they are at home, they will be abroad.

Your words are pence, but your deeds are pounds

David did not only speak, he practised what he preached. Men will count your words as pence, and your deeds as pounds. Your words are straw until your deeds become corn. What David said to others, he was prepared to do. The time for practise was long gone when he entered the valley. Some will say things out of fear and intimidation but not this young man, he speaks because of his faith in the Lord.

These words were spoken to assist whoever would enter into battle, seeking to assure them of a complete rout of the enemy, even before they take one step into the arena of conflict. We have in this short statement the alphabet for success in all future conflict. It is the formula made public for success. These words could have been David's opening line of a speech. If he had failed they could have been his famous last words. He could have returned and completed what he wanted to say, but he didn't, because the rest of what he wanted to utter was found in his action on the battlefield. Words are cheap, but they are very costly if it means giving your all to what you have said. He had to put his feet where his mouth was! You are the interpreter of your own words. Some speak well; yet after all the promise, they walk with a limp. There is no comparison between what they said and what they did. The test of what was said was in the next few hours. It is so easy to quote the promises of God, but how many will believe them? It would be such a pity if we only remember the shepherd turned warrior by these few utterances. We must add to them the fact that he slew a giant.

Be the same at the end as at the beginning

Bethlehem's boy was no 'turn coat'. He didn't wear his coat one way and when it didn't suit wear it another way. His coat was never turned inside out, or outside in for the grand occasion. He only had one dress, the shepherd's garb that he wore when entering the valley, and when he left it. Was this the beginning of all his writings, the Psalms and other writings attributed to David? If these few words were the beginning, then what a great commencement! Everything might have seemed dull after this battle speech, but no, wait a while and see, what he says becomes even greater. He became larger than his own words, larger than that challenge from the giant.

David was full of faith when he said 'Let no man's heart fail because of him.' Don't let circumstances melt your heart as ice in a fire. Whatever faces you, face it with the firm conviction that you have a heart that will not 'cave in'.[1] He believed, therefore he spoke that faith out of the abundance of his own heart. It is out of the abundance of the heart that the mouth speaks. If the well is deep, the waters will be pure and refreshing. People faint from exhaustion and lack of water during conflict, but the battle had not yet commenced. The very thought of facing a man the size of Goliath wilted some soldiers, men became midgets, leaders who should have been lions became frightened followers. When we 'faint' every pebble becomes a mountain we can't lift into the sling. That which is defined as small becomes tall. If it is tall then, in order to kill the giant, stand on it and reach him! That's what

David is saying. If there is optimism as treasure hidden in the heart then it will be revealed. Real pressure, as you face any foe, will squeeze out of you your thoughts and beliefs as you come to the most important part of your life. Your tongue and lips become the ready servants of fear and phobias. Under stress we say things, we really believe. A tree is not known by leaves or branches but by its fruit. Under great pressure what we are rises to the surface. We cannot hide what we believe when we are called into action. We need a battle, a temptation, to reveal the sourness or the sacredness of the human heart. As we stand to face any enemy with our own words we paint a picture with those words of our self. That which is spoken became a 'self portrait'. Others see us in our 'own' image, and after our 'own' likeness. The problem is some of us are not very good artists, and like children will we get the colours and shades mixed up.

It matters more how you say it than what is said

What the giant-slayer said was his 'maiden speech'. [2] He had done many things before and he had said much, but none were as important as these words. The troops listened to his comments, ready to receive orders. These words became his 'starting blocks', as he began his race for life. He obviously had listened to his Maker with a tuned ear. What the son of Israel said was not the babblings of a bad man or the incoherent expressions of a mad man. His convictions were being shaped into words and phrases. He spoke as one pointing out the way to a lost traveller. At this time in his life, he stood as another man of faith would stand in Jerusalem, recorded in the Acts of the Apostles, chapter 2, whose name was Peter.

There are times when it doesn't matter what is said, but here it did matter. The words were as bread to hungry hearts, as water to those thirsting for success in conflict. Are you midget, mouse or muscle quality? The words would linger in their hearts as the brave young man came closer to the giant. The Bethlehemite was not simply playing a part. There was no dressing up in a different costume for this theatre performance before the whole of the nation. He knew it was now or never! This was no poetic phrase or turn of speech, it was powerful and truthful. Words, and what we say are sometimes as important as drops of blood.

Come to every trial from a position of strength

Young David didn't want to approach the giant from a position of weakness, but of strength. As a child I used to say things to myself to give me confidence when walking along a lonely path or through a dark night. My words became as protecting angels and even the stars seemed to come down to earth to keep me company when I uttered a few words of prayer. This young man from the tribe of Judah was not going into the dark. He had light in his soul and he was going to move forward in that light. In making God his goal he was travelling towards the light. He could not face Gath's man as one quaking in his shoes and fearful. There is no evidence of him being 'tongue tied' with fear. 'Stage fright' had no stage here. If you do quake trembling, as you look temptation in the face, any pretence will drop off as you shake. Nothing fell from the beloved of God, only these lovely words formed into the victor's laurel before he entered into the onslaught. There would be those who didn't believe his words. When he slew the giant they all believed, no one doubted him. True faith is before, during and after the contest. The faith that takes you through any major difficulty must be enough to tend to you after the battle. The wonderful thing about this battle is that David had no wounds. Being fearful does not conquer fear, it multiplies it.

The best piece of armour for any other soldier to wear was to tread in the shepherd's footsteps in the words 'don't let your heart faint.' If only we can catch the spirit of what was uttered on that day. It was like a nerve pill to those who were nervous. It has been left on the pages of Holy Writ as a medicine for us to take and drink when we are about to enter our darkest moment, or face our greatest challenge. When children face examinations they can be very daunting, so daunting they want to take their mother with them! David took his Father with him!

Speak from a full heart the glories of God

The victory wasn't for the one who made the best speech. This was no Graduation Day speech, practised, polished, presented. The soldiers said nothing, they had empty hearts and heads. Within them they had nothing to cling to for hope or assurance. They were as reeds blowing in the wind-the wind of change. This was the young lad's 'acceptance speech'.[3]

The man about to challenge the superman in Goliath was not as a Roman General returning from a successful campaign travelling up the Appian Way,[4] known as the 'Queen of Roads' as scented flower petals were thrown among the crowd, and gifts given, as prisoners of war were paraded behind him. Soldiers were stationed near the chariot of the General, who had to shout the praises of the returning warrior. The son of Jesse spoke these words himself. He was no paid orator or mourner. He was the servant of the Most High. When you face a crisis you don't make a long speech. The need was so great, yet the words so few, because he wanted to reserve all his strength for the giant. Say little but do much. Don't have little to say because your heart is empty, say little because you are concentrating on the battle before you. Just a few words spoken to inspire others will suffice, something born out of your convictions. Let others remember you in flowers and not in weeds in the things you said and did! Great monuments with famous inscriptions are erected after a notable battle and victory. What the lad said was before the battle, but it was monumental!

The young man was acting as the Greeks when they introduced their 'cheer leader' to the crowd, in order to cheer some man after a great accomplishment. The Greeks knew what they were doing when a 'cheer leader' was introduced, they wanted to rouse to people to applaud greatness. There was no such thought in the heart of this giant-slayer. David, in speaking was trying to cheer the rest of the army on. This was not the Joker in the English King's palace, who was placed there to tell witty jokes in order to cheer the king when he felt down. It was the opposite with Jesse's son. He was telling winners that they were winners. The only 'joke' here was Goliath. When shepherds tried to get sheep to cross a swollen river they would sometimes lift a lamb onto their shoulder and call to the sheep to encourage them through a dangerous crossing.[5] They would shout words of encouragement not words of command, to get them to leave their safety and come to the other side. If they stayed where they were, they would die. They led the sheep from the front by their example. As one leaving home or the Bethlehem hillside, he said a few words of farewell. What he said tells us he will return! Our words do matter, for they will promote faith and strength or doom and gloom. There must be in every word a particle of God's glory, as there is in every new day dawning. Remember, Jesus Christ is called the Word of God, John 1:1. He speaks from a full heart, a heart full and overflowing with the goodness of God. The giant of Gath was large. The words of the youth of Israel were few but they dealt with a large topic-the giant of Gath!

Television programmes have those who could be termed 'cheer leaders'. They come onto the stage to warm up the people before the main event. Response must be roused. That potential within people must be set free. The hands so far apart, as far apart as continents must be brought together, to work together as they applaud. They act as one who acclimatises the audience, so they are not cold when the main artist appears. These 'cheer leaders' are lesser acts, making ready for the main event. Any preacher or public speaker will tell you of the importance of the one who is leading a meeting or service. They can either make it easy for the speaker or difficult. The words can have a calming effect or leave the listeners as a troubled sea, agitated and ready to sink as ships! For years the 'Salvation Army' has produced a magazine called 'The Battle Cry'. Let that spoken be as a trumpet blast, calling troops to go over the edge and into the unknown.

The work of the Holy Spirit is to inspire us

What the young shepherd said could describe the work of the Holy Spirit before we enter into conflict and while we are in the battle. In John chapter 16:7 He is referred to as a Comforter. He is the Paraclete. He was the Man with war experience, who had been on successful campaigns; an Orator Who was called alongside the soldiers. Those who are ready to surrender, whose hearts are so fearful they have turned white like the flag of surrender, need a prop putting under them. The Prop became the Prompter in the Paraclete. The Greeks sent for him if the army was dispirited. He was called alongside the troops to tell them of all the great battles in their history. He would remind them of their King, just as the Holy Spirit's work is to glorify Jesus Christ. Men of low spirits, whose passion and flame had diminished into a cinder had to be inspired to new and greater acts of heroism. David was fulfiling such an inspirational role. When others are passing through dark valleys and shaded areas, we are called to encourage them in the battles of life. The strong should bear the infirmities of the weak. What you say, and how you react makes you into a 'role model'. Leaders lead. If you want to know if you are a leader, look behind and see who is following. Leaders inspire! Every soldier chased a Philistine after listening to David and witnessing the conflict. Every blow against a Philistine was taken from the shepherd boy's action of swinging the sling. They acted out David in future battles.

A fire broke out in a tenement building. When the fire engine arrived they erected the ladder at the side of the building. A young fireman ascended the ladder and went into the smoke filled building. A few moments later he appeared at the top with a young child in his arms. However the fire and the smoke as he entered into the building affected him and as he stood at the edge of the building, with smoke and flames threatening to engulf both him and the child, he seemed to totter on the brink. He swayed backwards and forwards like a drunken man, he seemed to sway as if he couldn't make up his mind which way to fall. The crowd gathered below gasped. Some held their breath. Large beer-bellied men took burning cigarettes from their lips, and as they did so, the burning tobacco and the hand that held it went into suspended animation. Then someone in the crowd shouted 'Cheer him! Cheer him! The crowd cheered as if their team had scored a wining goal in the last gasp of the football match. Immediately, the young fire officer seemed to gather his strength and composure, he steadied himself, and then calmly took the young child, and began to descend the ladder. This is what David was doing when he spoke to those around him telling them not to be faint-hearted. He tightened their grip. Hands unconsciously returned to weapons and shields, as if the soldiers were puppets on strings.

You can encourage others engaged in warfare

The son of Israel wanted to cheer others into victory. His short speech would, after the battle be turned into songs of praise for him. He had to prove that it could be done then others would follow him into battle, knowing in the young combatant they had an example and a winner. There are those around you waiting for you to utter words of encouragement into their distressed souls. Words of comfort and challenge that they can take hold of as a drowning man takes hold of a plank of wood. Like Job, of whom it was said 'By my words, I have stood men on their feet.' [6]

In the word 'cheer' we have the suggestion of making the countenance glad, making the face smile, to turn a frown into a smile, and a languishing spirit into laughter. It becomes the forum for happiness. What you say can put a frown or a smile on the face of another. What is said can make men believe or become atheists! In Romans chapter 2:14-24 the writer says men blaspheme God because of those called 'believing' people. They saw how they lived, they watched them break their covenant with the Almighty, and this turned many against the Faith. What the stripling said to Saul might have put a smile on one side of some faces, but when David returned after defeating Goliath it would put a smile on the other side of the face. What could have been the midnight hour became noonday!

The valley on that day became as the 'Land of the Rising Sun'. A man about to enter a church met a friend, and simply said to him, 'Yours is the friendliest face I have seen all day, and this morning I sought the face of God!' I don't know if the man had sought the face of God, and found that is was frowning because of some failure or sin. I do know that the face of God is found in the revelation of Jesus Christ in the New Testament. Jesus is the friendly face of God. The friendliest face David saw that day was the face of the first Israelite he met after slaying this Titan. This same spirit of encouragement was in the believer who drew back the curtains after a dark night, and said, 'Good morning, good morning!'

Encouragement ministers into misery

David could have taken some of the spirit of Saul and his soldiers into himself, but he refused to do so. Who wants to sprinkle vinegar when they can diffuse scent? Listening to others would have been likened unto him taking Saul's armour. There was enough discouragement among both armies, to turn a champion into a coward. Enough pessimism to paint a yellow line down the back of the bravest soldier. Wholesome words had to be spoken to make a sick army whole. The future king didn't just look at the symptoms or speak of the danger and disaster that awaited the Israeli army. A doctor will write a prescription for a malady, this young man uttered words that would nerve every soldier and bless every saint. Wrap yourself in these words, and they will become a whole armoury to you! Listen to them, and love them because there is bravery in them. If you would do exploits, let these words be the mediation of your heart and the words of your mouth. Let what was said be as a manager or trainer to a losing team. Let this be your 'pep' talk. Read them, listen to them, then go on to win.

What you say can discourage the heart of another

What was said was so different to what happened when Israel entered into the Promised Land in Deuteronomy chapter 1:28. The spies brought back a bad report telling of all the dangers, and why they could never conquer the land, 'discouraged' the hearts of the people. What they said made the heart of the people 'melt', like the snows of Lebanon under warm sunshine. What was strong, solid and brave ran out like water from a broken vessel. A whole heart, strong, true and brave might be described as a mighty river. When we are discouraged that river runs everywhere, and loses its impact, lacking depth and direction. Who wants an eye with vision turned into tears, and making it incapable of functioning properly? What happens to the weeping eye is the opposite of that which was inspired by David, as he was about to go into battle. He spoke to those hearts that had melted, and moulded them into that which was faithful and true.

Famous athletes and sportsmen have sometimes a favourite line they quote before a competition. Those in the theatre have their own ritual they go through to help them get over 'stage nerves'. Footballers go through a ritual before entering into an important game. They even have lucky charms or a routine way of dressing to help them through the same. There was none of that in David. As far as we know he had never heard these words spoken before. He wasn't copying what another had said. This was no prayer from a prepared manuscript. It was a virgin utterance for a virgin battle because no one had ever fought with a giant of this size before. They might have told exaggerated stories of private conflicts and the size of the opponent or the beast they had wrestled with. Their stories might have seemed as wild and exaggerated as some of those stories we have heard from fishermen! This was not a private battle it was very public, with two armies and all the experts of war waiting to see what would happen. Would they have to call in the mortician for the boy challenger, or would they need wine and a song if he conquered the giant?

This was the parting of the way. Each soldier had to decide if it was true what David said, this youth who knew nothing of war. When the decision was taken, two pathways led from the Israeli camp, and only David walk on the one that led to the giant. One young man, not even a soldier, unskilled in military affairs, but schooled deeply in the affairs of the heart, believed that his destiny was in God. He must now walk the talk. It was a lonely pathway, the words he had spoken his only companions. He had no fond memories of earlier battles against any giant, only how to fight with a lion and a bear. Even Saul indecisive stayed where he was as ever. The decision to face and conquer the giant was left with the boy who had uttered the words. In a sense, the saying was being fulfiled 'Physician heal yourself.'[7] Prove to us what you have said is the truth, the whole truth and nothing but the truth. You must achieve for yourself.

Don't let any giant make you faint-hearted

The words of Israel's songster were loud and clear as a bell on a Sunday morning in rural England. 'Let no man's heart fail him because of this giant.' David carefully chooses his words. Even before the battle commenced, he reduced the giant to size by referring to Goliath as 'him'. 'Let no man's heart fail because of 'him'.' He was just another man, just another soldier among many. The lad proved that Goliath was so weak and puny: he couldn't even wrestle with a pebble.

Generals, when facing great battles have made great speeches. Presidents and Prime Ministers have done the same. Who can forget the Gettysburg Address given by President Abraham Lincoln of the United States of America! The words of Sir Winston Churchill's radio speeches during the time of England's conflict with Germany during the 1940 war. What David said was short, sure and simple. A few words about the heart from the heart of a young assailant. It was not to the head he spoke, but to the heart. It was heart language, spoken in the Mother Tongue of a Hebrew young man. It would appeal to every listener. A few words as the small loaves and fish that Jesus took and divided among so many, yet all were filled, with much left over.

'Let no man's heart fail'. When David uses that key word, 'fail' he is telling Israel and anyone reading this story in the Bible, not to be afraid. If I can do it, and I am but a boy, you full grown man or woman can. The word 'cannot' was not in his dictionary. No brain cell would accommodate it. The word 'faint' is used of anything that cannot bear the trial. It is the opposite to that which is real. It is feigned having been put on, and which can easily drop off. The young orator is appealing for reality in battles and warfare. The apostle Paul makes an appeal to young Timothy for 'unfeigned faith,' faith that is not covered up, and for excuses not to be made.

Challenge that which causes fainting fits

When we begin to faint, we can enter into regular 'fainting fits'. Any challenge, anything we don't want to face, we simply faint. Fainting knocks you off your feet, and you don't know where you are going to fall. It leaves you as a bundle on the ground. It arrests you, and makes you inactive. Trust in the living God was the cure for it. The word 'faint' is found in the word 'fall'. Don't fall to the ground as something lost from a pocket. Don't fall before the giant. Save your falling as you fall before your Master in worship. Do not give credence to that which is described as but a noise. Don't fall as a broken cup from its handle, to be smashed into uselessness. If you fall like this in fainting, then you fall as the giant fell. Learn this, one small stone used in God can trip up a giant! In I Samuel 4:18 this same Hebrew word *naphal*, which is translated 'faint', describes some one falling into a ditch. It is a picture of a horse and a rider in a battle. Suddenly the lance strikes the soldier and he 'falls' from his horse. Psalm 7:16 describes one falling into a snare. The same Hebrew word *naphal* describes a house decaying in Amos 9:11. It gives us an insight to someone falling sick in Exodus 21:18,19. It even is descriptive of an abortion, of a life being wasted into nothing.[8]

You become unbalanced when fear or unbelief is put on one side of the scales. Fainting means lying down, giving up, to be defeated before you even start. What is said can become as hoops of steel around you as you enter into a battle. Sometimes the giant isn't at the other end of the valley it is in you. It stands right where you are, as Saul stood next to David. What you overcome where you are, you overcome anywhere. That which is dealt with in the dark can also be overcome in the day.

Believe what you say, and say what you believe

Only the future king believed what he said. He alone was willing to venture on these words. The hurdle to be overcome was a large one, but God was larger and greater. This prince had far more to gain than lose. There were those who thought he could never win. The young lad thought he could not lose. You can meet with any temptation, and if you meet it with doubt, you will never win. If you can meet it with a stout heart then you cannot lose. There is far more for you than is arrayed against. The only way for Israel's youth to win others to his side to fight with him against the Philistines was to defeat the giant. In doing what he did, he was proving what he had said. His heart did not faint, falter or flicker. His words became larger than any giant. The sound of them was the trumpet call before the battle commenced. David stood as Minerva, the goddess of victory, seen with the shield by her side, and victory held high in her hands. Walking through the valley of Elah, if your heart does not faint you will be seen *Dwarfing Giants*.

Notes: -

1. Luke 18:1, the word 'faint' means to 'cave in'.
2. The first speech given by a member of the British Parliament.
3. Usually made after being elected to Office.
4. The main road going into Rome, that returning Generals travelled after a victorious campaign.
5. See author's book *Paths of Righteousness in Psalm 23*.
6. Job 29:8.
7. Luke 4:23.
8. See *Gesenius' Hebrew- Chaldee Lexicon of the Old Testament*. Published by Baker Book House.

Chapter

7

The Blood Boundary

The man of Bethlehem met with the man of Gath at *Shochoh*, an area which belonged to the tribe of Judah. The armies of Israel had erected their tents between *Shochoh* and *Azekah*. There was a small piece of land between the two named *Ephes-dammim*, meaning the 'place of blood'.[1] That is where David was stationed before he went to face the mound of flesh in the valley. This area became known as the 'blood boundary'. It immediately suggested the place of offering and sacrifice. It was probably where offerings were taken and slain, and their blood offered as part of the sacrifice. In the name of the place *Ephes-dammim* something had been 'cut off' which is a description of the crucifying of Jesus Christ.[2] From that which was severed or cut off, the young shepherd was moving to a place of healing and conquering. We too, with the knowledge of the One Who was 'cut off' from His Father that we might be reconciled to God, can see great achievements. Jesus was 'cut off' that you might be brought back to God, from Whom you were severed because of sin. It is called reconciliation. He gave up His place for you, that you might take His place and authority, and use it in your ministry of *Dwarfing Giants*.

We must challenge temptation from a place of strength, not weakness

David came to attack Goliath from a place that suggests the power of the blood. It had a boundary and a history that dealt with the shedding of blood without which there is no remission for sins. What the Lord Jesus Christ did when He died on the cross at Calvary is so important. This is your authority over evil and every temptation. Not all distresses are the size of a giant some are as small as a pebble or small as a piece of grit. Whether your predicament is large or small doesn't matter. One drop of blood answers to every assault. Every onslaught is to help you to become salt. Through His victory, we can have the victory when facing a giant in the valley. We can come against all the powers of darkness with that blood as our starting point. It is the finishing point for any evil. In the Lord's Prayer, Jesus spoke the words

'Deliver us from 'evil", i.e. the 'Evil One'.[3] There is destiny and deliverance in the power and reign of the blood of Jesus. Within the circle inside the 'blood boundary', there is a King waiting to be crowned. He is David's Greater Son. When we realise the full significance of the blood of Christ, we operate, not from a place of weakness, but of strength. From the cross, we cross out all that would cross us out. From the circle of blood, even from one drop, we advance to accomplish what has been started in *Ephes-dammim*. It was here that deserting troops heard the trumpet call and assembled to receive their weapons of war. Here they received their orders in new commands. If there was to be a victory it would commence here, and not simply on the battlefield. That blood is the source of all our victories. The 'blood boundary' means Satan can only come as far as we let him. Each drop of blood is the footprint of God. In that blood the sacrifice which was offered lives on. David must take its power even into the valley. If we live in that place spiritually, as David did geographically, then there is a circle drawn around us, put there by the One who has a circular crown on His head. We must take the power of the blood of Christ into the world. It will produce not one champion but many. 'They over came him by the word of their testimony, and the blood of the Lamb,' Revelation 12:11.

The youth came from the place of authority with authority. What Jesus did when He conquered all the powers of hell and earth, we are able to do. One drop of blood is enough to conquer all the armies of aliens arrayed against the believer. We do not come in our own strength, we come in the power and might of what He has already accomplished. The commencement of the crown, throne, kingdom, and the building of character, began with that which means 'the circle of blood'. If the future ruler of Israel had come from any other place, he might have failed. Here his plans were formed for the future. Victory commenced here, before it was taken into the dust of the valley. From this place came the power and plan for a new attack against evil, carried out with an army of one!

The sacrifice of Christ is our guarantee

The son of Jesse came after a sacrifice had been made, and the blood of the victim had flowed. Jesse's son came into the battle having already died to his own will and ambition. You can't kill a dead man. You might put him in a coffin and bury him, but you can't kill him because he is dead already. When conducting a funeral we are only dealing with the after effects of death. When we come against any temptation through the blood of God's Son, Jesus Christ, then we are on sure ground, and guaranteed a victory. When we fight in our own strength, we do not win. We become losers when we might have been winners. From the stench of sweat and battle, there came the aroma of a new victory. As each received a burnished sword and a polished shield that had been freshly anointed, along with bow and arrows, so from the blood of Christ we are armed. We are made strong enough to pull down strongholds. The hand of Jesus was nailed to a Roman gibbet; every other grip holding you in bondage must be loosed. That which is snatched from you must be returned, for the Day of Jubilee has come. There must be a starting point, a first step, and the moment of decision that you are going to win. When we read in the gospels what Jesus did on the cross, it makes victory a lot easier. The impossible becomes the possible. Spend time here; get to know God before going into battle, it will help you in future fights. After being here, each soldier was refreshed. They found their new rank and place in the army.

There is power to release you from captivity

John Trapp the Puritan preacher says, commenting on 1 Samuel 17:23 'The Philistine of Gath, Goliath by name which signifies captivity.'[4] The power of the blood of Christ is revealed in that it enables the believer to overcome all captivity, and to bring into that realm of captivity every evil imagination. It is not captivity to another but captivity to God. In being made a captive we are set free. When we fall in love with Christ, that love embraces us to set us free. The hand that holds the knife sets it free to cut and shape. It finds its ministry and usefulness in the hand that holds it. We are as a bird taken out of a snare, set free to fly in our native element. When temptation seems to close around you as a hand on a sponge to squeeze the very life out of you, as you mention the power of the blood, the hand slackens, and you are set free. It is the blood of Christ that unlocks all the treasure of truth. It is the Master's key, and the master key to anything you face. There will always be those things that will snare the soul and limit you, but as you do what David did, then you will conquer just like as he did. He might have appeared to be going into battle restricted, particularly when he tried to wear Saul's armour, but there was freedom to be himself here as nowhere else. It is the blood of Christ that paints the best and most accurate portrait of you, setting you in the most favourable light. This blood is better than all the weapons of war.

When Israel was brought out of Egypt, the 'House of Bondage', they had to take a sucking lamb and kill it.[5] Then they took hyssop, dipped it in that blood and then applied it to the lintel of the doorpost of their own home. When the Angel of Death passed through the land, smiting every firstborn child of the Egyptians, the Israeli houses were spared, because the blood had been applied to the cross member of the door. It was victory from within. The blood of the lamb acted as a cover. They had to 'strike' the blood against the doorpost so they might not be struck by the angel of death. This brought Israel out of bondage, into a new life in God, and into the Promised Land.

The blood in Exodus 12 is spoken of as a 'token'. It was a sign. That word 'token' is translated elsewhere 'flag' and 'beacon'.[6] We fight under this blood stained banner, and by the light of this beacon. Into the dark depths of the valley of shadows, and into every cave the light of the beacon must go. With the flame on the beacon you are able to ignite every other flame. It is as we walk in the light that the blood of God's Son, Jesus Christ cleanses (keeps cleansing) us from all sin. It was blood that brought them out to see the miracles, but it was their own self-will that took them into a wilderness for forty years.

New dimensions can take the place of restrictions.

The blood of the offering brought Israel into new dimensions of the power of God. The Red Sea was parted; the rock was split open in order that water could pour from it. The quails and the manna were sent into the camp to feed them.[7] Even their clothes did not wear out. It all stemmed from the blood being applied. Here, David was taking his stand on land that belonged to the tribe of Judah. That which means the 'blood boundary' would lead Israel as a nation into new freedom, out of bondage to the Philistines. They would be as free as sheep coming in and going out of new pasture, led by the shepherd and not fearing any wolf. It is amazing that from such an obscure area the future king emerged as some new creation from its shell. What the caterpillar calls death and the end, God calls a butterfly. David came out, before and after the battle as a beautiful flower emerging from a o,dﬔ f lud, folded leaf and withered stem. One drop of blood can release us from a giant, if we venture in faith. In 'Pilgrim's Progress', when Christian went into the castle of Giant Despair, the giant took hold of him, and was about to defeat him. He was locked up and imprisoned. Christian then wrestled the Key of Promise from his pocket, and was able to put it into the door lock of Doubting Castle. The door opened, and he made his escape.[8] Victory for you is to take the work and words from the cross, and let them work in your life. What David accomplished was private before it was public. It was witnessed in the valley before it was attested in the palace.

Your acceptance is not based on works

The surest place in the world is Calvary, where Jesus died. It assures us of a new life and victory wherever we are. The lad conquered, coming from the area of bloodshed and sacrifice offered. It was from the history of Israel. It had all happened in the past. David had nothing to do with that which suggested the 'blood shed'. All that happened to him, and how God helped in the battle was from this small place. The first step may be small, but it was a large step for Israel when David placed his foot on the head of the giant. Among Arabs the greatest insult is to hit another on the face with the sole of your shoe. David put his foot on the giant, putting all his weight onto the head of his challenger. The giant who had 'walked all over' Israel was now being 'walked all over', as David stood on Goliath's head. In fact all had been a 'walk over' for him in the conflict. The head of the man from Gath became the pillar for their future, and they began to build upon it. Very few are able to build a victory on a defeat, but Israel did.

When Israel's champion stepped forward, he was to be the living sacrifice offered on the altar of Elah. The valley became the altar, the place of offering. He was thrown as a piece of meat to a lion, named Goliath. God didn't close the mouth of this lion as He did with Daniel. He hit him in the head! David offered himself, not as Israel's substitute to this Titan, in his heart he was offering himself to God. It was not an offering of bits and pieces, something today, and a little later on. God never wants our bits and pieces He requires our all. The conflict demanded that they gave their all, just as the animal did when being sacrificed. God loves those acts of sacrifice telling of the fullness of honour and determination, love and devotion, because they are the shadow of God's substance. We need to be as a stone in the sling in our deep relationship with God. Every step David took was a walk with his Master of every situation. That which was pleasing to God, needed saving and was taken for future use in establishing a kingdom that would last forever. Where you are victorious, there the rule of God is ushered in. You become the answer to the Lord's Prayer 'Let your kingdom come.'

The only limitations are in you

The armies came together at *Shochoh*, meaning that which is 'shut in', fenced about and limited.[9] All your talents can be buried if you accept limitations. There was no way out, only through. The only way through the valley was to unhinge the huge door in the form of a giant standing menacingly at the other end. Anything blocking your view of God and the way out needs defeating. Blurred and barred vision needs re-focussing. Anything resisting you so that you cannot get to the throne or into your future requires killing. That giant the real temptation must not become the altar on which your life is offered in defeat. From that place of limitation, the 'blood boundary' would bring them into the freedom of roaming again throughout the Promised Land. It would be life lived without the daily challenge of the giant. That haunting voice had been the trumpet call to Israel.

When the apostle Peter was shut up in prison the saints prayed for him and the prison doors opened of their 'own accord'.[10] They opened 'automatically'. It is from the words 'own accord' that we obtain the English word 'automatic'. Any modern equipment described as 'automatic' comes from this Greek word 'automatos', 'of its own accord'. In Acts chapter 1:4,13,14 they had gathered 'with one accord' and from that oneness the doors opened of their 'own accord'. Miracles still happen to help us overcome our greatest enemies.

The shepherd's heart would return to shepherding, as he had done in the past. God never intended them to be bogged down in one small place. That which is made for the skies cannot be fenced in with wooden railings. The branches and perches must not limit a flying bird. Even the sheep pen is only for a time before they are set free to graze under the open face of the sun. The bondage here suggests that which is entwined, as if a rope of vine had been placed around a man and he couldn't obtain freedom until he came to the 'place of blood'. It was a limited freedom, the freedom of the horse at the end of a piece of rope, until Goliath was slain. Then it became the freedom of life. Goliath, using fear and intimidation had bound the army of Israel hand and foot. With their feet tied and their hearts limited they could not walk with God. From the Hebrew root word *suwk* comes the word *Shochoh*, found in 1 Samuel 17:1. The root word describes the way being stopped up before a person. They can go no further, they have reached their limitation. Once the giant was defeated there were no limits to where any child in Israel might go. Some would go back home, others would continue with Saul, but David would continue with his Lord. Yours is a journey, it is the Christian way that you are travelling. Be free to travel the whole road, and not just part. Get to Heaven having fully travelled the whole of the Christian way. Let there be such a depth about your experience in God that is unlimited. Have 'check points', where you can assess how far you have travelled in and with God. The Lord, as a time of preparation, uses some of the things we suffer deeply, just as the winter months prepare for the spring days, or the dark night prepares us for the light of a new day. The giant prepared them for the journey ahead that would contain many giants.

There is a panacea for all our pain

The army of Israel and the place that David came to defeat Goliath was between *Shochoh* and *Azekah*.[11] *Azekah* means that which is 'tilled like a field'. There has been a turning this way and that way. The soil is turned to let light into it, and this is the very reason we sometimes suffer. It is as if the plough blade has gone through it. It might suggest pain and deep hurt, just as it did when Jesus Christ gave His back to the smiters. Fields, as your faith, need to produce a crop. Every field is the farmer's and the shepherd's deposit box. When life has become a cutting place and we have been damaged we can go on to the next stage, which is one of sowing and reaping. Some of the things we suffer deeply are to prepare the clay for the Potter. There was nothing built upon it or planted in it until the servant of Saul defeated the opposition. God prepares the heart for sowing. It is then we need to dwell in the next place suggestive of blood given and shed. This place *Azekah* was just a field dug over with no sowing of seed, and no possibility of a harvest until David came through it. If you plant seeds, you will sow trust in the living God, and then reap a noble harvest. If you plant one seed it will develop grain and from that one ear of corn many fields can be sown. Find a nut on the side of the pathway, plant it, and give a future generation a forest to play in. This is what the man of Judah did when defeating the giant standing before him. It was when the young champion moved from one place to another that true liberty as a son of Israel was found. He has left you an example to follow, and footsteps for you to walk in so that you might overcome that evil arrayed against you. That ploughed field must be taken and used. Do not bury your ability here, mistaking the plough blade and the field for the real giant. There is no return pathway across a ploughed field. In the Old Testament the ploughing of a field was the final act of a bandit after the city was taken. It was done so that you might not thrive again. It describes our word 'bankrupt' meaning 'a broken bench'. When the field was ploughed, it suggested that you no longer existed you had been wiped off the face of the earth. In the New Testament the ploughing of the field was a metaphor for discipleship, Luke 9:62. That is only part of the story, because through ploughing, suffering and sowing, character can emerge in all the fullness of the glory of God.

There is power to produce something new

Had not God promised Israel a land flowing with milk and honey?[12] Where had those large grapes of Eschol gone? The milk had curdled, the honey had ceased, and the grapes had withered. The Gath man, along with the other Philistines, had stolen the benefits of the Promised Land. They had gleaned all the grapes, milked all the cows, and taken all the honey. They had sucked the promise dry. What had been ushered in through conquering had retreated from Israel. David wasn't here just to touch up the painting and make it look better. He was in the battle to defeat all things. He wanted to put the Name of God back into the land of Israel and into the hearts of the people, that they might speak it, know it, and see the power of God at work. That field, the location called *Azekah* must not be left as it was found. Faith, hope, victory, virtue, gladness, achievement, and the glory of God must all be sown in the tilled soil of the heart of every believer in Jesus Christ, until it brings forth abundantly.

There were many things that the future king discovered as he moved through each area. Note he did not just pass through *Ephes-dammim* he dwelt in it. Maybe he prayed here before he went into battle? That morning, the beloved of God, the man who was not only after God's heart but was the very heart-beat of God, came out from that place which suggests the 'place of the blood', to conquer the largest enemy that Israel had ever faced. Although it was known as the 'blood boundary', he did not know any limitations. The limitations and the boundary of evil commenced here. New frontiers would become his as he stepped forward with hope as a song in his heart.

All other powers can be limited by God's power

Here was the Red Sea and the River Jordan in another shape- giant shaped and giant-sized. The walls of Jericho were in the person of the Gathite. In that giant was the rock that had to be split so that water might gush from it, and the whole of Israel might be refreshed through such a great victory. This place was the *amarantos*, the name of a Greek flower. They are called *amarantos* because their petals never fade; they keep their shape, unlike other flowers retaining to the end much of their deep red colour. They became known as 'Love-lies-bleeding'. Typical of the saviour's death and the giving of His blood, as He yielded up His life for you. Hebrews chapter 1:12, reminds us that He does not change and as a garment He cannot be folded up. The blood of Christ is part of the Everlasting Covenant. Ten million years from now its power will not have diminished, withered or faded. It will be the same yesterday, today, tomorrow.

The blood and the cross of Christ work together

Israel then moved into the valley of *Elah*, where the battle was to be fought, and where Goliath daily challenged them. *Elah* is mentioned three times in 1 Samuel, 17:2,19; 21:9. *Elah*, suggesting the 'place of the tree', where it grows and matures sending out its branches for refuge. A tree in a valley where the armies met to decide the outcome of a war provided shade before they entered into battle as hot as the midday sun. The fullness of refuge is found here, as we see what David accomplished. The apostles Peter and Paul refer to the cross of Jesus Christ as a 'tree'.[13] From the cross, because of the cross, and under the cross of Jesus Christ we rise to prevail. It was and is the place of strength and growth. That growth can only be possible if the large mound of flesh at the end of the valley can be defeated. As the other youths of the day walked in the light and the smile of David's accomplishment, so as we walk in the light, the blood of God's Son, Jesus Christ, cleanses us from all sin. Our starting line and finishing mark is the cross of Christ. It will always accomplish what both the stone and the sling did. All the fruits of the tree called the cross are in our attempts at victory and achieving our objectives. Victory has a sweeter taste than any natural fruit from a tree.

Youthful desire will always win

The young boy did not come out to fight as the lion or the bear that had been overcome; he came out as a boy trusting in the living God. Blood bought and blood based victories are lasting accomplishments. He had just a pebble and a sling, but he had come through the 'blood area', and on to victory.

There were marvellous discoveries for the shepherd because of his association with *Ephes-dammim*, 'the blood circle'. There was the discovery of new armour from Goliath. A sword and a shield were his, not given to him, but won in battle. The best weapons are those taken in war. The greatest weapon you will ever possess is called experience. The greatest testimonies are those of trial and triumph. There was new weaponry here. God didn't expect the youth to continue to use the sling and stone in the future. A different weapon, a new approach was required in the next fight. God won the battle this time, but next time David must play a greater part. After the battle and victory he obtained more substantial weapons from the dead body of the slain. The power of God was seen in this area. God proved that He ruled here also. The Lord across the battle line is the same in the sunshine.

The first recruit of a new army that would trust the Sovereign Lord was seen on parade in the teenager. This was the beginning of the new David, not as a youth, or a stripling or a shepherd boy, but as a servant and a king. The faith he exhibited saved him from many things. The logistics of war were not to be dealt with by the lad. He didn't have to count soldiers as he had counted sheep. Was there enough food and water to last another day? There would be no need to care for the wounded and the dying. He didn't have to see that every man was armed, and knew how to keep rank. He was spared all these normal tributaries of war. The only one who had a headache was Goliath. While one lost his head, David kept his.

The boy-warrior discovered that life is more than bread and cheese. There must be some 'pebble' about it. If you are going to be a success, there are some things you must 'sling'. There are substantial things that the Lord needs to add to you, and He does it because of and through the blood of Christ.

Each trial and temptation presents a new exploit

Because of *Ephes-dammim* a line was drawn in the dust of the valley, stating that the Philistines had gone far enough and would be allowed no further. That line became a furrow or a grave into which the Philistines were pushed as they died. When you draw a line under anything, you do it to aid memory and for emphases, lest we forget. It wasn't the least line of resistance or appeasement that was drawn.

Mum's shopping list always had certain items underlined to remind us not to forget. When that line is drawn, you are going to write on it the new exploits you are going to attempt. It is the beginning of a new page and chapter, a new chapter in your life. Start with a line then at least you will know that you have started. Drawing a line, you are making a statement. When the line runs through it then it is finished; it is as a debt cancelled. Here, I intend to build, and start again. Where the line is drawn over, and through failure, disappointment and remorse, the glory of God begins to appear as seeds sown in the furrow of the line drawn. It was here that the decision was taken to fight to the death. In that valley one act was the defeat of a whole army. When Jesus Christ died on a cross, every sin and temptation was dealt the deathblow. Draw a line under your past and one through your sin with the blood of Jesus Christ. From the finish of that line begin a new future without the taunts of terror. Leave everything in the valley belonging to your despondency.

Strongholds can be toppled, can fall as flat as a pancake at the feet. These feet wanted to journey on as they followed the Lord into the next phase of the battle of life. Jesus drew in the sand when a woman taken in the act of adultery was brought before him.[14] He did this to suggest that she could begin to live a new life, commencing with the hand and person of Jesus Christ. She could start again with the finger of God. As that hand opened to draw the line, it covered all her sin. Jesus was saying 'Let me re-write all your life. I can remove the mistakes, the blots, and turn what has been a blank into a blessing.'

David had proved himself to be as the *Iphicratensians*- the best trained and the bravest of the Greek soldiers. They were named after their General, *Iphicrates*, an Athenian leader, who had a reputation as a fighter and a winner. David of Bethlehem before, during and after the contest was truly a 'merry man', not as one who has been drinking alcohol, but suggesting those who are fully trained, the bravest of all. Gallant soldiers were called 'merry men'. 'Merry weather' described a strong stiff wind. It is that which performed well in what it was designed to do. We think of exploits in English history and folklore of Robin Hood and his 'merry men'. Those who came to David in the cave of Adullam became known as David's 'merry men'.[15] He brought them to Adullam meaning a 'resting place'. It was in that rest that shepherds were turned into soldiers, peasants became pioneers. Men were discovered there who had kingdom ministries. In the shadow of their king, they found their true substance.

This youthful boy did all these things as he dwarfed a giant. They are written for our learning and admonition. We come to conquer when we come through the place of offering, sacrifice and blood. We must get to the other side of the valley and to future mountaintops. We can do it, as David did, by letting God's agenda become ours. The sibling fulfiled the old adage 'He who fears scars should not go to war.'

Every soldier after this battle stood in 'abeyance'-used of men standing with their mouths wide open in expectation of a sight about to appear. They knew only one person would return from this battle. David was coming out of the valley, but was he being chased? No, he was walking as a shepherd leading sheep. He did not come out running, but as one carrying a victory in his deportment. He came out of this combat with far more than he possessed when he went into battle. As they saw this, and as we read it, we say with them 'Now are we the sons of God, as we *Dwarf Giants*.'

Notes: -

1. 1 Samuel 17:1. See *Gesenius' Hebrew-Chaldee Lexicon.*
   Dr. James Strong Exhaustive Concordance. Barnes commentary
   on the Old Testament. Fausset's Bible Dictionary.
2. Isaiah 53:8.
3. Luke 11:4.
4. *John Trapp's Old Testament Commentary.*
5. Exodus chapter 12.
6. *Dr.James Strong, Hebrew Lexicon of the Old Testament Hebrew.*
7. The Book of Exodus.
8. *Pilgrims Progress. A Christian allegory,* written by John Bunyan
   while he was in prison.
9. 1 Samuel 17:1.
10. Acts 12:5,10.
11. 1 Samuel 17:1.
12. Exodus 3:8, 17; 13: 5; 33:3.
13. 1 Peter 2:24. Galatians 3:13. Acts 5:30; 10:39; 13:29.
14. John 8:3.
15. 1 Samuel 22:1.

Chapter

8

The Speaking of Your Faith

Varieties as the spice of life are soon recognised by the believer as those things arranged by Divine acts, and are well planned by God. Only God in His planning can square the circle or circle the square. These 'happenings' as we refer to them are so woven together, they form multiple patterns and are really the plans of God, conceived by the Almighty and appear to be as natural as forming part of the landscape. There is no such thing as a coincidence. The shepherd boy's victory over this Hercules was well planned and exquisitely executed. Coincidence and chance become the Sovereign's tools for changing an outlook. As He does He is able to change us until we begin to see as He sees, and to hear as He hears. Not a bird is disturbed, not a leaf flutters, but God is at work! What we see in part, God sees as the whole. It is of little use asking the trowel or the spade what is being erected or what the plans are to build; you must consult the architect. What appears as bits and pieces are really part of the whole. To David, the full picture and the final sentence are not uttered at the beginning of the battle, nor are they seen or heard during warfare, they are fully demonstrated through his faith at the end. The end is but the beginning to those who trust. When the Eternal opens His hand, it is to reveal a plan for your life written on His palm.

Faith sees and speaks of God's plan

In our lives, as God plans, it almost seems as if He is moving house. He brings in the furniture, some of it new, some antique. The sling had been used so often in the past. The stone might have been used as part of a game, and then tossed into the stream to be forgotten. It might have fallen from a hole in the shepherd's dress. When God makes arrangements, you can be sure that all is put in its proper place, and everything is brought in at the right time. God never re-organises anything. He makes all things possible, and in that possible, He makes all things new. The areas that are dark and need more light, that light is diffused into effulgence. Where other areas need specialist's attention, God works as the Carpenter of Nazareth or as the One who multiplies bread and fish. He is working in this battle before, behind and above the giant-slayer. When we have the faith of David and face Goliath, whatever is required, be it only a stone and a sling, God will lead us to the right weapons for victory. In the area where God is operating the weapons are prepared before we ever enter into conflict. Whatever stage of faith we have come to, the Master is still fitting pieces together, just as much as when Jesus put wheel to axle in the carpenter's shop at Nazareth. If you only tell part of the story of this conflict between large and small, you might tell the wrong part. Until the whole is fitted into place there can never be completion. For the King of Israel, it commences with a tricking brook followed by the putting of a stone into a sling. It progressed from there, but can you see how God added what was necessary for the occasion?[1] That article under surveillance and the Master's hand can never be used until that which is needed is added to make it complete. In the battle with the giant all things were made to 'work together for good',[2] because God was arranging it David trusted those arrangements, believing everything would result in success in the *Dwarfing of Giants*. When you have done all you can leave it with Jehovah.

Faith sees victory in battle

David is facing Goliath. This is not simply the stroke of an artist's paintbrush. The paint isn't scraped from the palate onto the canvass as he wills. The battle between David and Goliath is not arranged at the caprice of a fallen king. The Israelites and the Philistines may feel they have arranged this encounter of good against evil, but God has been moving the pawns in many directions. Every part of the puzzle has a Hand placed on it, so that the shepherd boy's faith might be spoken as he advances towards the man built like a mountain. It is not simply a young boy and a giant, but it is a battle of evil and good. Light and darkness are confronting each other as wrestlers, but there is only one winner! That which is allowed by God in giant form is meant to bring such utterances of faith from the lips of the future King of Israel. That reliance in a mere boy was larger than the tallest mountain in Israel.

When he speaks, it has long been decided in his heart. There was the communication of conviction, and that conviction would lead to commitment. What the mouth says is the over-spill from a full heart. Faith uses his lips as a dancing platform to perform its best before man and God.

That trust puts strength into David, fear into Goliath, and admiration into every Israeli soldier who watches the battle. David spoke his faith before he acted it out. It wasn't simply words or an uncertain sound as from a trumpet. These were not well-learned and well-worn phrases from a Shakespearean play. They were the passionate outburst from a heart in love with God. If David and the family of Jesse were to have a future, that future must be built in this valley, and it must be structured by faith. Here, the foundation of a future kingdom was laid by faith. Believing the Master will always bring that which threatens you down to your own level of understanding and obedience. Jehovah meets us where we are. On your knees praying and believing, He will meet you there.

Faith gives you something worth saying

God always gives those who believe Him something to say and something worth listening to. It is not only worth listening to, but worth repeating and using in future dark days. Every listening ear received those words of David as he approached his tormentor. 'I come against you in the name of the Lord!'[3] What David said at this time would echo along the corridors of the palace, right down the ages to remind him of the greatness of God in adverse times. There were those gathered around that belonged to Israel, who were operating in defeat and hearing what the youth said, would go on to achieve. When the king went into battle in the future he would rehearse the words of faith he spoke to Goliath of Gath on this memorable day. Great words and acts of faith are the children not just of a day but also of eternity. They have God as their Father. These words spoken were not as adopted children, but as those born within the family. There was room in the shepherd's heart for them.

Faith takes you into another, higher realm

The battle demanded faith of a higher order than the ability just to count sheep, go through a dark, shadowy night or trust God for a sunny day. It enabled the shepherd to move the sheep to new pastures. He required more than a sweet song by a stream to conquer the giant. Sometimes faithfulness is mixed up with faith. It was faithfulness that took the young stripling into battle and into the valley but it was faith that brought him to *Dwarfing Giants*. True faith brought him through to the other side of the valley of Elah. You might sing the 'blues' away, but not this huge Philistine bent on crushing you with one hand. This faith was not whistling in the dark. It could never be the barking of a dog at a mere shadow. There was no hope that things would get better apart from resting on God. The giant is so big, and David is so small, it demands that he needs the help of God. The order must be reversed. The *giant* must be *dwarfed* and the *dwarf* must be turned into a *giant*. It meant the young shepherd boy leaning on God, placing all his weight on Him, just as he had from day to day leaned on his own staff. When this same man writing in the Psalms speaks of 'trusting', the Hebrew word for 'trust' suggests rolling onto a bed and lying there,[4] putting all your weight on God.

Faith must baptise your words and works

This faith was not a matter of noise or words. It was the utterance of words that had first been baptised in faith. It was not naked truth, it was truth with the tunic of faith. The words spoken were used as a sword with four cutting edges. We can believe God with the assurance of stillness and quietness, as we can shout the Name of the Lord when we enter into battle. David had to believe God, as we have read in an earlier chapter, in the uncertain and the unknown.

When attacked by both lion and bear, probably when alone with the sheep he still trusted. The Lord so arranged the battle that the only thing for the lad to do was to rely. He believed what he trusted into receiving and being. It is in the unseen, the quiet moments, those times that are not seen as spectacular, that faith is developed until it is bigger than any Philistine army of giants. It had to be deeper than the valley he was passing through. It takes the same faith to conquer any Goliath as it takes to believe God to supply one pound.

Faith follows the plan of God

In a moment of crisis when you are facing the 'giant' things of life, what you really believe will not only be uttered, it will be effective. The shout, shine and the show will go together. You must be prepared to live for what you believe, and also die for it. By life or by death the Lord would be glorified, not in some magnificent way of riding into battle, as kings do, He came in on a pebble. Your faith will become an act. If David had never placed the stone into the sling there would have been no *Dwarfed Giant*. You must do your part and then God performs what He has promised. What I do in faith opens the door for all other things to come from God. As Noah opened the door of the ark many animals of all shapes and sizes entered and became his companions. In the moment of crises the human voice is capable of shouting so loud that is can shatter a drinking glass or smash a window. If your faith is weak, that shout might frighten the dog next door, but not the giant in your garden or heart. It wasn't just a shout, it was a command. Under the inspiration of the Holy Spirit you can reach octaves that have never been recognised by musicians! I knew of one lady who, to reach the high notes when singing, used to stand on her tiptoes. Faith spoken makes you just as tall as the rest. Goliath is hiding the throne that the son of Israel must be seated upon. David used God as a foundation and stepping-stone. When the Holy Spirit takes hold of our spirit we are capable of great utterances. When they asked Handel where he obtained the words for 'The Messiah', he used to point to the sky. We say and it happens. We can command, and it stands fast. Temptation can only go as far as we allow. What has been placed on the stage of your heart will be visible in order to display a confident faith in God. There needed to be such an impact and God arranged it so that two armies were watching Jesse's son at this time. It would make such an impression upon them.

Faith will always accomplish what others only think of doing

There was a movement in David's life when he moved from thinking to saying, to believing and doing. Many soldiers thought God might be able to help them, some freely discussed it, but while they were debating, putting their uniforms in place and sharpening their swords for a conventional attack, David was already running through the valley. While others were putting on their shoes, David was resting his feet on the head of the slain giant.[5] All the armoured men gathered in the valley of Elah thought God could deliver Israel, but only the son of Jesse did it! He had visions of conquest before he entered into combat. He slept, breathed and ate faith. The person who feeds on faith becomes strong. The man who knows valedictory before he takes one step, is sure.

Faith and works became his sword and spear. Faith turns thought into act, and act into facts. Faith births truth even out of fiction! Faith must always move from quiet meditation, from the Psalms with all their beauty into the Acts of the Apostles. That which was born in the shepherd while he tended the sheep, those deep convictions given to him by God came to full birth as he faced the giant of Gath. There had been training in the heart of the son of Jesse. He had not stood before a brass mirror practising for days what to say to the giant. It almost seems as if his fighting with the giant was impulsive. Faith is always like that. It never sits own and calculates how it can be done. Faith takes the leap, and then looks how far it has leapt. The history of it all what trust does, is seen later after the event. There was a Divine urgency about what he said and did. God was pushing the ship out into deeper waters to where the real storm was. When God is pushing from behind, and calling you from the front, you must go and do.

Faith can be both gentle and strong

In 1 Samuel 16:23, on to 1 Samuel 17, you will see the Sweet Psalmist of Israel went from playing a harp to killing a giant. That is what I call progress! That gentle hand which had plucked the harp, bringing sweet consolation to disturbed king Saul could kill anything that opposed the progress of God in his life. The faith that took the 'form of sound words' [6] was taken from within and used to inspire others. The mouth speaks out of the abundance of the heart. If you have a heart full of faith, and a giant jumps into that heart, there will be an over spill of what is in the heart. Such faith was in the man of Bethlehem's heart so that, in 1 Samuel 17:26, he discusses the reward of winning even before entering into the battle. If you follow David's conversation right through the battle you will hear remarkable words of faith. He is speaking God's will and heart on the matter. Each word is a heartbeat of the Eternal. What he says is not the cries of one for help. Those words are not heard as one going under the waves. This man's name is David (Beloved of God) not Moses! (Drawn from many waters).

He never grasps at straws, but he does catch hold of stones. There was a stream running through the valley of Elah. It moved along slowly, as if taking time to look at every shrub and tree. Each portion of water seemed to carry the sun with it, becoming a cup for that sunshine. Musical notes came from that stream. As the water bounced off each stone, there was a song and a message sent out. The valley had even witnessed the roar of the lion and the growl of the bear, the cry of the defeated and the vulture had often been heard here. That which had never echoed through it was heard in the words of David as he approached Goliath. It was a new language, the initial evidence of conquest. What was said was a combination of the architect's words with the words of solicitors and counsellors. They tell us to build, how to build, and to have it recorded forever. What the youth uttered as an echo of his Master's voice can and does live on in you as you face your destiny, even through many temptations.

Faith is more than providing answers

Goliath speaks as a natural man. The source of his inspiration is his natural ability. He seeks to belittle the young boy facing him. He can only record in speech what his natural eyes see, those things heard by his ears. He says what has been fed into his brain by time, sight and sense. His schooling is speaking. Beast and brute force are his axe and shield. What he has to say is simply roared at young David. The words come out like a burning, destroying fire. In contrast, the words of the young shepherd lad find God as their inspiration. The words said in faith are as a marshalled army. Each syllable uttered is a soldier and a sword. The words are from a deep well. They came from the same source as all the writings of David. The Spirit of God is using the Psalmist as an instrument, and He plays upon the soul and spirit of the coming king.

The words that Goliath speaks tell of what he will do with David, how he will destroy him, leaving Goliath with all the glory. Goliath tries to reduce the power of Jehovah as he curses David by his gods.[7] In contrast the words of the Bethlehemite tell what Jehovah will do, how Elohim will receive the glory. Four times the name of God is mentioned by Israel's warrior. The curse of Goliath is not received. His words, as fiery darts do not lodge in the heart of this boy attacker. No witness box was reserved for the accusation. The battle and the challenge of the giant are seen as a challenge to El-Shaddai. At the outcome, God will receive all the glory. It would all be Jehovah's. David is there as God's armour bearer to see the *Dwarfing of Giants*.

Faith is always more than natural abilities

The natural will always 'disdain' the spiritual. There will always be a tension between the flesh and the Spirit. One is the declared enemy of the other. The words uttered are meant to do this.[8] 'Disdain' is to reverse a miracle. It is to turn wine into water, healing into blindness. This is what the Pharisees of the New Testament did! To 'disdain' a thing is to make a man appear as a dog. It is the reversing of a noble creation into nothing, seeing every plant and tree reduced to a speck of dust. This dog bit the man! There is a suggestion in what Goliath said of David, that the shepherd was being trampled under foot, as swine trample on a pearl, whatever the intrinsic value. It was the turning of a soldier into a mercenary. Just doing it for the self-glory. Goliath in 'disdaining' God's warrior missed the intrinsic worth of the young man. He saw only David's staff, and thought he was chasing a dog. Unbelief never sees the God Who is in support of His warriors. David the giant-slayer saw beyond Goliath, while Goliath only saw to the end of his own nose. That which was within the believing Israeli, by using few words and little action overcame all things in the monster man.

Faith always sees the full picture. God doesn't see any struggle in part, He sees it as a whole. Trust is the remedy for the whole of your situation. You can meet Goliath of Gath in a quiet room, in a church or on the main street while shopping. From this story there are streams coursing out that we can bathe in and find refreshment for battle. The youngster is declared the winner by a head! There was a whole army inside David, placed there by previous encounters. The hug of the bear and the paw of the lion were there. Just as in the battle for Troy the wooden horse was wheeled into the city and at the right time the soldiers came out to attack, so in the faith of God's man there was such an army. When we speak of turning our faith loose we are letting the qualities of what we believe in free to do their work. Words that are spoken bring things into line and, like Jesus, David spoke words for the sake of those around him. The boy became what he believed. Words do not win battles, but they can give us courage to believe for the future.

Faith helps you to claim your covenant relationship

1 Samuel 17:31,32, note the words of the man of faith. 'Who is this uncircumcised Philistine?' There is no covenant with God for deliverance with this foreigner. He might mean a lot to his army of Philistines, but Goliath is not counted among God's sheep. That which is opposing you has no covenant relationship with God, and it should be removed. When temptation is overcome you have claimed more ground on which to stand. At the moment you may be standing on one leg. The space

and the place that the rebellious giant occupied became David's. Your words of faith will inspire deeds in others. What you say is taken and repeated. Saul did not have faith so he sent for the man of faith.

The shepherd boy could speak with the king and speak to a giant. The young man of Israel spoke to the mind of Goliath because the heart of the giant would not receive what God had to say. His mind was spoken to, but his head was taken! In his relationship with Providence, from this strong consolation, he went into battle. The battle never went inside David. Whether in the heat of the battle or in the heat of the desert, God was still the same, not to be melted or shrunk by opposing forces. Jehovah Jireh, (the Lord will provide) as in Psalm 23:1.

Within the hillsides of Bethlehem David had been building a platform for trusting God, in a deep relationship with Omnipotence. The battle before him was not a blind leap into the dark, it was a step into Light. The Light of that fellowship and friendship was with him. When other voices faded, when others could only discern the noise of the battle, David could still hear the voice of the Lord and understand it. He listened for that voice as he would listen for the call of the sheep. One false move and a thousand Philistines, besides the brothers of Goliath were waiting to pounce on him and crush him into the ground. He knew God was at the other end. If he leapt, God would catch him. His faith was an altar. Abraham always built an altar and then journeyed further.[9] The future king had that sort of experience, but his achievements weren't simply made into altars of stone and earth, he placed them into acts of faith. Altars can be cold as stone. Faith is a living thing. The growing boy had a reliance on God that can remove mountains-human ones. Faith lived within his heart. You can touch a mountain with your finger, it is unmoved and unmoveable. Touch it with faith, and it will be removed. This giant was a hindrance, and while he remained the soldiers of Israel would remain where they were. The soldiers were caged in fear of this Hercules. They felt like minnows with Triton. Goliath might have thought he held the keys to Israel's deliverance, but we know God holds all the keys and is the Key. Saul would remain as the weak king. Fear and trembling in the soldiers of Israel had to be turned into faith and adventure.

Faith said so little but accomplished everything

Goliath speaks forty-one words to David as a challenge. All David had to say was summed up in four words 'The Lord of Hosts'. Goliath had so much brass and metal about his body, while the boy trusted in his God. There are a number of 'I wills' and 'knows' that the boy from the hillside uses. 'This day 'will' the Lord deliver you into my hand.' I 'will' smite you. 'I 'will' give the carcasses to the fowls of the air. All the earth may 'know'. This assembly shall 'know". This is the tongue of faith speaking. It is the language of confidence knowing that God is more than able. These words come from one who saw God as more than a giant. Whatever opposes you the Almighty will be more powerful. God is presented as having feathers that we abide under. There is no armour like that of assurance in what God has said. Words like peace, joy, laughter, trust and calm are so small yet mean so much.

There comes a moment when even speech fails, and the man of action must move into action as an arrow loosed from the bow or a stone sent from the sling. Thrown as if it was going to strike the sun, but hitting the giant where it hurt the most. Every temptation has its Achilles' heel. All God's promises if used in faith, strike, and do what God intends. David came against the huge man of Gath in the Name of the 'Lord of Hosts'.[10] The God of the flag and the banner, the God of the marching army, and the innumerable multitude, who uses that number to conquer from every angle He chooses. Like the Roman army whose arrows were so plentiful that they darkened the sun, so that the opposing army falling over rocks in the dark, when the Roman arrows blackened the blue sky, attributed the eclipse to the god of the Romans.

The Name David used describes God as having all the armies of heaven in the palm of His hand. God has all power, yet He chose to use a stone! His real potency is seen in His choice. The Lord of Hosts was above and below, to the right and to the left. If Goliath had won, the sun and the stars would have fallen from the sky. God's Name is 'as ointment poured forth', but it is also power poured forth. When we have heard the words and the finest preaching, we must go to the 'action stations'. Written over the inside of some church doorways, seen as you leave the premises are the words 'Now your mission field begins.' Faith says little, it acts as if it is dumb, but it is so powerful it put the sun and the moon into the skies, and tells both when to rise and set.

When we speak faith, there is a whole language of love, life and victory. The ABC of faith is in that which is spoken. The words did not fall idly to the ground. They accomplished because they nerved the heart of

David. These words were as seeds being sown into hearts that God had prepared. All Heaven held its breath as the cheese-carrier advan-ced. Into that valley of defeat the young Israeli spoke conquest. 'The power of life and death are in the tongue.' What Goliath said spoke of death, what David had to say promised life. Words spoken in faith were a savour of life to some, the message of death to another. It was the end of a reign of terror. That which had haunted every soldier in Israel would be brought into the light of the Majesty of the Lord. What had been a ter- ror to children and to soldiers in their dreams was about to be destroyed. The first things God created in the Book of Genesis were spoken into being, but by faith David speaks the giant into that which is fallen and defeated as if it had never been created. When you haven't the strength to climb a tree, or chop it down to size, then by faith God can shrivel it into just a root! What the Devil proclaims to be a winner, the Power that works for you speaks it into defeat. When God wanted to make the giant stumble, He placed a stone in his head. If you were going to do that you would put a stone on the ground for him to stum- ble and fall over. You cannot be more defeated than to let the sword fall from your hand, to topple and fall at the feet of the challenger and lose your head to your own sword. This is *Dwarfing Giants*.

Faith speaks a language foreign to the natural man

There is a whole alphabet of language in faith. Faith teaches you that alphabet and that language if you wait in the secret place. Listen to what your heartbeats are telling you as God uses them to communicate truth. A class of children were asked to write and say what they would never be too old to do. One child wrote: 'I will never be too old to hold my daddy's hand!' We will never get beyond the need to feel the touch of the Master's hand.

When you 'speak the word only'[11] that tongue becomes as a ready- armed soldier. The Spirit of God whispered out loud into the young man's soul. David had to be as faithful under the inspiration of the Spirit as the musical instrument was to his own playing. It says of Israel as they came out of Egypt that they came out in 'ranks'. The margin of some Bibles says 'armed'. What you believe you say, and what this young man said made him fit to occupy a throne. Here is kingly (authoritative) speech before he sits on the throne. The young giant-slayer's armour is the words he speaks. The God that created him educated his tongue.

There are times when we need our tongues to be tuned again to truth. If God can conquer the tongue, then great things can follow. When and what you speak in faith will seem to some as if you are speaking Greek. There is a whole alphabet and language in believing, and it has more than twenty-six words to offer! In the controlling of what we say we have the key to the whole of the character. The first thing the Great Physician will ask to see is your tongue! From an examination of the tongue a physician can determine your health. The thing that tells of your spiritual health is what you say. It is a remarkable fact that David pacified a backslidden king Saul with his music, while he brought the giant to the ground with a stone. He handles the stones as well as he handles the harp! Sweet music to sour Saul!

Faith in the heart is more than armour of brass

'The pen is mightier than the sword.' What we think and what we write are more than the armour of armies. The steel in what David said became more than the brass that the giant wore. David's utterances came from his heart. There was the abundance of an armoury in his heart. That which was to be used in defence and attacked by Goliath was not from within, it was outward, worn as armour. The best armour is from the heart. As the future king faces the King of Largeness, listen to the elocution of faith, and the grammar of God. There is oratory in what was spoken. As we rely on the Almighty, we shall never lack an answer. Give ear to the salt spoken by God's man. The language, even before Goliath is defeated, is one of total control. As God controls the shepherd's tongue in what he says, he can control the rest of his body and actions. First God will control the tongue and then the stone, before toppling the giant. The huge giant as he lumbers towards the running youth is spoken to as if he was defeated already. There is a whole native language in that dictionary called God. When you don't know what to say in any situation, turn to Him the Word and you will find a whole page devoted to your problem. Some part of Jesus will deal with every part of the problem. I have noticed in writing this book, if you get the 'I' in the wrong place in the word 'faith' (fiath) it doesn't make sense. This boy knew how to speak to sheep and God in such a gentle manner, yet had reserved his strongest voice, his trumpet voice and choice words for the giant. His wasn't an empty head or an empty mouth. The Almighty had filled it with good things. Don't squeak and be 'mealy mouthed' when dealing with any opposition. Use your words as Noah used his hammer and saw when building the ark. Some things require forcing into place, others need knocking, whilst certain things you have to command, and through this you have the *Dwarfing of Giants*.

Faith utters words that enter into your heart

As you go through any trial, God will give you choice words, words that are held in reserve as precious china is hidden away for that special day of visitation. The heat of the temptation allows certain phrases to be seared onto the walls of your will. Words like butter, water or wine have been on your menu in the 'after dinner speech.' Notice David spoke in the language of his birth, but each word had a new birth within it provided by faith, old words with new meanings. He spoke in such a way that all those around fully understood what he meant. Whether we speak in English, Hebrew, German or French, let it be a language formed through your convictions that God can do it. Goliath certainly knew what David said and meant. David didn't have to learn the language of the Philistine to deal with him. He probably used the only language he knew, Hebrew. What he had said to the lion and the bear he now said to this man attacking the glory of God. Truth will place words as treasures in your heart. God will always use the language you have, and as you allow that to be spoken the Holy Spirit takes it and uses it as a weapon. When Jesus wanted to speak to Peter He used the language of the cock crowing.[12] Words of faith and truth, love and holiness are able to bring to your feet the foulest of fiends. These words of faith come from the alphabet of God. The confidence the shepherd boy had in God came clothed in the words he spoke. Boldness clothed every word, not one naked word was spoken. There was nothing idle or idol about that which was spoken. It was not the result of some theological training it was the outcome of a heart shaped to God's liking and through God's instructing.

The things around the young shepherd had taught him the language of life. It is not French, American or German; it is the true language of faith. That which was happening to him was not allowed to become his master, but his teacher.

1 Samuel 17:36,37 the speech of the young lad is not the silver tongued speech of the orator. 'Out of the mouth of babes and suckling' God has ordained praise.[13] The 'suckling' is the child leaning on the mother's breast for shelter and protection. Jesse's son listened, he heard words that he could repeat in battle. He listened to men of faith such as Samuel and kept their words in his heart so that they might grow with

him. What he said was never learned from his brothers or a fearful Israeli army on the run. He had been where success was the order of the day. What we receive in the summer can be used in the winter. While we are speaking words of faith we are not talking about another; we are not spending time with idle words that are seeking to impart their own idleness to us. David had to use the language he had been taught as a child. One of the first things changed at our conversion is our language. There was a fire, there was passion in his heart, and his tongue had been dipped into it. The words spilled out of his mouth as a volcano erupting. What he said made each soldier realise that God had been at work while they were in fear and trembling. God doesn't *Dwarf Giants* by making you into a dwarf. You are never made less by God. 'Your reach should outstretch your grasp or what is heaven for!'

Faith always takes something from the 'rock and hard place'

Everything the future king says is silver, the silver lining he had taken from the dark clouds, the silver from the 'rock and hard place'. Now he seeks to use it. David quotes from memory, inspiration and experience, a threefold cord that is not easily broken. 'This Philistine 'shall be' as the defeated lion or bear.' The Lord that 'delivered me,' He 'will deliver me.' If it has happened once it can happen a thousand times. What David said would have made a glorious acceptance speech for the day of his coronation, but that was later. There is a sense in which we grow up in our words. We become what we say. David has gone from childish talk and dreams of the early years into the full expression of faith. There is Someone putting these words into his mouth. What he has to say doesn't sound like some one speaking in public for the first time. He doesn't speak for effect. His heart is seen in pictures of words. He says what he believes and receives, in a defeated giant, what he has believed God for.

Faith is more than words, but it can make your tongue a ready instrument. If 'looks could kill,' David would have fallen dead as the giant glared at him in such a withering way. That look turns the plum into a prune! This battle was to prove that it is more than what we say or the armour we carry, it is God who gives the victory again and again. If God stands behind you nothing can push you back. In God you are in the biggest thing that shall ever be, from eternity to eternity. It is a matter of going on to conquer again and again.

Faith emphasises what is believed

Peter the apostle was exposed in the New Testament because of his Galilean accent.[14] How we say things tells where we have been, with whom we have associated, and what we are seeking to express. The 'accent' of this stripling was achievement, not accolade. There are words and phrases that I use given to me in the area where I live. When we are in great need we return to the language of our upbringing, because there are words we know which express just how we feel. Men, big strong men, in battle have been known to utter phrases and prayers they learned at their mother's knee, at the bedside. Other people may not fully understand their true meaning. Occasionally we return to our 'roots' and as we squeeze them things long forgotten and full of expression are revived again. David had been nurtured on faith, and from faith he had learned certain expressions. Some of them might have been when he defeated a lion and a bear these words lurking in the dark corners of his own heart, but they are brought out into the light of day as a challenge as he ventures into battle. What he said to Goliath was part of the honey found in the lion's carcass part of that which was taken from the bear he had killed. He had robbed the bear of its whelps. What God had made of him was fully expressed as he spoke to the giant of Gath.

Faith brings order out of disorder

It is always good to have a plan in your heart. I don't think that Israel's champion just ran into battle uttering all manner of words, like washing strung out on a line with the wind blowing it in all directions. If you read what he says it is a well thought out speech. It is equally as good as the sermon Peter preached in the Acts of the Apostles.[15] There is an introduction and a conclusion. It is not a mile long! It does not weary the feeble! It is as good in content as Paul's epistle to Philemon, the epistle of the heart from Paul the aged. The measure of what David said was small, but the content was great. He said things of an eternal nature that cannot be measured. Every Israeli child, every soldier, would hear these words repeated throughout history. When you include God in anything, placing Him at the very centre, there is no telling the length of influence. Include God in everything, and you will find Him in everything. He arrives in the sun and the showers, in joy and in sadness. There were many things that King David said that are long forgotten, trampled on by camels on their desert journeys. The battle might have seemed anything but conducted in an orderly manner. From the clouds of dust, and the many challenges offered, order appears as a rising sun.

Words of faith, language that tells of the longitude and latitude of God, live on forever. Here is a remarkable thing when we think of what we say in faith. Goliath and the Philistines have long gone. King Saul and his family are no more. We are not sure where the valley of Elah is. The sword, shield and spear have all disappeared. We have read from the Bible the very words of faith that the shepherd boy spoke. David lives on in Jesus Christ as stated in Acts 2. It is worth believing God, for it makes us part of Jesus Christ. It guarantees us a throne and an everlasting kingdom! That which is written in letters or books must perish. The language of faith is part of 1 Corinthians 13, which 'abides' and does not 'fade away'. The tongues of men and of angels are here, not as 'sounding brass' or 'tinkling cymbal,' but as faith, hope and love-these abide! They all need speech to express their true content. David does this and leaves Goliath dead at his feet. It is the first step to the throne of Israel. What might have been bits and pieces became the order of faith, all things working together for good, resulting in the *Dwarfing of Giants*.

Notes:

1. 1 Samuel 17:40.
2. Romans 8:28.
3. I Samuel 17:45.
4. Psalm 22:8.
5. 1 Samuel 17:51.
6. Titus 2:8.
7. 1 Samuel 17:43.
8. 1 Samuel 17:42.
9. Genesis 13:4.
10. 1 Samuel 17: 45.
11. Matthew 8:8.
12. Matthew 26:34,75.
13. Psalm 8:2.
14. Matthew 26:73.
15. Acts 2:14-26.

Chapter

9

The Lifting up of Stones Before Putting Giants Down

So many are wanting to be permanently at the top of the ladder, to hold it for others to ascend and descend. They hold to the doctrine of theology that you never have to commence small. They are never associated with infancy or puberty. When they aim for anything it must be the 'bulls eye', nothing short of that will satisfy. There is never the realisation that accomplishment comes to all of us through much practise, many mistakes, and that though we commence small we grow tall. Life is an obstacle race, and at times there appears to be more obstacles than race! It can become impediment-shaped, rather than life shaped in God.

Like David it must be pebble before real power. The lesser leads us to the greater. Learn to lift the small before you grow tall. By stretching and lifting we are maturing as we wrestle against our personal giants. There are some who forget that even a ladder has a bottom rung, that each great house has a solid foundation hidden from view. It is the training and straining that leads to reigning. Each rung of the ladder must be mastered before you can get to the top. On the way up you are taught rare and valuable lessons of faith. You learn where to tread and where not to put your feet. You can't walk on fresh air; your feet must touch the steps of the ladder. Your safety is in your surety. Your arms and legs are developed so that from the top you can stand with steady gaze and look around and down. This development helps you to help others who are following you. Those unnoticed periods, divided into hours, weeks, month and years are the most important seasons of your life in the strife. Many people who suddenly seem to have a claim to fame have been working unobserved during the training period.

David spent many solitary hours tuning his instruments, but not half as many days and years as God spent with him, maturing his life. On the hillside of Bethlehem he dreamed dreams, which became reality. Pebble power leads us to God's ability to reduce giants to dwarfs. That which is taken by the hand can be used for great things, as the small rod of Moses was.[1] They said to Jesus 'speak the word only'.[2] Just 'one' word, even as 'one' stone would be enough. That 'word' became the warrior of God. It is God's warriors who become winners in their work. God's pebbles are more powerful than Gath's giants!

You require much training

What you see now, as the boy from Bethlehem stands on the head of Gath's man, is the result of much training, sweat, blood and tears. As David had sweated, shed blood and wept, so these have become a part of him, changing him into an example for all to see and serve. We climb and claim by the things we suffer. It is through the crucible that the crown is formed. It is through straining to climb that muscles are made strong and find their true elasticity. The Penal System does not refer to a time spent in prison as a 'stretch' for nothing. That time is meant to discipline the offender. Something of the nature of the prison doors and bars is meant to enter into the character.

1 Samuel 17:40 and 49, the shepherd boy had to reach for broken pieces of rock in the valley, and beginning with something small he was able to accomplish much. Great writers can begin with but a small word, even smaller than this stone. Builders begin with a brick, great thinkers begin with a thought, and great singers or those who play instruments begin with a note. Even great discoveries are based on one idea. A great journey begins with one step hence the Chinese proverb: 'The journey of a thousand miles begins with one step.' Your greatest moments are all hidden in a small decision. The right thing at the right time will bring the right accomplishment. Written all over the small things in life such as these stones taken by David is your future. No matter how awkward or cutting if taken and used, this can be the means of your conquest. The training of the past was the laying of a foundation for the future. That small piece of granite contained all the workings of nature, storm, wind, rain, cloud, cold and sunshine all became part of the pebble.

If you want to grow tall then, begin small

These five pieces of stone had probably been broken off from a larger rock, thrown unceremoniously to the ground and then lifted to new heights as they were thrown from the hand of leather they were placed in. They mercilessly went through a growing process, as the water flowed around them acting as sharp instruments to cut and shape into destiny's pattern. If you would be great then commence small and, like this gravel, if you are driven and sent by Jehovah there is no measurement that can measure how far you will go. The final statement will be 'mission accomplished.' Taking hold of that which had been broken, victory was accomplished, as it was for the Church of Jesus Christ through the death of Jesus Christ. From the brokenness comes the building of a throne. Through the brokenness of a small stone came the healing of a nation by the death of a giant. From one stone comes the glory of the Kingdom of Israel. Never mind the giants; take care of the small stones! The stones will take care of those things defined as gigantic. Give yourself to the Supreme Being even as this small rock was given to the sling. Because it was a yielded object it had no problems entering the hand or the sling, or the giant's head! If it had been any larger it would have been rejected. God had to pare it down to the size of His requirement for ministry. The Lord brought it, by many means to His measure, to make it His treasure. It went where it was sent. It became an Apostle for Israel, a pioneer of fame out of shame and sham. It is little use measuring the stone if it is not part of the throne. All the ministry of the Master would have been wasted if the broken piece had not been placed into the sling. Stop counting the promises of the Almighty, and start using them!

God enlarges your smallness

Through a chipped piece of rock great unity was brought to Israel. In the hand of David it accomplished what no soldier could do with all his barrack square training. You will notice that God did not build a wall or a great fence around the young assailant, as He did with the tabernacle in the wilderness. There were no walls of Jericho placed around him keeping a distance between himself and the great giant. There was no policy of containment, only contentment used by Jehovah. There was nowhere to run or hide. The future king must not hide in the shadow of the former history of Israel. If this piece of stone failed to accomplish the will of God there was no second miracle awaiting the young shepherd. All there is of me must be given to all there is of the Creator. The Almighty had made no contingency plans. There was only one David, one Goliath, and one stone to be used. The stone became a reflection of the life of the music loving shepherd boy. What 'many' can never achieve, 'one' can sometimes do a much better work. Let the stone do the work for you. Take a promise from God, and let it so work that it reaches and touches realms that you can never hope to influence. When one stone is taken and used, another promise is waiting for your empty heart. That chip of rock grew from small beginnings into something larger than a nation and an army that couldn't defeat the opposition.

Maturity does not develop overnight

The man of God in the valley had to realise that you cannot conquer giants until you have learned to lift up stones. Small things must be dealt with first. He had to lift the stone before anything else. If your obedience to Jehovah causes you to stumble, you will never *Dwarf Giants*. That particle of rock would serve as ballast for everything else in the shepherd boy's life. We want to beat giants first and then lift stones. That is not God's order. The battle stratagem for all those struggling with the flesh or the world, seen as a great giant, is set out in this story for time and eternity. God displayed David's spirituality on a stone, heightened as the giant was toppled. You can only win by commencing at the starting line. If you are going to fellowship with great marksmen and those who achieve in God, then try aiming at smaller objects, until you become accomplished. You can leave everything else to God, whether it is large or small. The soldiers of the tribe of Benjamin who could strike a target within a hair's breadth must have missed many things by a mile at the first attempt, Judges 20:16. Make God your goal and you will strike everything else. We all want to start with the giant, but God wants us to commence our *warfare* and growth with the little stones lifted from a brook. We want to see the walls of Jericho fall flat and the Red Sea to open up before us, but that is not always God's order, and He is a God of order. Learn that the great is found in the small, and the conquest in surrender. Many want the flower in full bloom before the stem has had time to develop. How some people wait for a foetus to develop for nine months before being born I will never know! They want it 'here' and 'now', rather than 'there' and 'then'. We must have a definite target. The son of Jesse had a vision that was fulfiled. The stone wasn't sent anywhere everywhere and nowhere; it was part of a plan and a destiny. When the hand of the shepherd was wrapped in warmth around the small stone both had been well prepared for this hour of glory.

What you are in the dark you become in the light

How we take hold of the smaller things of life tells how we are going to deal with the larger. The future ruler gave all the power of his hand when taking the little rock. Half-hearted attempts never work. You can tell how some people will perform for God when you watch them saw wood, arrange flowers, vacuum the church floor, and wash dishes. If running with men wearies you, how are you going to run with horses? Lifting the small stones gives strength to meet the giants of life. Your spiritual muscles must be developed with small decisions that result in actions. Then you can go forward and defeat that which is defeating you. Holiness is made up of small decisions, and it is developed when you are alone. Lifting the stone makes you strong to lift the armour, sword and the head of Goliath. God's school was in that stone. All the deep teachings of God were in it. When the future king took the pebble, it was a private ceremony with no pomp or show. It was going to be the headstone for Goliath's grave. No epitaph would be written on it. The giant so strong and well known would die as the 'unknown soldier'. Private pains are always more important than public performance.

Ruling and reigning begins within

The first step to the throne was not when David amid all the praise and plaudits was crowned in Hebron and Jerusalem. It was right here in this story. God made known the heart of a young man, and He used a small stone to accomplish it. That jagged, small rock was the nature of the kingdom that would be, granite and grand in nature! In it was all the principles of a godly life. The lifting of the fallen piece of rock was the first step to the throne, the first jewel to be placed into the coming crown. If he can lift stones and sheep, he can help people. He can and would minister to the lame, those without legs or eyes. It would make him a servant to those who could not fight their own cause. He proved this in the way he dealt with Mephibosheth, the son of Saul, who was crippled in both feet, 2 Samuel 4:4;9:3. In the future, he would help those who were cast aside and forgotten. God's New Testament Kingdom has been built on broken bits of stone. If you can lift the small with care and love, then you can live 'in' God, 'with' God and 'for' God. The Supreme Being is working through what you consider to be the 'lesser things' of Christianity. Those small choices will make you great. It is the gentle touch of the potter's fingers and hand that produces the great vessel with its finely decorative pattern. It is the little things of life that we do wrong that cause giants to limit us to a valley experience.

The thing you do may be so small that it wouldn't fill a bird's beak or a fingernail, yet its true greatness is in God. Each play written must commence with one line on a page. If you don't believe me, ask William Shakespeare!

You can overcome using a promise

David didn't trip up on this stone. He didn't choose the weapons offered to him.[3] He accepted what was offered. He took from his surroundings and laid the man of great stature flat. That which nature had developed would be taken and used. So many failed to see any relevance between this stone and defeating a giant. In that small piece was embedded Israel's child's finest hour. All the storms of the valley and desert, plus the wild winds with their tearing power were in that one stone. It had been trained as any soldier for its work of winning. Some save memorabilia from great battles, but this was only a small parcel of rock. It became the epitaph, another Ebenezer, meaning 'The stone of help', also suggesting, 'The Lord has helped us so far'.[4] If it could have been used as a looking glass, the man fighting for the Lord would have seen all the future glory of his life and times, recorded by God.

In every small promise of God is the victory you require. Nature had brought the stone to where it was and laid it at the feet of the shepherd. Now he had to take it on a further journey. There will always be a Hand seeking to lift you into greater possibilities. Where in the past, wolves, bears and lions might have been his target, there was now a nobler target in Goliath, and a more glorious victory.

Everything we meet must be taken further, because it has been involved with us, and must go heavenward. He took it from obscurity into glory-the glory of a giant slain. This very stone was baptised in the blood of the enemy of the young warrior. It was going to be so placed that he would metaphorically walk on water. The giant's thought pattern was intact until a single stone riddled his brain, interrupted the pattern so rudely. If God's choice one had failed to take up the stones, he would have failed to kill Goliath of Gath. The will of the Almighty for David was to lift a stone and put it in a sling. There was nothing spectacular in that, but it was the first step of obedience. It was to lead to where true strength and greatness would be found. The mis-shaped rock didn't have to look for a target, the target came to the stone. If you want to see the small stones that God wants you to lift, then look around your church, see and hear the many needs. Get hold of a promise in prayer don't just stay writing psalms, singing songs or playing the flute. Let your spirituality become practical as you lay low a temptation. Expand into something like a giant! Don't just lift promises from the page of your Bible use them! Put them to greater use. People and animals had walked all over the small particle of rock yet through obedience and being lifted, it brought oppressive evil feet to a standstill in Goliath. Use a promise like a pebble to put a full stop after the name of Goliath. Use the small pebble as a pen, re-write any trial and turn it into a victory.

They might have presented barriers and hurdles to others, but not to the man of faith, who saw a challenge in every stone. These stones cry out against us. When they asked Jesus to stop the children crying out His praises, He replied that God was able to raise up children to Abraham through the stones.[5] This prophecy and words are gloriously fulfiled in this battle of Elah. A deed, some act of faith came from it. God can and will raise you up from the little stones that surround. The piece of stone can be the commencement of an altar that suggests death and sacrifice. The boy took up the pebble, but it was the man who stepped from it as the colossus sank low to become just another man. I knew a man named Howard Carter who travelled around the world, commencing his journey with one English penny!

In silence you speak volumes

God sees what we do in the menial tasks, and that speaks volumes. The child who can piece a puzzle together can go on to become an architect who puts buildings together. That little lad with his fishing rod can grow up to be a sea captain and sail the seven seas of the world. It is not the killing of a giant that spells true greatness, it is dealing with the stones that are sometimes thrown at us. It is how and what we build out of our hurt. It is not my temptation that decides what I shall be, but my reaction to all that happens to me. There is a certain colour in every crisis, and that colour has to enter into the character. Taking the little stones I can build faith and hope in others. Through you, others can realise that the Eternal can do such great things. Do we throw the rough edged pieces back at the person offending us, or do we take them, and encase them in leather, to be used in future days of challenge. The stone was with David only a short time. When you lift that which is going to bless you, and there is success, then pass it on to another. Declare the secrets of your heart. The prince in waiting could have tossed these pieces of rock back at Mother Nature who engraved them in the valley. David kept four stones in his pouch for future days and battles. Whatever you use, use it all! Give it your 'best shot'. Do something worth remembering and recording. It is not what is written on the page, but in the hearts of the nation. Taking that one stone David writes on the spirits of all those soldiers watching him enter into battle. The stone uttered no words, it made no threat, it never even prayed, it just brought the challenger tumbling down.

Burdens can become blessings

What family life, taunting brothers, bear and lion failed to do, the stone accomplished. The son of Jesse had to bend to lift the burden. Encased in that rock was a victory waiting to be released. It worked something in the future king before it ever touched the giant. David said 'I am willing to work with a stone.' How many builders or stone masons would be willing to work with one stone? There must be the development of a giant in you as you grow in faith and spirituality, before you slay the giant that opposes. That which falls at our feet as if shot with a stone, grows in our heart and is put to better use. God's giants are not born they are made! You can tell by the way people do something for God in a lesser role, how they will perform in the greater moment. If the bad things in stones are handled carefully, you will handle greater and public things in the same way. Take that stone, that suffering, and place them on the pathway, so that others following you might have an easier tread. Let them be as stones laid in shallow waters, to help another to walk through on dry land. No one would ever stumble over this stone, because a future king, as part of his training, removed it.

The man who wants to climb mountains and sail seas will be of little use if hills make him dizzy and a glass of water makes him seasick! He must learn to handle the lesser before touching the greater. How that estate is managed will reveal how you will react to greater things. If God can trust you with stones that cost so little and mean so little, He will also trust you with great riches and many precious stones that are part of your faith. Through your testimony, your preaching there will be precious truths, precious stones deposited in caskets that are open to receive true worth.

You need the discipline of obedience

Stones have to be removed from a field before seeds can be sown. In the removing of the stone the gateway is opened to a harvest. That harvest is in the stone. It is all in the discipline of removing the stones. In that discipline a way is cleared and the ground is prepared to receive the seeds of true greatness. Obedience to what God commands does all these things. We must take a promise from God and use it as David used that stone, and later the other stones also. That man who is used to handling great things must also discipline himself to handle smaller obstacles.

There is the discipline of obedience in this story of warfare. If the shepherd boy had put the stone into his hand instead of the sling, it would not have killed the King of Giants. If it had entered into his shoe, that would have made him lame. He had to use it. It had to be thrown away, given up and thrown away for it to gain more glory than the desert sands could ever glaze it with. In obedience we receive far more than we give. Far more is surrendered to us than we surrender to God. Sling a stone in obedience and receive something far greater in the head of a giant. Here is illustrated the principle of giving to receive, of surrendering to conquer. That which is taken and given is returned with great reward. The promise of God must be taken into the heart as the stone was placed into the sling. From the heart, what we believe is what is used. It was the fact that he came into battle with an empty hand which gave him a new sword. Once we empty ourselves there are many weapons of warfare that the Supreme wants to give. Both the sling and the hand were filled with a stone. A place was made for both in the battle. The promises of God were not made to be dormant, or placed in a stream in a valley. Use them and see them fulfil! They are there to be used, to make you useable and useful. What made this small rock useable was its surrender to the swirling waters around, then to David's hand, and into the giant' head, to be lost in its finest work. The stone was crowned with accomplishment as it entered the head.

You must see the battle through to the end

We all like to come in at the end of the battle. The end is not when the temptation appears, but when it falls. There is a certain type of person who wants to stand near the finishing line of a great race. There was a 'wag' at my school who would never run across the country as part of his physical training. He would find a place in a quiet hedge somewhere near the finishing line, sitting until the first runners appeared, then he would join them as fresh as a daisy.

When the giant was dead, so many of the soldiers felt they could have done the job even better than the victor. Many volunteers will carry the head of the monster. The problem is not in carrying the spoils of war it is in obtaining them! We must all start small before we can destroy that large obstacle presented to us. Strike the forehead before you take the head from the shoulders. Remove that great dark temptation that is blocking out the sunlight from your life and causing you to walk in shadows instead of sunshine. All David's powers of concentration were involved in throwing that object from the sling. He had eyes and hands only for that moment. He treated the opportunity as every opportunity must be treated, as if there will not be a second time. You, sometimes only get one shot.

The stone can be a stool to lift us to the place where we can strike the fatal blow. This giant might be lust or some other temptation, but unless it is brought to the ground defeated, we shall make no progress. Take this thought to heart that as the giant's body decomposed the ground was fertilised, and a barren valley became a fruitful field. If you see the battle through to the end you will know the full glory. You can then look back through every action of success. Keep looking forward and be forward looking. The end comes only when you are proclaimed victorious. Don't make a shrine of your history. Don't worship the past. Jacob said 'with this staff I have passed over this Jordan, Genesis 32:10. In Hebrews 11:21, he worshipped leaning on the top of his staff. The staff stayed with him to the end. He kept his original vision as he leant on that staff.

Here is true greatness God overcame the greatest thing in the Philistine army, Goliath, with the smallest and newest recruit to the Israeli army, a pebble! Here and now the battle finishes for us. We stop when we don't think the small things that make us holy are necessary. Small nails hold great pieces of wood together. Small rivets help an aeroplane to fly. The referee can direct twenty-two men in an English football match. The power of that small whistle between his lips is unbelievable. The train guard stands at the station with a small flag and, as he waves it, the train with its thirty carriages begins to move out of the station. The policeman, as he raises a small hand commands many vehicles to come to a halt. The power of the smaller controls the greater. It is one of the fundamental principles of life. That which has no will of its own, a small hard thing defeated that which was full of its own self-will and importance in the man from Gath. That piece of broken rock became the full stop to the life and times of Gath's son.

Your destiny is in the small issues of life

Maybe you have thought I would like to conquer a giant! Can you? You can! Can you, as they say in Lincolnshire, England 'carry corn'? Can you drive a nail straight into a piece of wood, or saw in a straight line? We never overcome anything until our hand is empty and we are willing to help with the secular and the ordinary. The fact that God used this stone proves it was no ordinary thing that the future king did when he bent down to pick it up. Your destiny is in the small issues of life. There was gold in this rock, of a different nature to what the natural man thinks. David picked up a small object and in doing so he received the beginnings of a kingdom. Your future might look as dull and as unpromising as this pebble, but if God is in it, there is a lustre waiting to be discovered. Find a pebble, and somewhere you will find an ocean, then a continent, a tribe and a nation. The glory of the small is revealed as it strikes the forehead of the giant. It only takes a small decision to do the right thing.

Your weapons are not carnal

The true weapons of the soldier of God were not in the hand of Saul or with the Israeli Army. They are not found in 'conventional' wisdom. The 'corridors of power' have no power at all. The unconventional strikes as an adder's bite at the heart of conventional. The weapons of our warfare are not carnal, as a thought process or a natural disposition. They are not brought from a steel kiln or made out of the best steel. They have not been taken to the flint to be sharpened. Nobody would have ever thought of putting stones into a shepherd's bag to win a battle, but God did. There is no natural wisdom here. All Saul's regiments were held in check as it was revealed what should bring about more than a shout, a great victory.

As you lift the stone, and do the small thing, the weapons you require are under that burden which you feel has become part of you. Your arsenal is under the stone, lift it and find the help you require. What stumbled horse and rider, soldier and warrior was taken and used. The minister of death to Goliath became the minister of life and hope to the young lad and to Israel.

One of the unwritten sayings of Jesus is 'Lift the stone and I am there.' In the writings of David in Psalm 55:22, he records 'Cast your 'burden' on the Lord.' 'Cast' it, as you would throw a stone into a pond. They cast gifts into the treasury in the New Testament. The word for 'burden' in Psalm 55:22 is 'gift'. In a broken spirit there can be such a gift from God. This precious gift is in that very stone you are lifting. You will feel the full weight of the burden lifted. There is a weapon in every stone. When you give it to God it is made into something useful. It becomes pointed, sharp and hard. Your best weapons are forged in the fires of valley and depression formed in the very heart of your crushed disappointments. They grow out of the scattered seeds of a lost cause, which may even be the last cause.

You must recognise opportunities even in stones

Like the jawbone of an ass that Samson used to deliver Israel, the stone had lain in the valley. Probably the feet of thousands of soldiers had trampled over it yet no one had ever realised its potential or realised that God could use it to emancipate. It is having a vision within when what you have destroys a giant and a Philistine army. The deliverance and the stone were where the future king was in the valley. The stone didn't need to be imported through Hiram, as when Solomon was building the temple. This was the 'Stone of Scone' that was placed under the throne used for crowning English monarchs in Westminster Abbey. The Kings of Scotland used the same stone. The 'Stone of Help' (Ezel)[6] was right within David's circumstances, and he took it as he believed in the Almighty to perform. Ezel is the stone that 'shows the way'. No other stone no matter how beautiful would have done what this one had to do. You can garnish it, polish it, paint it, but the deliverance is within the problem. As David ran towards the giant he was practising his athletic skills ready for the time when he would chase the Philistines. There is nothing quite like being prepared! Each happening in your life is a train-ing period for the next giant. God's opportunities are at your feet right where you are, waiting as a pebble to be used.

Asking in prayer and using a promise like a small stone makes you taller than the tallest giant. When you begin small with a stone, you can see over mountains into the future. When commencing small with one jagged rock, you make way for others to follow in your footsteps, just as Jesus did when He rolled away a larger stone at the resurrection from the dead. Death was a Goliath that He conquered.

You must be God's man to strike God's targets

God's man was obedient. Even if he had been blind and deaf he could not have missed the object of God's wrath. All heaven was willing that small object to its target. When we have poor vision and even less zeal, the Greatest enlarges the target so that we cannot miss. We do miss however if there is a mote in our own eye that needs casting out in order to give us a clearer vision of the real enemy we face. Goliath was built like a mound of earth, yet God took a segment of earth to bring him down to earth, even a piece of chipped rock, a rock which others had trodden on many times. A small stone crushed Goliath of Gath as it landed where God had determined.

There are times when you must wait

With the stone gone from the sling the youth had to wait for the giant to fall. Even when we receive a promise from the Lord it takes the patience of time to see it completed. Sometimes the answer comes all at once, at other times it comes little by little. It must have seemed like an eter-nity until the giant fell at his feet. The stone flew through the air swifter than the giant fell. The stone was flying to give life to Israel, while Goliath was falling into the sleep of death. The stone grew so large when it entered into his head, yet the man became so small when his head was removed. All this earth's glory felled by a folic of rock! He fell as quickly as the stone travelled from the sling with its message of death. The stone, as any promise from the Book (brook) did its work valiantly. It did not 'shilly-shally' or make a detour on the way. It was not found wanting. It was a stone, a weight by which God measured the might of the man of Gath. If only we could be as successful as this rock in our work for God. It had to be used just once. No shouting, ranting, cursing or upbraiding, just quiet obedience brought success.

The weapon was lifted up and placed where it would be the most useful, in a sling. When we are centred in the hand of God we cannot help but do our work in a successful way. From the small particle of rock we move onto greater things. Everything that came from that small fragment was increased. Whatever the stone may represent, throw it away. Pluck it from you as if throwing from a sling, and God will give you a dead giant in its place. When we can handle smaller things, larger happenings will replace them. That which can happen out-grew the stone. It travelled from being small to large because the rock was lost in the temple of the giant. New armour, greater armour than one weapon was presented to David. He took possession of the armour because he first took possession of a small rock. He trusted God, and all his trust was seen as he picked up what would be the weapon of his warfare. He was able to handle a pebble then a giant. How you handle the insignificant will reveal how you will manage the great. The smaller is the discipline for the larger. We must commence with the small to conclude with the large. If you can fish for minnows with a net in a shallow stream, then you can be trusted with a rod and line in deep seas.

Make yourself available to the mercy of God. That mercy will never leave you to the mercy of any temptation. Your best weapons and hopes of overcoming are found in the valley of experience as you 'pass through'. Psalm 23: 4,'Though 'I walk through' the valley of the shadow of death'.[7] The God who used the sun on one occasion,[8] on another the stars were used in battle,[9] granted us a great insight to humility when He used this little stone. Make me that stone! If He grants you the request you have made, you too will be found *Dwarfing Giants*.

Notes:-

1 Exodus 4:2,4,17,20.
2 Matthew 8:8.
3 1 Samuel 17:38,39.
4 1 Samuel 7:12.
5 Luke 3:8.
6 1 Samuel 20:19.
7 See author's book, *Paths of Righteousness in Psalm 23*.
8 Joshua 10:12.
9 Judges 5:20.

Chapter

10

The Sling and the Stone Working Together

God rarely uses a crowd. The magnificence of the many can deny God the glory found in the few. The crowd brings the strength of many. The individual considered weak brings glory to God. The glory of the potter is not in the mound of clay but in the individual pots created with beauty and design. Throughout the Scriptures it is Noah, Moses, Elijah and Elisha who were used by God, and all the law and the prophets hang on them. When we look for the crowd and the great army we miss the very purpose of Destiny in using the small to defeat the great. The things considered 'feeble' become 'well able' in the work of the Eternal. It is the person with a single purpose who accomplishes most for God. The principle is illustrated in the army of Gideon. The Lord had to reduce it to the measure of His glory.[1] Here, in this battle it was a sling and a stone that accomplished for God. One was useless without the other. The two fitted together into the purposes of God, to find their true meaning in life.

The stone presented a new open door

The word sling in the Hebrew language can suggest a door.[2] It certainly became a door of opportunity to a nation, yet it became a closed door to the challenger from the Philistines. That door had long been slammed in the face of Israel. A nation was being turned into a crowd. A giant named Goliath had put his foot to that closed door, holding it firmly shut with his heavy chain armour. He was challenging the Lord God of Israel from within the land of Israel. Through that door, and the little stone, Israeli soldiers were able to march to freedom, to reclaim the land stolen from them by the Philistines. There are such great possibilities in small things. They house such potential, enough to allow Israel to march into a future, instead of being chased into a dark past by the fear of a foe.

The sling presented the ability to overcome

The word used to describe the sling *(kiblah)* can suggest that which is carving a piece of wood with a knife in a swinging motion. This would describe David swinging the leather thongs through the air before releasing the stone and defeating the enemy. Gesenius in his Hebrew-Chaldee Lexicon of the Bible says the word sling suggests 'the sailing of a ship', as it sends the waves to the right and to the left, parting them with its prow. It can describe that which, by its action moves obstacles. This is seen in the action of the sling as it whirls through the air, the passage of a ship as it parts the waves of the sea. The same action of the sling can mean 'to engrave,' as the engraver's tool moves from right to left, up and down digging deep, as the sling would pass easily through the air. There are many ways that God can write on the tablets of the heart. There are lessons that not only need learning, but need to be engraved, as with a tool upon the heart. Can you see both happening in this battle? New ships would sail from this port when the sling had done its work. Through that sling, God is writing something upon the heart of every soldier. It would be a day they would never forget. It was the location of defeat for one, the finding of a destiny for another.

The stone and the sling, like you and God, moved together, worked together to complete a task. What no hand or sword could do, the stone with the sling accomplished, each weapon causing its own wound, and in a unique way contributing to the winning of the battle. You have a contribution to make when *Dwarfing Giants* that no other can make.

The stone had no gem qualities

The stone used by David had no gem qualities; it contained only a few minerals. It wasn't chosen for its value or glitter. There was no intrinsic value in the piece of hard core. If you saw it, you would have just kicked it onto one side or thrown it into a pond to entertain yourself with the ripples it caused as it sank into oblivion beneath murky, disturbed waters. This was not chosen, as you were not chosen, because you were polished to perfection and shining, described as diamond or pearl. This 'stone warrior' found in a pebble from a brook is mentioned three times in the battle. 1 Samuel 17:49,49,50, a threefold cord that is not easily broken. Some things are never mentioned three times in Scripture, only once or twice. To be mentioned three times brings the glory of unity and strength into the influence of this pebble. The meaning of the word stone is 'to build'. God had to build the weakened army of Israel. He had to build both faith and hope again. A kingdom had to be built. The word stone means a stone of any kind whether polished, rough, small or large. From and through this very stone the House of Israel would be built, and the House of David would be part of it. It became a wedge of rock to enable the glory of Shalom to enter. It would become a stepping-stone for anyone who was facing great odds. As they heard what the shepherd boy accomplished, they would say, 'I too, am an Israelite!' In future days, when they felt their feet were being placed on uncertain ground, they would remember this stone, and their tread would be more assured. It was a foundation stone. It became just as important as the stones Israel brought with them out of the River Jordan.[3] Later in another extreme circumstance, this shepherd poet wrote, 'My feet had well nigh slipped.'[4] The memory of what this stone accomplished kept David's feet intact in slippery places. The memory of what happened lived on during his reign as king. When choosing soldiers or making appointments he would always remember the small. Those rejected can be winners if given the opportunity to serve. This stone represents hope for all those who feel rejected and hopeless. It was glorified through service. Although it might have been a dull colour, into every dark valley it would shine as a bright light, to be used by future pilgrims.

The stone and the sling were foolish weapons

The armoury of God as unusual as that which has not yet been discovered. This sling and stone was part of the 'foolish things' of this world that God chooses to confound the wise and the mighty.[5] The Eternal didn't have to move far or reach long to find such a weapon to win His war. He went to the 'off-scouring' of this world. The Holy One went to the 'trash heap' of nature. What nature had thrown unceremoniously on one side, God picked up. Nature had tossed it about as a rubber ball throwing it here and there. It landed where the Lord of all glory finds us. No one would have ever conceived the idea that a sling and a stone might work together, fulfil part of a great plan, and reveal the Divine mind. God's tools are shaped by nature. All the elements are brought into their own capacity when the Almighty takes them and uses them to confront His enemies. The ravages of nature, and all the feet that had trodden on this small particle would be released as it flew into the giants head, as a missile to its target, or as the eagle to its prey. All it suffered became part of it, more part of it than brush strokes become part of a master painting. This small object could only ever be but a stone, but it was a glorified one. It would never be an eagle, sweeping and diving, or a fish that swam around in the stream. It was swifter and surer in God's hands and plans than the striking head of the Cobra. If the Eternal had taken and used conventional weapons then He would have gone to the army of Israel. Samuel had taught Israel a great lesson when a king was required to succeed Saul. He was told not to look on the outward, but on the heart, and the son of Jesse was chosen.[6] Can you see how God works, as the Master Player, and moves the pawns into place long before they are required? Every time the Eternal wants a weapon in a man or a woman, long before they are taken and sharpened ready for use, God has been training them in some quiet back street, and sometimes in the depths of their despair.

Nothing just happens in God. He never puts sand or seed into a bag and allows it to run through a small hole, falling anywhere and everywhere. When the power of God organises a life, it is an order above what we call organisation. David was chosen long before the stone was found or even the sling was made. In God's timing they were all brought together, and the whole account becomes a beautiful mosaic. God didn't look for the splendid shield or the blood stained sword. He never entered the Sandhurst College of the day where Generals are trained. He took hold of a shepherd boy by the heartstrings and said, 'I will make you into a king, using a stone and a sling.' The first materials He used were men, and He still uses Mankind, but He is not limited to one type of material, He will use every part of His creation as a musician will use every string on an instrument, or the full vocal range of musical notes. Just as the singing voice will go through the whole range of notes, so the Supreme uses all His capabilities to make you capable. The speck is made spectacular. The world is His factory and workshop, and there are some magnificent things produced from what already exists. The Carpenter of Nazareth doesn't only look to men for His materials; He uses wood, stone, fish, bread, crumbs and spittle. David took bread and cheese to his brothers, but he took a sling loaded with a stone to a giant.

The stone and the sling brought success

The purpose of God for every life is to take that life and let it be ruled by Jesus Christ as King, a King in every situation of life. Each talent we have is both sling and stone. Each gift from God can be found in these two small things. Success is not in greatness. If it was, then Goliath wins every time. There is great (giant) glory when the feeble become strong, and the stone finds its strength in a sling. The very things that we 'disdain' look down upon God lifts up. Rejects are of better quality for God to use than any masterpiece. It is better to have the finger marks of God all over your life than the thumbprints of the famous. The hand of God shapes as its touches. The hand of the Supreme is softer and more sure than the feet or the heel of a man. His hands never tremble and they don't let anything fall to the ground. What God takes and what He catches, He keeps! What we feel the Lord could never use, He takes and uses fully. God had a Son, defined as 'the stone that the builders rejected,'[7] and men didn't receive Him. He became the Head of the corner. Wherever we are the throne of righteousness and power needs to be established. The Eternal will do it where He wants, and He will use such 'foolish' things. These two locked and lost in one another, the sling with the stone are a perfect description of unity. One was waiting for the other to act. They were placed together in friendship, fellowship, as those that were meant for one another. Being close together, almost knitted together, they saw a giant fall apart.

The sling and the stone can suggest so many things. The things that Jehovah uses to overcome our enemies, as we believe Him, are seen in what happened. Remember it was faith that knitted together these two instruments of war. They came together, and were closest when placed in a hand. It is the Hand of the Eternal that brings things of opposite nature together to fight in a battle. Faith went into that sling and obedience followed it. That is why it was such a great success. These two became the twins of success. In the corner of every heart, deep valley battles are en-acted as the enemy of the soul is engaged, but battles are won in God's way and using His methods. Those things in your past that you thought had worked against you need bringing together. Take whatever is useful from your present or your past, and use it in your future. Turn future happenings that might have been difficult into something achievable. That which is against you can be used as it is turned towards you working as the needle, to embroider a pattern in the grace that has been supplied. God creates many things from the broken bits of life. See the bits of grit, gathered by a bird at the seashore turned into a beautiful and multi-coloured shell that hold a future for a young bird that is housed in the egg. The pebble could do nothing without the piece of leather. If this stone could cry out it would say what you should say about your Lord, 'Without You I have no strength or ability to accomplish anything. You are my lifting power. I serve You as a stone in a sling.' One depended on the other for victory. The more the sling was turned through the air, the closer together they came. It is the same when we suffer. In the experience we are thrown together and come closer to our Lord. After the conflict one was not recognised without the other. They were both essential ingredients for success.

If we take Jehovah's stone and sling, whatever that may suggest to us, then we shall be crowned as winners. We go into the battle a boy and come out a king. God's methods are still the best methods. They have been tried and they work! Such a large thing was defeated by something so small-this is the hand of God! This is the way He works. The evidences of faith and grace are woven into this story. What the stone with the sling may represent are small things in life that help us to achieve our goals. Such a small thing as the song of a bird in the Dawn Chorus, which seems to fill every hedge and tree when we are feeling so alone. The dawning of a new day is another small thing, after a worrying night. The smile on a child's face, as it is turned towards us, when we have been furrowed by worry. A word said in the form of encouragement. These things become our sling and stone when we *Dwarf Giants*.

The stone and the sling were unconventional

If conventional weapons of horses, spears, shields, lances and bows were used, then the glory would have gone to men and weapons. The blacksmith or the forger of weapons would have been crowned. Soldiers and armies would have ordered these weapons that were able to defeat giants. If conventional weapons had been used the mark of the weapon maker would have been on each instrument of war. The blacksmiths who had forged the arsenal would have received the glory. They would have said 'it was my spear or sword that laid the giant flat.' There would have been no requirement to trust the Lord. When the sling and the stone were brought together, if other giants had been lined up they would also have fallen. Saul, if he had succeeded would have had this accomplishment engraved onto every spear and sword. Everyone would have wanted to wear his armour! Using the sling and stone God gives to us a great principle. Use something that men look down upon, such as the word of God or a promise for the heart, that men think will fail, and if you succeed, God will receive all the praise and the glory. It seemed so impossible as to be mad. It all looked so silly, a little shepherd lad, facing a great big giant, but God poured His wisdom into it for our teaching and for us to learn from that teaching. Using such basic weapons Jehovah blesses. Attempt something so impossible that when you bring it to maturity all will be amazed, and their faith will be increased because of your winning ways. It took a hand to bring them together. The hand of God is able to unite all the loose and broken qualities of life. He can restore one broken piece to another until they form a whole and become useful. With a stone and sling, God has an army that numbers just two! They will be as Caleb and Joshua the only two spies sent into the Promise Land who brought back a good report.

The valley of Elah can become your schoolroom where valuable lessons are taught, not simply chalk on a blackboard, or something written in a textbook. This was Shakespearian drama, happening before their eyes! All power and victory must be traced back to its source, and the fountainhead of this victory was not traced back to Saul or David, but to the Giver of all good gifts. Jehovah used the useable to its full capacity and beyond. Your gifting may be small but there are no limits with the Sovereign. Without the Eternal it could never have been performed. The stone, thrown away by nature was caught and trained for war by the hand of God. Little fragments of desire, the size of a pebble can be used. Small faith in a sling can grow into the size of the giant it topples. Your life lost in God as the stone was in the sling can attain the unattainable. Thongs produced songs, 'David has slain his ten thousands.' Pebbles can produce praise for God.

The stone and the sling are your weapons

When we lack a natural ability, to provide the answers to any affront, we are thrown back on God. When we have no answer, He provides the answer through Jesus Christ. We tend to dig very deep into mind and heart in order to find a solution, but we have to go deeper until we find ourselves with the mind of God, and the armoury of answers that God has chosen for us to use. To know that the Almighty has spoken to you, even if the message is as small as a pebble, the noise of His voice like the whirling of a sling, that is enough to bring you great assurance. To have heard and understood is the best piece of armoury for your soul. With conviction that you are right you can scale every mountain of flesh. Giants and opposition can rant and rave, but if God is on your side it means that you are armoured on every side. The enemy may say many things, but the most eloquent speech was heard in that which was never spoken represented by two weapons, the stone and the sling.

If you listed on paper the weapons that the future king used and compared them to Goliath the natural man would choose Goliath of Gath every time. We can all achieve goals on paper. The glory and thinking of this world was encased in Goliath's armour. The power and thinking of God was as free as a stone loosed from a sling. A hand captured it, the hand of the man of God, to set it free forever with a greater liberty to accomplish greater things. It was that surrender that brought about its valedictory. The stone didn't even know where it was going; it didn't know a thing about the battle, it just did as the hand and sling commanded. Its true direction and mission was left to another. That hand of the Lord can become your springboard into victory.

When we have the same convictions about our King as the stone had about the sling, then we shall achieve our objectives. We shall readily say, 'Lord, I can only go where you send me, and if I am unwilling to go, thrust me into the battle as the sling thrust the stone. When I am as one dead, cold, lifeless, having lost my first love, take me and turn me as a stone in a sling, and send me on a mission into another sphere. Don't let me settled down; keep inspiring me to go on. When I lose my life and purpose, and become as a fallen broken stone, grant me new purpose, the purpose that requires as much zeal as a stone requires from a piece of leather. When I lose my sense of direction and will not go forward, be as a Sling to me.'

The stone and the sling introduced God

The stone and the sling bring us into a new concept of God and His ways. He will not only reveal His glory in the large objects of nature such as stars and storms. The smaller was hidden in the larger. The way God does anything is by using small-unnoticed objects. These instruments are so 'everyday' that they are hardly noticed. The eyes of the natural man don't always see what God wants them to see. They pass over such gifts as a sling and a stone. The glare and the trumpet blowing, the loud noise and the great show belong to Goliath's camp. God's method is a man who moved as silently but as surely as a stone from a sling.

That person must be dedicated. If they are given to one cause with one heart and mind for the glory of God, they will prevail. There will be no falling to the ground or stopping short. They will succeed where more gifted people have failed. As the sling went around with the stone within its grasp, it made the sound of many bees looking for honey. That honey was in the defeat of the Philistine. This was the only trumpet that God blew on that day, heard in the sound of the sling. Something that men would not give a second glance is the very object that is taken and used. 'Boy beats the best of the Philistines!' This would have been the 'Valley Journal' headline that day.

The stone and the sling were small, not great

The One above uses the small and not the great. It takes the Almighty to accomplish something out of nothing. The One that put the light of His eyes into stars also put power into something inanimate. The Lord takes the small things that are broken as stones. When broken in spirit we are candidates for glory. Being small, unnoticed and unknown become your credentials. When He is looking for weapons to fight His wars He goes to the bottom of the pile. What is obvious and on top of the list, He demotes in favour of that which is so small it is ready to slip off the page. When the inventory is made slings and stones are not counted as weapons. They don't come within the first ten. The very things that would have been toys to the young shepherd boy, Jehovah took and used to establish the principles of His Kingdom. These articles of war were not even included in the weapons that soldiers were given, yet were included in God's armoury. His arsenal is filled with small items that He calls great things. Things like snails, conies, badgers, the cry of a baby in Moses, the rod in his hand, the blowing of trumpets and the smashing of vessels, digging ditches, bread and fish, a mite in the hand of a widow woman, a piece of bread in another's hand. The list is endless of the small things that the Eternal has used to accomplish great things. God is not tied down to our choice or the weapons that we think are great. He steps aside from those things that we pray for, with which we hope to overcome giants. When the Almighty shops for weapons, it is the ones left off His list that we need to discount. The sling and the stone are at the top of His list.

David already had the sling; he needed to be balanced by a stone. We all require something to balance us, so that we will not wobble or be blown off course. We require the stones of life, just as the bee does when flying in the wind, and carrying a small piece of grit to keep it balanced. David already had one weapon, but the next article of war had to be found. God adds to what we already have and, in doing so, He adds to everything. Your gift might be just like the pebble at the bottom of a stream lost to the cause in a deep valley of depression. It is sometimes, the very things we don't ask for, the things we fail to recognise as having potential that He uses. There are some talents that we don't have to pray about. Just use what you have, make them available. Sometimes you are asked to lay aside your natural endowments so that He can place that which He has wrought in His heart into your heart. Then the heart is stretched. The heart is 'full and running over,' as in Psalm 23.

The stone and the sling were of a different nature

David killed Goliath because two items different natures were willing to get wrapped up in one another and lost in each other's cause. There was no competition, they were complimentary. One could do what the other could not. Looking at the sling you would not see the stone inside. It would be as Moses being covered in a rock by the hand of God in Exodus 33:22. There wasn't a hair's breadth between them. The faster the sling whirled through the air, the closer together they came. The sling was lost in the power of the stone, and the stone was lost in the power of the sling. Two missions merged into one, hand and heart. These two were seen as one, as one was lost in the other's cause. One was friend and helper to the other. They would live, fly and die for one another. The stone would only travel as far as the sling took it.

They parted company once their mission was complete. The stone was just used once. It then made way for other stones to do their work in defeating Goliath's brothers. The sling was taken and used many times. Work, for some, is completed in just a short space of time, while others are called to serve the Lord of Hosts for a lifetime. This is true relationship, describing two ships sailing side by side as in a convoy. Not as shallow as 'skin deep' but as deep as the heart. These two were workers together for the glory of God. In this incident there is such a beautiful illustration of real unity, and what it will accomplish. Unity is not conformity, each had its own distinction that was used to compliment and complete the other.

If you can get so involved with your church, your sister or brother as these two inseparable friends did, then all will be well. The sling alone and the stone alone win no battles. It is 'cold stone' without the hand and the sling. The sling was as empty as an empty head without the stone. It was socket with the eye. The stone must not become a wall of partition. It must lose its identity in another's ministry. It must be willing to be hidden before it could be revealed. The leather sling has to put up with the coarse shape of the stone. It allowed itself to be moulded to the shape of the stone. Its port and sea were of the same nature. Losers became winners. The stone and the sling, as far as we know had never faced a giant before. The stone must surrender its freedom to the sling before action can take place. Both must pass through the hand of a king.

The stone and the sling were brought together in battle

It was a battle that brought these two implements of war together. There are times when troubles of gigantic proportions bring us together. United they conquered, divided they must fall. It is Goliath who must fall. One without the other was like a bird with one wing or an aeroplane without an engine. What we suffer, and what we must take our stand against should bring us so closely together that not even skin separates us. Locked into another's vision and purpose they excelled even as we can. Each lived and existed to serve the other. They went the same way, faced the same direction. The work of one was the work of the other. The burden of the work and the battle was equally shared. They did what they were best at doing. After coming together as the stone and the sling they were separated only when the temptation fell. The sling would be used again, but the pebble died as it entered the giant's temple it made the supreme sacrifice. The sling would go on to do something else. The stone had but one opportunity. It had to do its best on this one occasion. It sank with all the force and dedication it knew into the cranium of the Gathite. The stone stopped where the Gath man fell, lodged in his temple. It took the temptation to where the king could put his feet on it. It took that cruel, mocking giant right down to the earth for it to be buried forever.

The stone and the sling were from different backgrounds

The sling might have been part of the body of the lion or the bear that were killed earlier. With gut used as the strands or even pieces of cut leather and hide used as thongs. The sling came from one area, while the stones came from the valley. The stone had been a free agent for the sun and rains to kiss, the winds to blow softly upon its face. When it was placed in the sling, it gained a new liberty. It might seem as if it would be restricted or even incarcerated as it was placed within the confines of the sling, but in losing its life it found it. The sling might have seemed like a coffin to the stone that was hidden in it, yet from that leather coffin the sling, came the resurrection and life of Israel. The freedom of surrender is found here. It could only rise to new heights through submission. It could only fight and win when it surrendered to another. It knew the limitations of its service while it operated alone without the influence of another. Without being used, it could never rise above the earth's surface, could never come out of the valley. Once a stone, always a stone, alone. It could have stayed where it was forever but for the hand of the king. Unless we recognise the service and the qualities of another, we ourselves must fail. What that brother or sister possesses might not fit into what I think is service, but they serve God and not man. The very ministry you find objectionable can become the object of your love and service. One can never do what the other must do neither the sling nor the stone acting alone can overcome the giant. There was a rising into power as the sling embraced the stone. It was fellowship for just a moment, yet it would reap a harvest that was to last forever. When we lose our lives, we find them. What we think is a stone in a sling that will limit us, is the very thing that will bring us achievement. Let each talent fulfil its potential.

The stone gathered strength from the sling

We are not very happy or ready to face the discipline of the cross that releases the true you and me into our destiny. We think devotion to another's cause will limit us, when the reversal is true. One gathers strength from the other. One provides what another cannot provide. The sling gave the stone an almighty push. That sling was a new source of life. We need one another for accomplishment, as these two needed one another. Alone, you will never strike your target; you will never overcome the real giants of life. The sling will be left whirling around, and the stone will be still and silent with no message from God to Goliath of Gath. Without others we become quite useless. Love others they are the other part of your soul. Each brother and sister is a segment, as part of the whole. Together you are as a sweet orange, but alone you are only peel or pip!

I must be dependent on you and you on me, working together as ball to joint or thought and brain. We two together can accomplish great things for the Supreme. The stone had to get lost in the sling before it could lose itself in the forehead of the giant. The deeper it sank into the leather the further it would go and the deeper it would sink into its target. It is always one step at a time. The placing of a stone and companion together was the beginning of imparted strength. One did something for the other. They must be as a horse and carriage, a hand in a glove. 'Where you cannot go, I will lift you,' says the sling to the stone. 'I can't swirl around in circles at great speed but I can lay here in your arms as clay in the hands of the potter,' replies the stone. 'I am here for you to do with me as you require.' There was an interchanging of plans, a sharing of what they must do. They, who have no will of their own, were operated by a greater will. The 'stony' burden was lifted by something else. The stone must get some of the dye and colour of the leather into it. The smell, and maybe a little of the colour of the sling was taken by the stone into the head of the giant. The victory belonged to the two of them and to the Eternal Who allowed it all to happen. The giant never felt the sling, but he certainly felt the stone! When that arrived, he knew he had been visited!

The stone and the sling had to become one

While these two stood afar off from one another, one would remain forever in the valley. That would be the sum of its achievement. The sling would remain with the memory of the blood of lion and bear, but not of a giant. You may stand in grand isolation, but you will win no battles until God and His weapons become your partners. When the Knights of the Round Table returned from battle without scars, they were sent back to produce evidence that they had been in a fight!

There is a verse in Proverbs 18:1, that states, 'The isolationist only thinks of himself.' As a Church, as a company of people we are better and greater when we forget our differences and are together. The talent of another helps us to achieve and mature. They save us from being ordinary and selfish. You become part of another, as you share your gift with others. The Church is a great area for taking and using what you are and what has been given to you. In Manchester, England, there is a famous prison called 'Strangeways'. The name means 'the gathering together of many different waters'. The Church is where those who are prisoners are set free, as with so many gifts they come together as 'many waters'. When we fellowship, we become like the wine distillers in Leeds, West Yorkshire, England. They take many different sorts of weak and cheap wines and through a process of mixing together produce a good, palatable wine. The secret is found in the mixing together, one weak or poor wine giving what it has to another, until they are blended into one.

The stone and the sling required closeness for success

When revival unity comes the giants we war against had better watch out! The success and the secret of it came as they clung together. These two were twin brothers in the same womb. The closer they were, and you can't get much closer than a stone in a sling, the better work they were able to accomplish. When we realise our total dependence on one another, then we strike our targets as our vision is revealed. One felt the weight of companionship, as the stone felt the surge of the zeal from the sling. Neither was just decorative armour, or there, as some of the soldiers were from each army, just to see the battle, and wonder what the outcome would be. They were at the battle scene in order to enter into the battle. God has reserves ready to be released into the battle of your heart. There are as those who serve yet only stand and wait. There were no limits attached to their commitment to one another. It was true, rare and full. It took them all the way with each other. You will share my blessings and victory. There was a common enemy, a common objective. The killing of the giant and the resisting of temptation will be attributed to both of these instruments.

The call they received came in the hand that took them and used them. When they were lost in that hand, then they were used. All our accolades come because of the Hand that guides and governs us. Anybody looking for the sling and the stone would see neither as they were held in the hand. The sling was in the girdle of the shepherd, and the stone was hidden inside the shepherd's bag. The glory of these two weapons of warfare was the future king's hand. All that blood stained hand (it had killed many beasts) did was to present them with an opportunity for service, just as the two nailed hands of Jesus outstretched on a cross did for us. Without the hand, they were stone and leather and that is all they would ever be. They lacked identity, purpose and vision for past, present or future. It is the hand of the Lord of Hosts that provides such remarkable victories. There was a greater Hand at work than the hand of a youth. That Hand was a closed door when it was closed as a fist, but presented a door of opportunity when it opened. To 'bare the 'palm' to the best' was used by the Romans to depict the successful gladiator, who opened his hand and revealed the palm, to receive a branch from a palm tree after a notable victory or great achievement.

The stone left the hand with far greater speed than the dove left the hand of Noah to see if the earth was dry. The stone was mad about its mission. Its zeal to travel to the target was never in question. Could it travel that far? Alone, it could not travel at all, but with the other weapon it could. What would the stone accomplish at the end of its journey? That was left with God. 'Caleb 'wholly' followed the Lord.'[8] In the word 'wholly' is the figure of the eagle seeing the prey, and swooping to take it on the run. The wings of the bird with its talons outstretched, its eyes on only one object is a full picture of devotion to a cause. It is the intensity of the bird that concentrates its whole body on the prey before it. The eagle goes for the prey as if it is its first and last meal. Its desires are all in that one act. The stone travelled in the same manner, and is an illustration of the word dedication. It went to its target as with a fixation.

The stone and the sling were weak when alone

The mission would not have been accomplished if these two pioneers in stone and sling had remained as they were. Both had to be disturbed and taken from where they were. There is real achievement and dedication when we feel that we are being used, and that our service is part of another's service. At the end of the battle, if Jehovah and David get the glory, the stone and the sling don't mind. They have been available, and the greatest thing you can do with any sling, is to take it and use it. Both were made to feel needed. They had strengths and weaknesses, but the strength of one cancelled out the weakness of others. God had a large purpose for something so small as a stone in its armour of leather. The stone that is taken as a weapon of war or to build with has all the achievements necessary.

Both instruments were taken from a blank past and introduced to a future of glory in God. From being quite useless, the stone was taken into service. It proved to both what could be achieved if they were in the right place at the right time. The 'servant heart' must be as stone, unmoved by opinions, if it is to arrive at the scene of its calling. Make your calling and election sure, as sure as a stone, by striking the target and defeating the failure or temptation. As the sling had to be spun around almost like the clay on the potter's wheel it brought it into another dimension. Both were involved in something far bigger than they were. Aim for the sky, and hit a giant who stands in the way! They had justified their existence. When the roll of honour is called, these unusual weapons will be mentioned. It was glory based on a sling and stone. Two of the smallest things in the Israeli weaponry were the cause of the victory. It was their commitment that paid dividend. This would be their finest hour and would lead to them becoming part of all future celebrations when the accomplishments of the nation were mentioned.

The stone and the sling rank among the greatest weapons

Anyone hearing the story must have known that there was a greater Power involved in such a victory. This will rank as one of the greatest victories in the history of Israel. There are many such victories, where people have been facing tremendous odds, but Power has brought them through. Their achievements in God never became their Achilles' heel. They gave God the glory. As they were laid on one side, the Glory moved on to some other challenge. Next time the weapons would be quite different, but both weapons and targets would be part of a future battle. This sling loaded with a stone was ranked among the 'helps' listed in the ministries of 1 Corinthians 12:28. In Acts 27:17 the word 'helps' is used to describe the 'under girding' of a ship. These were cables that passed under the ship to strengthen it during a time of storm.

When God is looking for a great army it may only consist of two or three, but those two or three make everything count. The stone must not be seen, or its coarse make-up, so it hides in the sling. The same doctrine applies to us as we hide in Jesus Christ. Stones can be handled well, they are swift and they have no will of their own. That is the secret of their success. The greater glory of this battle belonged to these two, these twins of armour who brought such success through their devotion to a cause. History records for all time that together they *Dwarfed Giants*.

Notes

1. Judges 7.
2. See *Dr James Strong Exhaustive Concordance* and H. W. F. Gesenius' *Hebrew-Chaldee Lexicon*. Both published by Baker.
3. Joshua 4:3-8.
4. Psalm 73:2.
5. 1 Corinthians 1:27.
6. 1 Samuel 16:10.
7. Luke 20:17.
8. Deuteronomy 1:36.

Chapter

11

The Hand in the Bag

Passing through the valley David encountered many things that had never happened to him before. What happened to him happens to all who seek to faithfully follow the Lord. Sometimes things you are called to go through are like a hand being placed into the blackness of a bag. When the hand of the future king entered that pouch there was nothing in his hand, but when it was withdrawn it was clutching a precious stone that would lead to victory. Such granite is being placed into our character as we pass through the darkness. The hand of the shepherd had to disappear into his scrip before the hand of God was seen. It was the surrendering of the youth's hand, to be replaced by a greater Hand.

As we pass through the thorns of life we catch some of the scent of the roses, and that scent remains with us. If we will lift up small pieces however fragmented even from a shattered life, those small fragments can be used to form the mosaic picture of what we shall be and do in God. Greatness is not found in the grandeur of palaces or much trumpet blowing, but in the hard knock when you come up against the stones of life. The Sovereign Lord is always at work, even in our indecisive moments. The Lord's man was being monitored and tutored.

Jehovah God builds with the small stones and the small decisions. They result in great acts. He builds slowly but surely, just as the 'mills of God grind' and what He built reigned in Israel for over forty years. We need to take whatever happens, and let it blend together to make us into the person that we should be. You will only be what you allow to work into your life. Every wooden figure has had to pass under the paring knife in the hands of the designer, before the model appears.

Experiences must be hand gathered

Coming through every valley, as the sun breaks out from its hiding place and clouds part as curtains, there must be the gathering of stones into the bag. As they were taken, broken, yet part of a whole and put into a bag, so the Lord would take a life, and put it into the depths of His love for safekeeping. There must be that 'hand gathered' as you travel the hills of life. Like the armour of Gath, they cannot be passed on. There will always be that which is around you, and is at your feet waiting for you to take and use.

These were not old stones which had been used many times before; they were new ones that the son of Jesse picked up as he moved to the battlefront, to where he could see the form of the giant. The old happenings just become 'old hat' and 'old shoe'. It is the new things that must be made to count when character is being formed, and being weighed in the balances and found wanting. These pieces of granite had never been in the shepherd's hand or bag before. Character is more than a shout from a giant or the blast from a trumpet. You must know the stones; they must be hand picked. The promises of God must be your Friends, knowing them better than you know what is assailing you. The time that the stone or the hand spent in the bag wasn't wasted. What the Lord gives, is given to help you. It must be fully used up.

What is given today is your 'daily bread', and will sustain you just as these stones strengthened the servant. Every ounce of your life needs to be used in God's warfare. Do not return from the battlefront with weapons that have never been drawn or used. So many promises of the Eternal can be turned into 'picture postcards'. For some they contain only a picture of the power of God. The stones in the valley weren't meant to be placed in order, as an artisan might take and use them. They need to be mustered as soldiers and servant, each having a glory of its own. Being an artisan is better than being a mere scribbler, using gold paint to scribble with. We are not here to count the numbers of promises; we are here to use them! Act on what the Lord has said! Find out if the stones will work! To do that you have to put your hand into the bag, and take from your spirit what your Defender has placed in it. Don't bring out the darkness of the bag; bring out things of an eternal nature. There is the 'plan of the pebble' in the shepherd's container. There must be something in the heart before, during and after the event. Stones were used in the Temptation of Christ to illustrate the power of God, Matthew 4:3,4.

What happens today is preparation for tomorrow

There is a future, a glorious future in the experiences of today. Realise that what is happening to you is of Designer quality. The Elohim who laid out the hills, planted the shrubs and taught the fish to swim is planning and planting His design for you. Each stone had its own design. David, the man of God's choice took these stones with the thought in his heart that they might be needed sometime in the future. He had an eye to the future. He didn't look to the soldiers of Israel, to king Saul or to the giant, but to God. There his eyes found true rest for his heart. The plan of attack and conquest was already being conceived. From one small sling, through the stone and the bag came a great victory. Your conquest may commence very small, but it will grow and grow.

Out of the failures of yesterday be prepared to build for a better tomorrow. David's hand was prepared to adventure itself into the darkness of the sack that the stones were housed in. From the momentary darkness came his very weapons of war. Here and now you may commence building your future with stones, precious (valued above value) promises. The future giant-slayer had to touch another realm, and he did this when his hand was buried in the bag. He thrust himself where the potential for victory was found.

God's army only numbered one!

It was a fair exchange, one stone and one promise for a giant. In that giant was all the pride of Philistia. The Lord of Hosts formed His army, numbering one, David of Bethlehem in order to bring the giant down! Things don't stand in the way forever, for there is that within your heart love, zeal, faith and choice that make up five stones for attack. You can win with just one being used, but it must be fully used. It went into the bag as a pebble, yet because of the attack upon the giant and the victory, it came out a pearl. A true pearl of wisdom came from the bag, declaring the wisdom and knowledge of God in battles. As the hand clasp the stone, so the stone must take hold of the work it was sent to do. What David's hand entered into was a full dedication, totally given to the sling, to a small rock and the bag. He filled his hand with one thing at a time. From a confined space, something was set free to fulfil a mission.

Be the person that God has chosen you to be

There would always be a need in David for God to perfect. You are only what God, your Commander in Chief has desired, when temptation, be it small or great is lying dead, without breath or head and the eyes closed at your feet. The stones are not in the bag to balance the young man, as the promises of God are not in the Bible to act as ballast. He could have filled the leather shape with more stones. It is the storing up, as the squirrel does with nuts or the dog burying the bone so that they can return to the past, and use it in the present and in the future. These stones were better than gold nuggets; the bag was better than a jewel casket.

There are so many small things, the size of a small stone in the hand that need keeping to be used in the coming days. The days when, in Goliath, the shadow and the substance of that great mound of flesh seen and known as a temptation threatens you. Whatever happens to you, do not reject it keep it for the coming days. It may seem only as important as a part chipped from a rock, but wait until the plan for your life is developed. It is then that each happening in your days of tribulation will be pieced together as parts of a puzzle. If you can't find the centrepiece don't throw away all the other pieces. Wait until the Divine hand brings them together. Wait until you have passed through the valley and the dark night has been etched with the light of another day. There is fragmentation that needs storing to be used in time of crisis. If you haven't learned to pray, you will be weak when suddenly you have to pray as you face great odds.

David had collected valuables from the path of life. What he took, he reserved, ready for the hand to enter the bag and use its dark secrets. His treasures and your treasures are not in this world's gems, they are found in the deep hurts and happenings of life, wrestling with lions and bears as suggestions of temptation, and 'walking through' valleys. You have in your heart what you have passed through. There are great fish in the sea that gather plankton for strength as they sweep through waters. There is a certain blending that takes place as unkind and kind meet together. The rough and the smooth are interwoven in the stone and the hand coming together, held together by the sides of the scrip. The things we learn and those things that teach us can be as hurtful as a point of the diamond engraving the rock, or as rough as a broken stone. When it has finished its 'plough work' the message of what has been written remains forever. Winds cannot blow it out storms with their rains cannot wash it out. Whether they are stones or roses, it matters not. You have collected something from everything you met, as you make every challenge serve you.

We obtain weapons when passing through the valley

The skin of the bear and lion was made useful in the tent of the young warrior. David picked up the stone in the valley, not on the mountaintop. It is not in the glamour and the adulation of life that we gain, it is in the rough and the rugged; between the furrows where the blade of the plough has passed that real seeds are scattered and sown in the hope of a future harvest. Your darkest moments can become your dearest moments. These stones were the silver lining in the dark cloud for the warrior. Each pain we suffer is another adventure knocking at the heart's door, saying 'Please let me in.' The young prince in waiting didn't just take from experience for himself. The pieces of rock were placed into his reservoir, but they were taken out to help, and in helping himself he helped others.

We are not aware when weapons are being formed and found

It might appear to be a casual happening when it says that David took five smooth stones, 1 Samuel 17:40. It was as ordinary as coughing among the shepherds of the nation. It was so 'every day' that is was 'every day'! Yet something ordinary had to be converted into something far more glorious. You will always have to see deeper than the bag. There is the need to receive a revelation from the Sovereign Lord to understand some things, while He understands all things. You can never judge the end or the outcome of any matter by the beginning. Like us, the young shepherd boy knew that to keep is not to waste. He knew what to throw away. This stone could be as the stone that Jacob set up for a pillar, and dreamed dreams with his head resting securely upon it.[1] Goliath would be slain. It would become part of his crown as future king. When Israel crossed the River Jordan they had to lift stones from the riverbed as evidence.[2]

This was such a stone, picked up and used for the building of the character of the nation in stone. It contained more glory than the stones that fell from Jericho's walls. It had a more enduring quality than those 'fished up' from the bottom of the River Jordan. With this stone bridges would be built. It became a stepping-stone through the flood of opposition. It would be the first stone in a wall to keep the Philistines at bay. The hand had to take hold of it and it could only do that by moving alongside. When we speak of things being kept 'at bay', as Goliath was kept 'at bay' until the boy killed the man, we mean that the giant was kept out of the harbour bay until permission was granted. In 'keeping at bay' we see a ship waiting to enter the harbour. In the days of yore it could not come into the harbour until the flag was raised as a signal for entry. It was kept 'at bay', in 'abeyance' until it received further instructions. 'Keeping at bay' can also refer to keeping the hounds back or on the leash, chasing you as temptation, waiting to overtake and destroy. If the hounds are kept 'at bay' the stag knows that it is still alive. Baying hounds are not feeding hounds. It is not wrong to be tempted, even Jesus was tempted.[3] The wrong is to let the hounds come beyond the 'baying', it is then you are destroyed. The future Light of Israel did not simply resist evil; he slew it in the name of the Lord.

When we are empty we shall be filled

David came with an empty hand to lift up something and put it into his scrip. The only thing that filled the cavity was darkness. It could have been filled with junk. It could have become as a little boy's pocket, full of all manner of things such as string, chalk, a rubber, some cotton and even a nail! In that scrip he kept his cheese sandwich. What a good diet for soldiers of the King, and what a menu for a future king, cheese sandwiches and stones! We all need opposites such as bread, cheese and stones.

Was the bag made from the skin of the lion? If it was, here was a testimony of what slaying a lion could do in providing the sack that contained the victory. Little did David realise how necessary that, which he had taken and made part of him would be so useful in the future! With an empty bag, as with an empty heart, we are vulnerable when under attack. If it is not full, it can be filled with emptiness and darkness. The best way to keep other things out is to put something in. Let your heart be filled with the promises and presence of the Eternal. Let your fellowship be so real and deep that you fly forward in zeal to perform the word of the Lord of Hosts.

We require the right weapons for the right moment

There might have been no thought of battle or conquest in the shepherd boy's young heart as he picked up the stone. He picked it up as young boys do, but God was in that one act. He would take it in case he needed it. Small incidents lead to great acts. It is when we take to heart all that happens, we take to ourselves what William Shakespeare called 'hoops of steel'. That stone was as good as any arrow, in fact it was better because it was the right thing for the moment. Later, he would slay others with the sword of Goliath. The weapons are many, but at the moment it is the small thing that will count when we are facing great odds. It is having the right word at the right time. It is so safe when facing great odds to have a promise from God for that one occasion. Each stone in the bag was taken by the hand, and used in a different manner. Each had a service to render, a plan to fulfil.

Many might have taken the stones, deposited them, and then forgotten all about them. The hand must be at full stretch for it to count. There are so many periods of suffering, some large, some small, of many varying shapes. Lasting for many years, or for only a few weeks. God allows things to happen to every Christian, so that we might not forget. They come to us as stones. He has to apply the stone to keep it in our hearts and memories, to be used in the future. At the right moment the hand went into the bag, and there were reserves on that day. The hand being dipped into the bag shows the commitment of that hand to the vehicle holding the stones. One is prepared to get involved with the other. You have to be the springboard, and the pebble will be the swimmer.

The son of Jesse had nothing else in his hand, so it easily fitted into that which contained the required piece of strata. When giving yourself give all there is of you. The fingers, the palm and the nails, the whole structure of the hand were given. It was almost as if the hand was created for the stone. That hand became the throne that the stone would rule from, and from the presence of the hand it went on into service and conflict. There was no staying there in the warmth and security of the palm.

The promises of God are our weapons

There are some things that need to be used as weapons; other things need sending with great force to accomplish their desired end. We must mean what we say and do what we must do. It is not enough to 'flick' a promise at the adversary. Half hearted attempts mean half hearted results. Life and victory does not commence until the hand goes deeply into the satchel. Sometimes we have to speak the Word of God with the force of a stone being sent from a sling. Our convictions must be sure. There must be zeal, as there was in this battle, as we shall discover in a further chapter.

There were only five stones in the pouch. When David took one, another four were left. The decision as to which stone should be used was left with the hand. You must let the Lord choose. At the first dip he did not take everything out of the bag. Don't use all your weapons at once, choose the text or the promise that is relevant for the occasion and the battle. You may go to God time and time again, and you will never reduce or run out of the resources of the Eternal. There is so much in God that you can never even reach the fingertips of the Everlasting Arms! Too much or too little was never taken from the pocket of leather. At one grasp enough was taken because it held a supply there. Just enough was taken to win the day. He returned to it as something that had been placed in reserve for such a time as this. The stone, and those left in the wallet were as riches indeed. Anything is 'rich' that assists you to conquer vile circumstances. Riches are not in money or jewels, stocks and shares, they are the very things that meet the need at the moment of challenge. Each pebble was more rare and more assuring than all the wealth in the king's treasury. Nobody else, including king Saul had any of these hard rocks. When David reached out his hand he made them his own.

The promises of God need placing in the heart

The promises of God are there, and are meant to be taken by you. God loves to see an empty bag. All that is within the pouch is within the human heart, placed there waiting to be used. You do that when you believe. How many stones, how many promises can you believe Him for? Have a heart as full of the Word of God as this pocket was with pebbles. There are as many and more promises in the Bible as there were stones in this sack just waiting for you to put your hand in and take them out to be used. All the stone required was a helping hand to lift and use it by slinging it through the air. The young lad never took the stone out of the scrip just to give it an airing, or to let it see the scenery! There was no time for a 'trial run'. He took it out of reserve because it had been put there for this moment. When the promises of the Almighty and His hand come together, there will be the *Dwarfing of Giants*. All the Lord has and is must enter you before it enters the giant. The stone went from the bag to the head of the beast. This object put Goliath's 'light out', but lit with brilliance a shepherd boy.

There are reserves for you. All you need do is to put your hand into the bag. Face the darkness and the unknown in the bag. In that darkness within its folds there is light. There is a Power at your side. You never know what determination might uncover or discover! Jesus Christ came to earth and lived a full life, filling it with so many things that you might take and use in adverse situations. The deeper you go, as the hand of David went deep into the bag, the more there is. Jehovah Jireh has provided you with so much to be used when facing the enemy. Why fight with the sticks and the brooms from your own imagination when real stones and a sling with the power of God have been provided? Do not use the lesser, or yesterday's means for today's battles, use that which is freshly provided in your own heart. Do as was commanded in the New Testament: 'Loose him and let him go!'[4]

The stone required both the hand and the scrip. Without that hand lifting it, there was no power. It would, by nature, have fallen to the ground. The scrip was required to carry the stone to the place where it would be most effective. Using it too early would be as bad as using it too late. Wait until the precise moment of attack, when you have a full frontal view of the enemy, then quote the Word and see that evil fall as an axed tree.

We will call him Robert (that is not his real name). He had attended his church one Sunday evening in Eccles, Lancashire, England. He stopped to catch a bus home when a strong, large young man approached him and demanded money from him. Robert only had £1.50 and his bus ticket home. Rather than be smashed to the ground he surrendered both money and ticket. The thief snatched them from him. As he took them Robert said, 'I am a Christian and I love the Lord Jesus Christ. I have been to church, and am on my way home.' When he mentioned the name of Jesus, the assailant immediately gave him back his money and the ticket! Then while sitting on the bus with him, the assailant asked Robert to tell him more about this Jesus.

We are sometimes like that stone, we tend to gravitate, and become belittling of ourselves. What we cannot reach, the Hand can. What we cannot do the Hand can do in all circumstances, reaching where we can only look. What God has said is effective, we make of none effect by our lack of faith. 'Has God said?'[5] This robs you of the ability to demonstrate conquest. While we have clouds of doubt the Sun of accomplishment will never shine upon us. Pessimism can become our demeanour, yet God says we can be as that stone in the bag. Hidden in Him, like the stone in the pouch, for Him to reveal and help you to make your mark. That life of yours is made to count for every ounce. Every gram of the piece of grit counted in the conquest. You can make your mark even in giants. What seems like a fortress of flesh can be opened to you, and a small weapon can open up the great and the strong. The small tin opener will open a large tin! The bottle-opener will reveal the contents of the bottle when it is applied. The stone will topple the tyrant. There is that which is made of stone which will be needed in future days. The promises of God are not cast in straw, leaves, flower heads or chaff, but in stone. The Asda Super Stores in Lancashire have a huge rock placed outside each store. They have written on each rock their promises to keep prices down forever. Written in stone (the Resurrection Stone) are the promises of God, in order that you might be reminded of the character of the One who has promised.

Some lessons are difficult to learn

Stone will always overcome the flesh as seen in this giant. This was one stone that a giant could not lift or shift. There are hard lessons of stone quality that need to enter into your bag, things difficult to learn, but once they have been learned then they are priced above rubies. It is useless leaving stones on the floor, you need to pick things out of what is happening to you, and keep them in reserve. Not every loose stone was taken, only the five that would count in conflict. God allows the stick and the stones, the 'thick and the 'thin' because He knows the quality of what will be required of you in the future. We only see stones in a bag, carried by a young man who doesn't really know what he is doing. There are segments of suffering that can be taken and used. David had seen these stones at work before, he knew they could do the job again and again. Tools of the trade become tools of truth, weapons of our warfare. Weapons are forged in the fires of your own temptations.

Our enemies are right where we are

In our scrip we have the Scriptures, and the things written are there for our learning and admonition. There are so many miracles and happenings for us to take hold of, as we believe the Giver of the promise to overcome the Goliath at the end of the bed or at the bottom of the stairs. He even comes into the office or into the crowd that we stand among. Remember some of David's greatest enemies were not simply in a giant, they were in those of his own familiar friends and family.[6] Some of his brothers had already taunted him and accused him of pride because he had come to 'see' the battle. How wrong they were! He never came to 'look' at the battle he came to 'leap into' it! The person who wins has learned to resist using what God has granted. After the storm suffering souls have snatched something from the lightening, and placed it in their own soul. Colours from the rainbow are taken to decorate and illuminate their own bland souls.

The stone had a work to do

There wasn't a lot of variety in the bag but there was enough to kill a giant. Life itself is first one stone after another, one giant after another. Giants come in all shapes and sizes; they are not all from Gath. There is a stone for every giant. The fact that Jesus rolled away the stone when He rose from the dead should give you great confidence. That same resurrection stone was meant to crush all that would break you into pieces. The piece of rock David used had all the security it required both in the bag and in the giant. It was put into the compartment, not to remain as a stone soldier or statue. It wasn't put there for comfort, to remain there forever. Part of its training for reigning was in the dark corner of the bag being squeezed by the hand that collected it. The hand that found it used it, taking it to its ultimate destiny. It was held in reserve not retired! It was waiting not sleeping, awaiting resurrection into new life. It was going to become the partner of a king! The bag, as the heart, must not become a bed for the Word of God. It must become a factory, where it produces something through us. It was in that leather wallet as a reserve soldier, ready to be 'called up' at any moment. It had received much training as it lay in the stream allowing the storms the cold and the sunshine to pass over it as a brush adding glaze effect. You can have so many stones, so many good things, yes, far more good things in your life than the number of stars or moonbeams, but if you never use them they will become pictures and as useful as a paintbrush in war. If you never put your hand to the plough, you will never plough any acre. The stone without the hand is the plough without a plan.

The promises of God are of stone quality

The stone that could kill would also deliver and it did. What God has given you is choice. It is of stone, not string nor has it straw quality. It was better than the finest brass or the furnace wrought steel of the day. It was sharper and more powerful than Goliath's sword. The time spent unnoticed in the leather pocket gave it its cutting edge, its ability to win.

The Everlasting One allows the challenge to you, so that you could be taken and used. The storm has been allowed, so that the wilting part might be renewed. The bag must be full not empty. Jehovah has so many ways of filling a stream, bag and the human heart. The streams and the stars with the stones of God are many, too many to number. God once took the grains of sand from the seashore and used them to help Abraham to conquer. Streams as they flow uproot many shrubs and weeds, carrying them away by force. The stones remain the same whether they are in the stream or in the parcel of leather. They remain, as God does, true to their nature. That which was wrapped in leather was a present fit for a giant!

When we use one promise we are given another

The Supreme One will always ensure the stones are not too many nor too heavy. We are allowed enough grace for a day at a time. He gives us enough for one battle. For the next conflict, the content of the pouch may have to be renewed. You will have to do some more stone gathering. In doing so, lifting these stones will make way for the seeds sown from the Word of God to grow into a harvest. When you lift stones, you make a way for a new seed to be planted in the very place where the stone was static. When you lift a stone in suffering or take a promise from the Word, as you lift it, the promise lifts you. Ask King David! He will assure you that this is true. You can witness these assurances in all the kingdoms he conquered, and the many vessels of silver and gold that he was able to amass. Whatever his glory, it could all be traced back to this one stone. The moment he began with only the size of one small fragment, he began to believe God. Giants fell and once one fell, the man of Gath's brothers soon followed the same fate.[7] A whole line of dominoes or playing cards standing upright can be flattened by a flick of a small finger.

The ability to overcome is with you within your heart. As one stone was used, the next stone came into line, waiting to be taken. God has hidden His word in your heart, not only that you might not sin, but also that you might overcome every army standing against you. Overcoming all the Philistines commenced with overcoming one. That stone within can defeat that which is without. 'Greater is he that is within you than he that is in the world.'[8] An army is that which is organised, and evil is an evil organisation. It is one stone, one thought, one deed that fragments the best organised temptation. The promise rips the army apart. It doesn't commence with the weakest link in the Philistine army, but with the strongest and the best. In toppling Goliath, the pride of the Philistines was punctured. All their power lay at David's feet. The master in the giant became the servant of the boy. His first servant was a stone, his second a giant.

We can always triumph over the worst

To triumph over the worst is always within your reach. The name of the Lord is a sure stone to be used on any attack. That is why David records in one Psalm, 'This poor man cried, and the Lord delivered him out of all his fears.'[9] Putting your hand into the bag or going to the Word of God is not an admission of weakness. The hand in the scrip was a sign of surrender. It was a hand searching for something new. It never reached the bottom of God's grace. Lose your hand in order to find His. When a soldier goes to the arsenal for new ammunition before entering into a battle, that is not considered weak, it is good common sense. Go to the place of help, where you have been before. Close this book and go there right now! We go to the Word, as David went to the bag, because it made him into a king. In each trial there is a vein of silver and gold. Each difficulty contains precious properties. In each, there is a Hand held out waiting to take us further. It is the same Hand that wrote on a wall,[10] and wrote forgiveness in the soil.[11] There is honey in the rock. This small pebble contained the sweetness of success. In the Word there are thousands of promises. Sometimes, as with this one stone, it is one promise that is able to vanquish. That stone must be yours, you must have held it and let it be stationed by the Holy Spirit in your heart. A heart lined with promises as this pouch was with stones is a strong heart indeed! The promises of the Holy One are always stationed and ready. Your hand can be so full of a sling and a sword that there is no room for what God has said. The Word of God is smooth and rounded like any well-worn stone. It is effective for the purpose of overcoming giants. Keep what you have available near to hand. That Hand takes what you have and puts it where it will become useful and powerful.

We are called upon to make great decisions

When any great decision was to be made in Israel they placed stones in a bag.[12] The Greeks did the same using stones of different colours. Sometimes seashells were used. One colour was used for rejection, white conveyed acceptance, as it came out of the sachet. Jesus in the book of Revelation promises the 'white stone' (small pebble) to the over-comer.[13] In the Old and New Covenant when they 'cast lots' it was the stone that came out, or the marker with the person's name on it who was chosen. Written all over this stone, invisible to the naked eye was Conquest and Victory. This one was a winner! It was as different to other stones as the Word of God is different to any other word ever spoken or written. God's choice will resurrect that which is buried, and that which is long forgotten. Buried in a bag it will be remembered. It will come out of its corner fighting. The biggest decision was to take hold of the stone; but it led to many other events.

The pouch was loaded before the attack came. Take time to let God put within you that which will take you through every valley and over every mountain. When the Lord has put something in you, you will put something into giants, like a stone that will see them lying as flat as a pancake at your feet. The Gath-man was as large as any mountain, and, in the natural you would have to climb it, but because of this victory, you can walk over any threat. When God lets His word come into us He is building a person for future conflict, yet not only conflict, but also victory. It is the conflict that helps us to handle victory with dignity. These stones would keep David well balanced in future years when temptation lasting longer than Goliath would come in the form of king Saul. Some things are dealt with swiftly, while others require much time.

What we surrender never makes us vulnerable

There may be that person, who says 'I have put my hand into the bag, but there was nothing there.' What if the man of Gath attacks while my hand is in the leather package? You have your voice which can be used to pray. When the English wedding ceremony takes place the groom stands at the bride's side in such a way as to leave his hand free, ready to draw his sword if he is attacked. The Eternal is never empty. If there is nothing in the heart, then we must allow what God says to enter it and give it fullness.

You will not be diminished by what you give. Your power to achieve will be increased as you surrender your ability. If there is not one promise, one stone that you can use with assurance, then go back to the valley and the dark difficulty until the stones are formed and found. If you have put your hand in the bag, put it in a little deeper, and when it almost seems as if you are lost, there you will touch the heart of God. At the bottom of the bag is the plan of God. You will feel the burden of Jesus Christ, Who is able to raise up children from stones.[14] Underneath, are the Everlasting arms, you cannot go below those arms. Putting your hand into the bag, into the Bible, is like Jesus asking Peter, when there were no fish to be found, to launch out into the deep.[15] Suddenly there were so many their nets nearly broke! They certainly had a full bag! When Jesus wanted to feed the five thousand He took small fish and bread; the bag seemed so empty. When He had prayed the bag or basket in the New Covenant story was so full that all were filled, and afterwards they gathered twelve baskets of what remained.[16] We find in the pouch what we expect to find. Seek and you will find. Neither 'seeking' nor 'finding' are measured and limited. If you come with large faith, it will make your hand larger to accept what has been put where you need it. If it is stones you need, then it is stones that God will provide. The measure of the need is the measure of Jehovah's supply.

The power of God is reserved for you

It is reserved for you, as God's power was locked into those stones. In taking a stone, he was taking part of God's creation. When the hand is hidden in the bag, it speaks of going into such power, reserves and wealth that the hand can only handle one at a time. One promise is large enough for any hand. Get familiar with the stone you have before you look for others. There are choices to be made, but you must make the right choice. You will always come up with something. The Eternal never leaves the open hand empty. That which is filled before it comes to the wallet He leaves it full, and passes it by. It is a perfect picture of Goliath in all his armour of brass. He filled the armour. God didn't fill the giant, He felled him!

The Everlasting One has said 'Open your mouth (Hebrew, open it wide) and I will fill it.'[17] This is taken from the funeral ceremony and the work of the mortician, when they used to put precious jewels into the mouth of the dead person. In this context God is saying 'When you are prepared to die to yourself, then I will fill your mouth with precious things to say.' The young man with the ruddy complexion was fully active and committed. One hand in the leather wallet the other carrying the sling. All the youth and immaturity of youth was given to the Lord of Hosts. His heart was involved with God, and that contained faith most of all. In David was all the zeal of 'first love' for God. It can accomplish all things.

Time spent with the promises of God is not wasted

David had to make time to put his hand into the bag. Time spent with God's promises is not wasted time. The builder must give time to let the concrete or the mortar set, as the carpenter gives time for glued joints to harden. There has to be dedication to the lesser in order to meet the need of the greater. The way his hand went into the bag told its own story and wrote its own verse about the man after God's own heart. A hand had to be stretched in a leather pouch, before the giant could be stretched on the floor. He plunged his hand in with no reserve. One finger followed another like swimmers from a diving board into the deep, unknown waters. It was not just the giving of a finger and thumb, but the whole that had been slipped into the unknown. It is the unknown we move into that brings the remedy for the enemy that we know. That enemy who has shouted into our spirits both morning and night must be defeated. The Solid Rock and the stones of Scripture are 'well able' to do this. If we live in fear we live in the echoes of what has been said by that which is wanting to strangle the birth of a King within and we need to hide in the bag (in God) like a hand placed in it. That time given to the leather pouch was just as necessary as the time spent slaying lion, bear or Goliath. There has to be a time of preparation, a moment when we let all else go, so that we might believe what God has said, does say, and will say to us in the future. That word from God is as sure as a stone. It is waiting for you to come and collect, as a hand going into a bag to take out a stone. God's storehouse, as a leather container was so close to David he simply had to reach out.

As with all the promises of God, you can never tell the devastation they can bring to any fleshly lust or grave temptation. If only we had gone to the promises first, as David went to the collected stones, then the story of any life might be a different story. Stones were often used to mark a spiritual experience or great deliverance. Whenever there was a spiritual awakening a stone was placed there forever[18], as this stone was planted into the head of Goliath of Gath. As he faced Goliath, David knew he had a reserve in stones. They didn't seem much to anybody else but David had every confidence that the God Who created these stones would own them again. He would grasp and use part of His creation for another purpose.

One promise is as good as another

Any one of these particles of rock would have defeated Goliath. The stones were available for any young shepherd lad or soldier. The difference is this young shepherd took them intending to use them. When we come to the Book, one promise is as good as another. They are all 'promises'. From that word 'promise' we have the word 'promisor' 'promissory' meaning 'that sent forward'. The promise must send us on a mission. It can be sent as the spies were sent into Canaan, to spy out the land. This stone had to take the land. They must not be left in the brook where green slime forms on them or they become just museum pieces. Promises that only garnish the Book are no promises at all. They stay there as arrows in the quiver, not used on any target. A stone as a promise only means something when the hand goes into the bag. It becomes its call into action. Take it, use it, slay with it. Learn to lie in His hand as a stone in a hand. Any hand, as any life that commits itself to God, will always return with something that will meet the need of the moment. With a full Book of promises, it must be difficult not to take one of them. Any word, if God owns it will become a promise. In that small measure of leather was the crown and destiny of a future king. A shepherd boy was being turned into a king. As the hand and the stone came together, somewhere between the two was a crown. The hand that entered the bag will lift the crown after *Giants* are *Dwarfed*.

Notes: -

1. Genesis 28:11.
2. Joshua 4:8.
3. Hebrews 2:18.
4. John 11:44. Mark 11:4.
5. Genesis 3:1.
6. Psalm 55.
7. 2 Samuel 21:19. 1 Chro 20:5.
8. 1 John 4:4.
9. Psalm 34:6.
10. Daniel 5:5.
11. John 8:6.
12. Numbers 26:55.
13. Revelation 2:17.
14. Luke 3:8.
15. Luke 15:4.
16. Mark 6:43.
17. Psalm 81:10.
18. Genesis 28:18.

Chapter

12

There was no Sword in his Hand

Nothing could be as weak as a little boy facing a giant without any weapon of war. To the natural man it is like a small child trying to empty the sea with a seashell, or expecting to take a grain of sand and attempting to reduce the Rock of Gibraltar to a seashore. Yet this young boy accomplished it in the Lord. David was facing great odds, to prove that God is greater than the greatest opposition. He defeated those things arrayed against him without any sword or the sayings of the day.

The sword has many uses, whether it is broad, flat, long, short as used by the Roman soldiers or just sharp, it speaks of natural skill, human wisdom and achievement. It describes natural talent. The abilities you are born with can make you successful in the natural. The sword is an emblem of judgment and vengeance. It can also suggest authority and power. Soldiers were servants of the sword.

By our own will we can bring about devastation using the tongue as our main soldier in the battle. We can kill, hurt and maim; yet this is not God's method. In Matthew chapter 5:1-48 we find the Beatitudes, where we conquer without the sword in the hand. There has to be total trust in your Master. As sheep trusted the shepherd to bring them through dark valleys and swollen streams, so David had to rely upon Jehovah. It is saying and doing what the Lord asks of you. Obedience fully arms you for the fray, there is no requirement to use natural ability. All the training with the sword that David might have experienced was of little use when facing a giant. Inspiration imparted became his implement of war. David was not a man of the sword; he wanted to be a man of God. His national and natural instincts did not lead him into battle. If he had relied upon the natural, it would have been like the bear or the wolf leading the sheep into its den.

When we use the Word of God as our Sword, then it is described as 'Ice-brook', meaning 'of the very best quality'. The Spaniards used to plunge their swords and weapons while hot from the forge into the brook Salo, to harden them, for the brook had very cold waters. This gave the sword a natural hardness, and helped it to keep its cutting edge. The Sword of the Spirit which is the Word of God is a Delphic sword, it cuts both ways. All we have to do is what this young king did. He carried such a conviction in his heart about the ability of God to win. This confidence was more pointed, more sharp than all the swords of an army. Trusting the Almighty was better than the sword of Edward the Confessor. His sword was called Curtana-the cutter. 'For the word of God is quick, and powerful, and sharper than any two edged sword, piercing even to the dividing asunder of soul and spirit, of the joints and marrow, and is a discerner of the thoughts and intents of the heart,' Hebrews 4:12.

Let God be your destroying instrument

The soldier who has been trained takes up the sword. The meaning of the word 'sword' is 'destroying instrument' just as much as a famine or drought. What the young Bethlehemite accomplished through resting on God brought about more than a drought or famine. Moving outside the realm of a steel sword, he saw the Lord provide a miracle equal to those witnessed when Israel as a nation trusted their God as they entered the Promised Land. It killed a killer and destroyed a destroyer. Let the sheath of your sword be the Holy Spirit.

There would be a famine of giants in the land of the Philistines, caused by a small boy believing God! Instead of throwing stones into a stream or at a bird, he decided to throw one at a giant. God took what might have been a 'plaything' to defeat a real thing. David had such a strong faith that he did not feel vulnerable. His natural ability, and all he had learned about warfare had to be surrendered as he opened his hand. He surrendered everything that any man had to offer in the shape of a sword. He was going to use something larger called God. Natural attainment and the glory of it, were left with the soldiers. In leaving that earthly glory, he was rendering to Caesar what was Caesar's, and to God what was God's. When your own will has to be represented in a cutting edge and you submit to the Lord, you begin to move in the power of God, not in the persuasions of men.

It is written, 'There was no sword in his hand' so that we might understand that God does not save by swords. There are times in every life when God ushers in a new method of attack in order to overcome. This method had never been used before. There were no dead giants toppled by a stone in the museums of Israel. It would become a first time exploit, to be used by many when discussing attacking and defeating giants. From that open hand rolled the future strategy of war. History books had blank pages when recording such events in the past. David was going to change all that!

This is God's record of this battle; 'There was no sword in his hand.'[1] A great victory in so few words. It is like those New Covenant miracles, so much is expressed in that one word 'miracle'. Having nothing between his fingers or gripped by the palm of his hand does not tell you what was in his heart. There was something there more cutting and longer lasting than any weapon of war. A sword could fall from his hand and be broken or blunted by warfare, but these heart assurances would never buckle or break whatever the impact. With little means the victory was won.

This sort of thing happened in the wars of England as the Spanish Armada sailed up the English Channel. It was assembled and sent by Philip II of Spain in 1588. The Spaniards sent 'fireboats' against the British, but the wind blew in the opposite direction and those same 'fireboats' destroyed the Spanish fleet. A coin was minted to commemorate what God had done. What happened could be described in modern terms: 'No visible means of support.' What about the 'invisible means of support?' Miracles accomplished without natural swords, are equivalent to the English word 'hurrah'. It was used as a term of attack. This is the word that was shouted when entering into battle. Psalm 100 begins with this Hebrew word 'hurrah' translated 'shout joyfully,' Psalm 100:1, and occurs in many other Psalms. It is not a sword, but as the shout was given it put fear into the enemy. The enemy thought that God had come into their midst when they heard the shout of triumph, and they ran away. David said what he believed, and that was enough. The Word of God became his sword. Without a sword the shepherd of Israel appeared to have surrendered before he commenced. Here is the secret of his success. From the place of submission, he conquered. The resistance removed, he made a way for Jehovah to work.

Let your convictions triumph

There is no explaining what was in David's heart. Principles, spirituality and trust in the living God filled his life. He had convictions that put sharp edges onto 'smooth' stones. He was a winner before he became a starter! The person who knows they will win before they start is never a loser. He could see the giant at his feet before he had taken one step. He lived in the victory before he had the victory. Without a sword and from a distance victory was obtained. When you know that Jehovah is on your side, you fight with all your might. Convictions about success become as real as a stone being swung around in a sling. Already, in his mind, he was making a space in his tent for the armour of the man from Gath.

These spiritual principles were not so much in his hand they were as part of him as an influence that came from his very heart. When this youngster began to move into battle with a seemingly empty hand, there were those who just stood and gazed with their mouth wide open. They thought David couldn't win, he knew he couldn't lose. They thought David had an empty head because he had no metal in his fist, but in fact it was in his soul, deposited there by God. Without the natural thoughts of men or their way of doing things we can still win. 'The meek shall inherit the earth.'[2] The sword has no need to become your weapon of defence or attack. You do not require a 'standing' while leaning on God. What you are committed to helps you to overcome. Love achieves the 'all things' of 1 Corinthians 13:7. Jehovah must put only that which is in the hand of the shepherd apart from his staff and rod, or there will be open shame, sorry desertion. We can have natural ability and stand with Saul and his sorry soldiers, or stay with this swordless warrior. I want to march with a man who has convictions about his cause. You can have the best methods, the latest fads or doctrines, and still be a loser, standing at the feet of Goliath rather than at the head of a dead body.

Natural ability does not guarantee spiritual success

We all want familiar things in life that we think will bring us success, especially when facing temptation. We turn to our history rather than our spirituality. We become as Samson who said, 'I will arise as at other times.' He didn't know that the Spirit of the Lord had departed from him, Judges 16:20. That steel armour belonging to king Saul, who was 'head and shoulders above others', when measured with David didn't rise to the level of David's shoes. If we can get a grip of that sword with two cutting edges and a point to war with, then we feel sure that we shall stab something. We become like Peter in the Garden of Gethsemane. We ask others to listen to us, and then chop off their ears by what we say, so they can neither listen nor respond. This was the way Saul fought. We can't copy others in our personal battles. We must carry in our hearts our own convictions. What has been a victory for one might not apply to you. God might want you to do something different, to have a new approach. So many times with or own sword or our own will we do not chase away the darkness and the fears, we simply stab at the darkness, as one would stab a shadow. We make no in-roads, we have no progress. The 'sword' has always been a figure of the human will. George Matheson wrote: 'Force me to render up my sword, and I shall conqueror be.'[3] The empty hand without a sword was a token of complete surrender. After a European war, the defeated General offered his hand to his victor. The victor turned the hand aside and said, 'It is your sword I require, not your hand!' We all have carnal ideas, small swords found in human thinking that need surrendering.

The empty hand is a token of surrender

With an empty hand it means 'I hold nothing against you, I come as one with the token of surrender.' All I have in the form of a weapon is an open palm. When we are weak we are made strong. With no carnal articles of war in our hand, we have left all in the Hands of the great Creator. As that palm was left open, so all the failures of the past slid from it. Destiny in the hands of David was let slip to the ground. Past failures were let go. The doubts and fears that ensnared the soldiers of Israel were released. The failures of the past could not last. This young lad would not be robbed of a future. Anything David had kept for himself and anything imprisoned within the fingers of his hand was being released, as in the Day of Jubilee, where everything was returned to its rightful owner. There is so much that we imprison within our own hands. When we open that hand we release it into the battle of the Lord, we let loose all our influences. The hand commits most deeds, good or evil. The empty hand was needed to take the armour from the Philistine and to build God's kingdom. When we appear defenceless, He covers our defenceless head.

Whatever there might have been of discouragement was let fall to the ground, and left where it fell. Past hurts must not fall from the open hand of surrender, simply to be gathered at a later date, or fall to be sown as seeds. National pride, family taunts have to be surrendered. When you let it go, you can then move forward in another direction. Part of your

ministry is in your hand and when you release it you are free to commence another work for God. Give that which is broken and crushed to
the Potter. He will make out of it something new, something just large
enough for you to handle. When Noah had placed one plank of wood in
the ark, during construction, he took another piece. That new piece of
wood might have been part of the door of the ark, or the floor or the roof,
for Noah had a plan from God. Every piece was part of the plan. God
doesn't run out of service for you when you run out of ideas for your own
life. Give Him the shattered splinters, the broken bits, and leave the Lord
with an empty hand, your hand. What the Lord has for you will not fit into
a hand that is already full. The plans for the future will find no place if
you don't open your hand to let other ideas fall to the ground. The empty
hand was always used when making a plea of innocence. It was used
as a disclaimer of any deed. 'This slaying of the man of Gath is the
Lord's doing, not mine; my hand is not in this deed.' It is a symbol of giving and receiving. The future king gave far less by not taking a sword
than he received at the end of the skirmish with the giant. That which is
kept you lose, and that which is given you keep, to be multiplied by the
power of God. David never had a sword of his own to surrender. He
received something far more significant in the sword of the giant. There
comes a time to lay the sword on one side in order to and see how God
will work it out.

There came a moment of 'sweet release'

What might have been part of the shepherd was set free, while what
belonged to Goliath was brought to that hand to be controlled. David
had often opened his hand, to lead sheep to roam into new pastures.
He had fed sheep, removed rocks with his hand, sweet music had been
produced through his fingers running along the musical reed. All were
surrendered in order to produce. This is what would happen here. Away
from the dry and barren into the green of victory with all its appeal.[4] We
surrender the lesser in the open hand, to receive such fullness; the
glory of it cannot be measured. One sword was exchang-ed for the
glory of the Lord of Hosts. Do not measure the sunshine of the Creator
by the number of clouds in your life. Do not even measure the size of
the sky by the number of stars. We paint the size of our Father by the
number of blessings we receive. The full hand and the blest life are the
natural man's way of calculating spirituality. Where there is nothing,
there is everything in God. Even the past history of the rod and staff, the

memories of slaying a lion and a bear were released from his power. It wasn't enough to hold onto the past as a child holds onto a toy. New achievements can enter the empty hand. That which is wrought of God can come and fill the hand as it can fill the heart. There are some things we must leave to God, as this stripling did. We must not open our mouths and let what we have to say become a sharp two-edged sword, cutting into ribbons, and taking ears off right, left and centre. With your own power you might kill what the Eternal wants to keep alive. There is always the conviction that we need to 'put our own oar' into the swirling waters. We find ourselves going off course, and the current takes over. Desert the plan of the captain, and we find ourselves floating on the surface of the swirling waters. When we put our own oar into the water we have stained our own sword, particularly if the cause is not just. Instead of being limited by surrendering the historical weapons of war, we are advanced. The greatest army that ever marched was always stronger when on its knees before God.

Do not chop and slash others with your sword

Praying hands are empty hands. When we pray for others we must not use a sword to cut and shape them in their absence. Sometimes there is the temptation to cut others 'down to size' by our prayers. There must be no criticism of another through prayers. Give God the thorny branch. He will give back to you a rose. When you have no sword in your hand, you appear quite defenceless. You have no scheme of your own without this weapon, yet it is then that you discover a greater plan that comes from the Planner. Your heart is God's Planning Department. When, in prayer, we offer to the Almighty what seems like vinegar in our spirits, He gives it back as 'new wine'. There must be no 'cutting edge' in your prayer life, as you seek God for others. Your will does not enter the equation. When you have lost your sword, God uses His sword to accomplish. At that moment the phrase from the Lord's Prayer is completed 'Let Your will be done on earth, as it is in heaven.' Use any 'cutting edge' against the Adversary, but not against your brother. This is clearly defined in the response of David to the taunts of his brothers[5]. The New Testament adage is 'live by the sword and die by the sword.' [6] Criticisms you offer against others will come back to haunt you. Make sure your natural sword is not stained with the blood of brother or sister. God doesn't change people with a sword, cutting off bits here and there. The Lord does it from within, it is an everlasting work. That which has been chopped off with a natural sword or word can grow again, ten times larger and stronger than before! It is far better to see some grave temptation dead at your feet rather than cutting little bits from it here and there, like a child using a pair of scissors to cut paper.

We win when we surrender

The future king of Israel was not less of a soldier or a man by not having a sword in his hand. God had another weapon He wanted to use. Laying down one thing opens the door to another. That which God ushers in is far more powerful, and with it you can accomplish so much more. The victory was in following the Maker.

There is that within our own power, such as our will that need surrendering before we can take a step forward into the giant territory. When we surrender, we take more territory than the giant of Gath ever possessed. One step for the right is might in any fight. A sword had already been offered to him[7], for in the thinking of the day you were not a true soldier unless you were bowed down with weapons. For the lion-slayer that would have meant bowing down to those weapons, and making them into idols. The best weapon was his surrender, not his ability to be a soldier. As he fought, he was worshipping his Lord, for a moment, with an outstretched hand.

King David wrote in Psalm 18:2,30, and again in 2 Samuel 22:31,'The Lord is a 'shield' and 'buckler' to those who trust in Him.' David saw God as a shield with a central buckle which covered the heart and vital organs of the body. That form of defence saved the soldier from the penetration of the arrow or the sharp point of the spear and javelin. So God would protect those who trusted in Him. God is also the Sword that was not in David's hand. In the hand of God that instrument is sharper and more deadly accurate than it would ever be in the hands of a mere man. In the hands of a man it might squash a gnat or wound a soldier, but in the hands of the Almighty, giants are toppled, armies are routed, and a nation is delivered! That sword of the Lord became the bridge all Israel soldiers were to walk over to safety.

Emptiness must be replaced by fullness

The list of endless 'carnal weapons' includes spear, bow, arrow, chariot, javelin, buckler and shield, and could be expanded. We in the West have made our God too small. A closed hand is our emblem, and a clenched fist is the figure of an aggressive world. When some people want to 'make a point', they stand with a clenched upturned fist. There is nothing in the clenched fist of aggression, and there never will be. The clenched fist never conquers anything. It doesn't even point the way forward as a pointing finger does. We adopt the clenched fist, when it should be a hand stretched forth to heal granting signs and wonders by His holy child Jesus.[8] There was another occasion when the Lord of Hosts gave Israel a great victory through an empty hand. It was when Gideon led his men to drink water.[9] They had to lap as dogs from an upturned palm. The Lord becomes all things to all men when He becomes their weapon of warfare. Jesus is made unto us wisdom, righteousness, sanctification and redemption, but also in our challenges, He becomes the very weapon that the empty hand needs to make further progress.

He is saying, 'You can win with Me.' There are weapons and armour of the heart that God's Spirit grants us. The weapon is the ability to overcome. It might not be made of steel or wrought in a furnace, burnished by the blacksmith, and polished in the broken bits of a life. When we are nothing, the Eternal is everything. Your weapons are found in the Coronation Sword used by British monarchs as they are crowned. It is an emblem, not of war, but of mercy. Words like peace, forgiveness, patience, forbearance and kindness are all part of your weaponry. The largest sword you will every carry is the sword of obedience.

The empty hand means you can receive something more, this time by using God's methods, once you have turned aside the methods of men as David did. He was not following convention, but moving with conviction. Normal convention would never have won this battle. New temptations need new methods to defeat them. The next idea must come from the Lord. The methods may change, but remember that whatever the method used to bring you into victory, God is still the same. Necessity becomes the 'Mother of Invention' in this battle, and the 'Mother of Invention' must become the 'Mother of Intention'. Was it the first time Israel had encountered a giant of these proportions? It certainly was the first time that a major battle would be won by a simple open hand. That same hand wrote its testimony in the history of the nation of Israel.

'There was no sword in his hand,' but what mighty influences came from it. The hand that was empty was filled with such a large conquest. God placed a giant into the hand to receive it. We must make way and give space to what will become our most sublime conquest in God. With the palm open the finger can be pointed to show the way to all who would follow and defeat strongholds. Let your faith be exercised and stretched as the finger of an open hand.

Having taken the sling and the stone in his hands, they could be trusted with the head and armour of Goliath. If, through your open hand you can handle a small stone, you will be trusted to handle the sword and armour of a defeated foe. Those hands would soon handle a crown, the crown of a king. These hands could be so gentle when playing the harp or the flute and so strong when defeating a giant. In the tenderness and the strength of this Bethlehemite you can see the very character of his God. You cannot commence battle with anything more common or everyday than an empty hand. Any cause is advanced by even a little finger being committed. Here it was a whole hand of fingers given as a band of ready, willing and able men. With the Spirit of God taking and using them accomplishments were achieved.

Whatever a hand accomplishes, it must always start empty. It might be filled with many things later. Can God trust you with the empty before He trusts you with the full? Can you be trusted with your palm and fingers, empty before God fills them? How will you operate in the quiet and unspectacular? Will you handle fullness as well as you handle the ordinary things of life? To be useful with one can lead to another. That which is so ordinary can lead to the extra-ordinary. When your palm and fingers obey Him, there is every possibility that the heart will do the same. The Lord of Hosts wants to discover these things from you. He knows it already, but He requires additional proof. He wants to see that proof demonstrated as clearly as a play from written script is demonstration as actors, perform the words. Coming into any temptation without a sword means that outside of God, we have no defence, no champion. The words 'Cover my defenceless head, hangs my helpless soul on Thee', become so significant.

The empty hand suggests the guileless

There is nothing in life that will harm us, if we have openness as open as sincere as the open palm of the hand. The open hand is a metaphor of the guileless person, suggesting the sincere and frank heart. The New Testament word for 'guile' is 'without bait'.[10] Nothing hidden or shut up, as open as a hand taking a sling and a stone. The opposite to 'guile' is to be 'shut up' with all the doors closed the self-defenses in place. There was no pretence, hidden. Hypocrisy had been hissed off the stage. The hypocrite could not find one facemask. That which is false is so far removed from faith that it becomes atheistic. As Jesse's son went towards his enemy, it was like a little boy going for a walk and a frolic with his father. The fingers are empty, waiting for the father to take hold of them and give them a squeeze for sweet assurance.

There is something so simple in the Jesse' representative as he goes forward to meet 'more than a handful', without any weapon. There is the quality of surrendering in his action, even before the battle has commenced. New things can be written on the open palm. Instead of reading your natural history, wait and see what the Divine scribe will write about your future victories. If we have an empty hand and proclaim before we commence that we have no power at all within us, if we can send out a signal to the rest of the world that we have only limited power, then that guarantees us the help of God.

Note the hands did not hang limp by the side as one defeated or weary. It wasn't weary hands he had it was waiting hands. It wasn't his hands that required lifting up. They simply mastered no sword. It was not the picture of one surrendering through weariness, or the sign of the sagging coward. The sword was not David's way of doing anything, and neither was it God's. Jehovah has a large sword in the shape of His power that stretches from world to world and shore to shore, touching both the Generals of the army and the soldiers. It is able to operate even when unbelief sheathes our weapons. When Jehovah is 'dull', He is sharper than our sharpest weapons. When we have lost the helmet of salvation, the sword of the Spirit and the shield of Faith, God steps in with mercy and loving-kindness. King David had not lost his sword. That which was natural glory He chose to lie on one side. In Philippians chapter 2, Jesus Christ laid aside His glory that He might conquer. David had been offered the sabre of Saul, but he declined because he was persuaded that his Lord had something better for him. The weapon of war would have already been moulded into steel, but that which was in the hand and heart of the shepherd from Bethlehem could be moulded into victory.

Jesus never resorted to using a sword

The greater Son of David, the Lord Jesus Christ, never used a sword. There was no 'guile' in Him.[11] He died on a cross with hands wide open. When He ministered it was with empty hands and in doing so, He defeated all the power of the enemy. Each time a miracle was performed by Jesus, it came as from an empty hand that possessed the power of God. There was no sword or knife in His hand when He divided the loaves and the fishes. When He looked up to heaven and broke bread, there was no sword involved, only His hands. When the strings of the tongue of the dumb were loosened no weapon was used to sever those strings, and loose them into the glory of speaking. Scales fell from the eyes of the blind, but there was no surgeon's tool or soldier's weapon. Peter felt pain as the eyes of Jesus as they gazed upon him with deep penetration[12]. When Lazarus was loosed from the bands of death there was no sword in the hand of Christ Jesus. The miracles of Christ needed no weapon of war. David's tools of war and ours are mighty through God to the pulling down of strongholds and the casting down of imaginations. He put all things under His feet without using a sword. 'Men of the Word' serve Him, not 'Men of the Sword'.

There came a moment, as we shall discover in a later chapter, when the slayer of Goliath had to take up the sword. It was the best weapon in the future but the empty hand with no weapon was required at this time as if to confuse the human mind. We must all learn that no weapon, word or thought is necessary for the Eternal God to win the battle. Learn this, that giants can be toppled with an empty hand but not without trust in the living Lord.

What the young lad lacked in an empty hand, he made up for in a full heart, a heart that was in love with God. Love for God can believe, endure, and do all things. There was enough armour in his heart through his trust in the living God to overcome all the Philistine army. His heart of faith was larger than Goliath's and larger than the valley they operated in. It only takes a little faith to overcome a great obstacle. If we come with emptiness, then God has something that will fill it. In this battle the relative of Christ had to appear as a hand without a sword, vulnerable and helpless.

Let your hand be empty ready to receive

Without the weapon being gripped by his fingers there was the message going forward that here was a man with a loose grip and with an empty palm, waiting to see what the Eternal would send into his hand. If we don't grip natural abilities or hold onto something, we think we are weak. We are at our strongest when we are at our weakest. It was the head of the giant that waited to confront him. The fact that the sharp cutting instrument was missing means that David would not rely on the extension of his natural powers, as the sword is an extension of the hand. There would be nothing in this battle that was hand-based. The future king was not involved with holding a sword. The sling and the stone were meant to become the family crest, not the sword and the shield.

To use a modern phrase there would be nothing that he was committed to 'up to the hilt'. In a vacated palm, there is always room for something else to be added. The throne of the Almighty could be established in that hand. God brought a kingdom to the shepherd. The open fist didn't stay empty, at this time it was not the will of the Lord of Hosts that the hand should become a sheath for the sword. God doesn't always conquer using man's dexterity. He does it with those who are open to Him. That is another suggestion of the open hand. There is nothing hidden, no sin of Adam who tried to hide from God. Try to get a child to open its hand! It needs great persistence and much coaxing, particularly if that child is holding something detrimental to itself.

Strength and time spent to burnish the sword could be spent in listening to the voice of God. When that voice was heard, it was listened to with the thought of obeying. That is why in the New Testament the word 'believe' has the intrinsic idea of 'hearing' and 'obeying'. To obey is better than to sacrifice, even a sword, by leaving it out of the hand. When the piece of shining metal became too heavy, then David would trust in the Living One to touch what he could never reach. What he could not cut, with this instrument, he would trust God to convict. If he could not fell the giant like one of the Cedars of Lebanon, then his Almighty could. Without this weapon men would see him incomplete, but they forgot the completeness that God provides.

Faith always conquers in adversity

David is only one of God's army of warriors who had won battles without using a sword. Another was David's relative, Benaiah, who came into a pit on a snowy day and defeated a lion with his bare hands. He also came against an Egyptian while unarmed, took the spear from him, and killed the Egyptian with his own weapon, 1 Chronicles 11:22. These were men of quality who served God with all their endeavours. Hebrews 11:38, says 'of whom the world was not worthy.'

This battle with the giant, as with your battles, was not the sword's, but it was the Lord's. David had determined that he would never get a grip on anything else, be it a sword, spear or shield, as he had on the Almighty of Israel. The metal stick in the hand could break, become blunt, get too heavy to wield, but the God of Israel in character ever remains the same, with a cutting edge of steel, and as sharp as the day He was first known. Let go of things that don't really matter, reach with a full reach and grasp for God. In taking hold of the Almighty you take the giant's achievements to make them part of yourself.

When going for God you take the Greater to defeat the large in Goliath of Gath. The fly may not have the wings of an eagle, but it does fly. The ant does not have wings but it can ride in the eagle's feathers, soaring and flying to mountain crags and over the seas.

The sword and a steely nature must not become your ensign

The sword and the steely nature must not become the emblems of this new dynasty. The flag of the nation must not fly from a metal pole, but from an open hand, telling all that through the surrender of those unclasped fingers they could win their battles. Some of the disciples of Jesus wanted to call fire down on certain people.[13] This would have been the same as having a sword in the hand. They even brought swords to the garden of Gethsemane. Jesus conquered death using a stone when it was rolled away, as recorded in Mark 16. You can defeat every temptation by yielding, not to the onslaught but to God. You sink into His arms to find His hands. The boy's natural weapons would never be stained with his own success. It was the blood of the giant that the

Deliverer used to stain the stone. The first question Goliath must have asked, when he fell when the stone struck him and he was succumbing to death, was 'Who threw that?'

The diminutive was not depending on what others had done before him. He would not draw the battle plan in the sand; he would receive it from the heart of God, to be written on his empty palm. To know God is better than any other form of defence. To love Him is better than four sharp edges and a point of steel. A sword would have limited by the space in the hand it occupied what God had to write on that palm. He didn't need the steel of the strong, human resistance to win. He would not depend on the methods of Saul or the soldiers of Israel. Their faith was in their weapons, while this young man's faith was in God. They could never rise above their weapons, and, therefore, they could never rise high enough to strike a deathblow at Goliath of Gath. The Eternal brought the sword down to the size of a pebble, because that is the only thing that passed through those open fingers. When everything is reduced in humility, as we are, then we can win. If you are small, as small as a hand without a sword, and the enemy sends an attack, you will be so small it will go over your head and strike Goliath who is standing behind you. The words that reverberated around the valley coming from the lips of awe struck soldiers were 'He did it with nothing!'

There is a greater role for you

In England, when knights are accredited by the Queen's outstretched sword, there is no sword in the knight's hand. By the means of a gentle tap on both shoulders your life is changed forever. A Mister or Master becomes a Sir. Even soldiers on parade will turn their sword or gun upside down when walking with their leader. In this story of David and Goliath, is the making of a knight. The word 'knight' means simply a 'boy'. Boys were used as servants, and a 'knight' was the servant of the realm. Those who served the feudal kings bore arms were the king's knights. It became a title of honour. In modern Latin the term 'knight' means 'golden' taken from the gilt spurs which were worn. Always remember that the 'enthusiast', that this young lad revealed means 'one who believes he is in God, and God is in him.' The word 'inspired' is similar because it means 'in the Spirit' (capital 'S' is mine!). These were the qualities exhibited by the man of God who fought, and won without a sword in his hand. It is not enough to fight, only to win. It is not enough to face temptation with a steely countenance; it is only enough to overcome it. Open hands and hand slapping is a token of a child at play, and yet that is the very thing that the One above chooses to mention in the Scriptures when the Divine recorder records the events that changed both a man and a nation for the better.

Our weapons are not carnal but central

In the New Testament the word for 'weapons', 'armour', 'battle' and 'warfare' are the same word. In John 18:3, the word *hoplon* is used of a weapon. The word meant the tool that prepared any weapon for war. David was the 'tool' prepared by God and he didn't need a sword in his hand. He was that sharp threshing instrument as he yielded himself to his Master. This root word for 'weapon' is used in 1 Peter 4:1, to 'arm' yourself with the same mind as Jesus Christ. It is the same *hoplon* that is translated 'instruments,' Romans 6:13. Our weapons are not carnal; they are not swords and spears, guns and missiles. We have but one weapon, God. The Gospel of Jesus Christ is God at work as a weapon, not to kill people but to set them free. Such a victory as David's is seen in every soul won to Christ. The giant within another is defeated. When Christ enters a life through faith we say, 'Greater is He that is within you than he that is within the world.'

When you give Him your empty hand, just as they did when joining the army to swear allegiance, He fills it with success. The hand of the shepherd might look empty, but the God of Israel can fit into the palm of the hand. Yet the heaven of heavens cannot contain Him. The sword and natural abilities must not be in the hand, God wants to fill that empty hand with greater things than stones, sheep, sling or sword. He wants to give you such success you could not have gained it yourself. You know that God gave it to you. Your natural achievements could be written on the nail of your little finger, while what the Almighty grants you needs a whole palm for it to be written on, 'There was no sword in his hand.' This is the battle stratagem for *Dwarfing Giants*.

Notes: -

1. 1 Samuel 17:50.
2. Matthew 5:5, part of God's armoury.
3. George Matheson, the hymn writer who was blind.
4. See author's book *Paths of Righteousness in Psalm 23*.
5. 1 Samuel 17:25.
6. Matthew 26:52.
7. 1 Samuel 17:38,39.
8. Acts 4:30.
9. Judges 7:5,6.
10. John 1:47.
11. 1 Peter 2:22.
12. Luke 22:62.
13. Luke 9:54.

Chapter

13

The Name of the Lord

Before entering into battle the king of the nation would always present himself to his fighting troops. They wanted to know if he was still alive and active. They wanted to physically see the man at the front of the Forces. A look on his face or the mention of his name would be enough to inspire the troops to new endeavours and everlasting acts. This is why Jesus Christ made thirteen resurrection appearances after He arose from the dead.[1] There will always be pride in the name of a leader. Some fight for one cause, others for another, some just fight. The human leader was left in the safety of the covered ground, away from the scene of the hottest part of the battle.

David knew his God, and that relationship went with him into this war. It was developed before Goliath ever appeared. Out of that relationship faith and power were conceived and born. God was not left on the touchline to cheer and encourage; the Almighty was at the forefront with David. Whatever your battles in life, you cannot go where God is not, you cannot arrive where the Almighty has not been. His presence sometimes is as a table spread in a wilderness, right where your enemies are, Psalm 23:5.

Extreme opposition demands extreme measures

Extreme opposition demands extreme measures. If the future king had just looked after sheep, happy to hear them bleat in the same old way, and watch the brook glide gently by as he played on his harp, there would have been no champion to be discovered in his character. He required a new challenge, as any archer would require a new arrow when an old one has warped or broken. This new challenge would further change the coming king. David had to move forward, out of the pastoral scene and the easy life. Just over the hill beyond the problem, the Lord of Hosts is waiting for you to hear the battle cry. God will arrange all sorts of giants so that you might call upon His Name. It is the fiery temptation that drives you to the Lord. It is in the darkness that you seek the light. There will be times when you have conviction that you have nowhere else to go but to the Lord. Another giant, after the bear and the lion appeared in another form. It appeared in David's son Absalom, it manifested itself in Bathsheba, then in Doeg, and so the list goes on. This is not the end of conquest for the young man, it is the continuation. It is not the beginning of the ending, it is a part of the whole battle of life.

It is the Name of the Lord of Hosts, or any other cognomen belonging to Him that suits you best in your situation. Here, for the youth it was the Name of the Lord of Hosts. Shouting it was the shouting of the battle cry, sending troops to their weapons and stations. That Name became a rallying point for every soldier. They called upon it and came to it as wounded men to ointment and medicine. The Names of God are like stars with many facets, every facet providing light. The son of Israel was allowed to move where he could prove that his God was the only winner when it came to facing any foe. Goliath came against Jesse's son with a sword, spear and a shield,[2] but David had Someone Who had far greater power than any well-armed army. That Name, The Lord of Hosts, has so many weapons in it, released as a hail of bullets with missiles as we believe. There is no power greater than that found in God. Medicine, science or astronomy owes all their powers to The Lord of Hosts. He is a 'host of things' to so many. The exploding volcano, the mighty clap of thunder, the river torrents with their cataract falls come from Him. There is no retreat in this Name, only attack.

We are familiar with the statement of a pirate being 'fully armed to the teeth,' and this aptly describes Jehovah. It is the taking and using of that description that gives it its cutting edge. There were many other occasions when the Lord of Hosts had mustered the troops and snatched victory from the jaws of defeat. What comes through that Name strikes the target hard and deep every time. The Lord of Hosts identifies the Lord with the soldiers and the encampment. He is the God of battle and the battling God. Each army had a favourite phrase that they shouted as they entered into battle. That phrase was borrowed from a previous victorious encounter. Something of a previous victory was supposed to enter into every soldier as he shouted out a phrase or name. Jehovah becomes one with the defeated and the weary as that Name is shouted loud and clear. In the hush that entered the valley it went out as clear as a morning shout. He comes into battle with a crown and a throne. The medals He gives are found in your achievements. You are distinguished by what you accomplish in the Lord.

Each member of the army will have a crown and a throne when the Lord of Hosts displays His power. God comes to us in our distress to share with us what He has. His Name alone can feed the hunger for victory as manifest in pangs during any battle when a soldier feels faint. The longings and visions of the soldiers are met in His accomplishments. Believe that there is no part left in you for unbelief to hide. Lean so heavily that His imprint is left upon your soul.

The power and purposes of God do not change

The sword could break and bend, the spear could be thrown into oblivion, could disappear over the next hill and be lost. The shield could be lost in the rush and push of any battle, smashed by the horse's feet and trodden on until it was churned into mud. The sword, javelin, and spear could all cut and injure, but David required something that could kill a giant, turn the taunts of the man of Gath into sweet victory songs, that would become the Songs of Zion. Such accomplishment, through this encounter, would turn tears into wine, and pain into plaudits.

The servant of God needed something that would out-last a thousand armies and their arsenal. A choice must be made. He chose the Name of his God. In it, through it and because of it the hearts of the defeated troops were optimised. That which was limp and weary to the point of surrender was turned and suddenly nerved again. The flapping flag in the breeze was caught by that breeze and taken into a full display of colour.

He had the Name of the Lord and he used it to come against Goliath. He had probably used other weapons when he fought the lion and the bear, but the best article of war is saved until this moment of triumph. If you are going to crown God the Lord of every part of your life, then crown Him with His great Name. The 'stripling' used a small pebble, but behind that small piece of shattered rock was the character of God. Unlike Goliath's weapons that could be seen and handled, that which David had was invisible yet it revealed itself in tremendous power large enough to create mountains, but small enough to throw a stone. He is ever as large as the need, and as small as humility. The very God that shaped the leaves and branches of trees and even this stone, could be such a power as to defeat the enemy. It was the loneliest place in the Universe as David stood before the giant, yet the young prince was not isolated from the Lord of the Universe. God even occupies that space.

David only appeared to be alone, even as you seem to be alone, but he had God for his Companion and Armour Bearer. Israel required the same delivering Jehovah as Moses and Joshua. This, to the shepherd lad was another Red Sea and crossing of the River Jordan. The man might be different but the Eternal was the same. If all the nations are a drop in a bucket, then even a giant occupies a small area.

God needs to lead and we need to follow

What the shepherd boy uttered placed God back on the throne of Israel, at the helm of the marching army. The army was in disarray and dispirited. Every one of them would not have made a good seed sower let alone a warrior. The training Israel received during the wilderness journey, turning shepherds into soldiers, had been forgotten. The lessons had only been drawn on the wilderness sand, they had not entered into the heart of the people. These soldiers gathered to fight with Goliath were the grandchildren of those who had travelled through the wilderness of Sin. God wants to teach truth, for truth is eternal and will never be forgotten if it enters into the heart and spirit of a nation. For victory to be achieved a new idea, a leap of faith had to take place. The heart of God had to be reached by a human voice as this Name was called upon. The Eternal's battle plan had to be sketched on the heart of a young shepherd. The best way to prove that this was from God was to attempt to put the plan into operation. In throwing something at Goliath, David was throwing back the insults and accusations.

The Lord of Hosts was Israel's God of war, and He was about to prove that beyond all doubt. If you want a battle, to seem to be in the past, then use this Name. It was Goliath's gods against David's God. It is the same for all of us. It is the Lord against the lord of the Philistines. Dagon, their deity, had to be carried into battle, and then returned to his place, or he would have stayed where they placed him. The Lord of Hosts was before the army of Israel, reigning from on high. It is the discovery that your God can prevail whatever the giant may represent, that brings victory. There is a Name above all names.

The God that David served was the same Lord that Saul served. The difference was, and always is, one had faith while the other had none. Saul would have leaped into the dark, urged onwards with bit and spur to be defeated by some evil spirit. He would have operated as a natural man. David was carried by the Lord into battle as a lamb in the arms of the Shepherd, not to be slaughtered, but to be hand fed and reared. The Light shone the greatest and the best at the heart of the skirmish. However great the temptation you are never shut out of the love of God. Facing a great shadow and deep suffering we are still sons and daughters of God. David wasn't any less a son of Jesse because he was engaged in warfare and temptation. There was trust in armour and natural things from one quarter, while there was that child-like faith in the lad. It meant a leap into the arms of God, leaving Him to do the rest. If you think like men you will act like men and count like men. If you look like a man then you will see like a man, and your eyes will rest on the problem rather than on the source of victory. Begin to pray, speak, think and act like a man of God. The Lord of Hosts became the Sovereign of the servant.

The Lord of Hosts is His Name

The name you use if you are defeated will be that of a man, and not of God. You will then discover how far short the names of great men fall when dealing with every day domestic things. The name of a famous product or some television show or soap opera will not meet the deep longings of the human heart for victory as high as a mountain and as low as a valley, a victory of such magnitude that the angels hardly dare to breathe. What happened on this day would stretch from one end of Israel to the other and would be proclaimed from Dan and Beersheba.[3]

One took to cursing and commanding, while David took to his lips the Name of the Lord of Hosts. It was more satisfying and fiery than the latest alcohol beverage. He took something from the Lord and used it. What the young prince in waiting did was to quote the word of God and use one of God's Names that was so well known in Israel. Everything must be brought into line with that Name of holiness and power. The finest bow and the latest sharpened sword could never strike like this Name. Some would have used any old stick to fight with, but the shepherd chose a golden sceptre in the Name of the Lord. The shepherd's rod was all right for dealing with sheep, it was no good when dealing with a giant goat!

Saul as a natural man may lend you his armour for a day, or for this battle, but what will you do when he takes it back? The army and its leader had so backslid that the Name meant nothing, it was as hollow as a shell without a pearl. What good is a scarecrow when you require real soldiers? That which is uttered must not be a blunt axe head or a sword with rust found buried in a grave. It had to become more than just a Name. It had to be more than a saying. It is not enough to quote His Name; it only contains the power we have faith to believe for in our circumstances. Where faith goes, the Lord ventures forth, riding high and mighty. When unbelief prevails, there the Lord stops, because He does not recognise it as one of His attributes. The need must be met in an explosive fashion, as dramatic as any miracle. It wasn't the first thing that came into David's head, but it was the first thing that sprang from his heart. Almost like an arrow resting in the bow it had to be released to prove its worth.

One phrase or religious saying is as good as another, until we face a giant in a valley, then we discover the weakness or the strength of what we believe. So many religious formulas and phrases become hackneyed with use. They are so over-used the label drops off, and you can't tell what it means. We require the zeal of youth and first love to say something that means something. In the shadows of the valley we need to discover sunshine. Somewhere among those rocks and boulders is the victory trumpet that has fallen from the lips of the bugler. This valley tests your reliability on God. The Name of the Lord was made to count beyond where the sword cuts and the spear penetrates. There was no sword long enough to reach the giant's head. If God were not the Lord, here, then He would be Lord nowhere. God is only Sovereign in the places where you let Him reign. Whether in the palace or in the pastureland, He must be the Sovereign Lord. The stone, the small pebble must come under His authority as well as the large giant. The secret is to surrender and have obedience if it is only the size of that pebble. If that is what the Almighty requires, then you will go on to defeat giants.

His throne and kingdom is never established in despondency. The power of God is only where we allow that power to be displayed. Let Him turn every cloud into a chariot. What would bring rain to drown you let it bring water to refresh you in the heat of the battle. The darkness can provide a new dawn. From the sour and the sagging let a new song of Zion ascend into the deep, sounding out into every part of life. For the composer of many psalms, the time had come, not for singing but for slinging. A new phrase sprang from his lips like that held back as a coiled spring- the Lord of Hosts.

Your destiny is ever before you

We hold the 'trump card' in our own hands. Your destiny is ever before you, waiting patiently, yet sometimes knocking to gain admittance into your life. The next step Jesse's son took led to victory. Within the circumference of that step victory was found and gained. A man of war needs the Almighty to prove Himself where he is, in the hottest part of the battle. The future king must 'bear the brunt', for this word 'brunt' describes the 'hottest part of the battle'. It is where the temptations are the greatest, where it is as if we are being burned alive by passion and we need God to come to our aid. We must always lean on the Almighty, take all that He is and use it to conquer all that we are not. That which is missing in you describes your weakness in battle. The answer is found in the strength that He imparts. We call 'on' the Lord, and we call 'for' the same God when we require reinforcements.

The very term 'Lord' suggests that God rules in authority where He is. It was a matter of claiming the land back that God had promised Israel through Abraham, the piece of land where Goliath now stood, and the army of the Philistines were waiting. The whole area belonged to Israel. The son of Jesse had to claim the valley where the battle was being fought, and in the valley, 'down in the dumps' establish his own throne as he established God's throne. It is of little use Him being Lord of everything, if He becomes Lord of nothing because of our limitations of Him, as we make Him into a limited company. He must never be the God of convention or convenience. Your victory is tied in with God, as much as any parcel is tied together, and how much you believe Him, will determine how much you receive from Him. He must be the Lord of the grain of sand, the Lord of the stars and of everything else in between.

Their concept of the Lord was stale. I am so glad that the Lord didn't choose to use an old method, thereby confirming what they believed Him to be, the God of history. The Lord has many facets to His Lordship, and a new one appeared in this valley. In you there is so little while in Jehovah there is so much. Lordship will become the measure of your throne, royalty and power. The servant of Saul had proven himself in so many other realms, now he had to prove that his God was right where he was. He would never be greater than he could be now. That Name had to be taken and applied. The King must be crowned in the battle. If

Jehovah wasn't the Covenant Keeper here, He was not the covenant keeper anywhere. He must be 'Jehovah Shama', the 'Lord is here'. Every knee must bow, giants must fall, toppling into oblivion. The Name of the Lord must be used. The wealthiest person in the world is poor if he never spends what he possesses. It possesses him. We must use all that is within the Name of God.

The glory of the Lord needs restoring

The glory of the Lord could be lost in battle, but that same glory could be found and return through a battle won.[4] Names distinguishes us from each other. It is the name that marks one animal from another, and one sea or river from another. A name gives value and power. In that name are all the qualities of the person, their history and their future. This Name lets others see the works of the Lord. Those works and wonders were all contained in the Name of the Lord of Hosts. The power that Goliath thought he had was put back into the nation of Israel. He made people tremble and the ground to shake as he challenged daily all to come and fight with him. Israel had not a man strong enough to fight and destroy Goliath, but like you, they had a God. He had degenerated into a historical figure and a museum piece, as useful as the statue in the market square at Bethlehem. He had fallen to the level of the idol because of Israel's idolatry.

Israel, along with David took the mantle from the shoulders of this great giant. As David had challenged the Gath man, the soldiers would challenge others. They caught the echo of David's voice and used it in future battles. Here come the giant killers! When this happened it would be as if they had found an old shield and weapon, which brought a triumphant shout to any soldier. As the American cowboys cut notches into their guns, so each weapon was stained with some memory of the past. The triumph of a nation was in these weapons. All their past glory and future prospects were in the Lord.

When David mentioned the appellation of the Lord of Hosts, every soldier knew what it meant. It was the Name of the God of battle. It was on every young man's lips as he took the sacred oath when entering into the ranks to become a soldier. All their past achievements had been in this Name. This was the new Day of Jubilee.[5] It referred to the old, golden days of triumph under Moses and Joshua, when Israel was so successful as they marched into the Promised Land. Later, it continued through Samuel the prophet. That description must be proven to work in battle as well as in the home. It wasn't a dead, powerless, religious name. It is not enough to be a king in a palace or in the Church, we must be the same in the highways and bye-ways of life. The Name of the Lord of Hosts had to be powerful in Gath, Elah, Bethlehem, Israel- this is true revival! It had to be the same in the shepherd boy's heart. We can attest to His power in the river and the large rock, but that power must become relevant in a strong temptation.

God's best medicines are found in temptation.

Wherever there is a hurting heart there must be a believing saint. Some of God's best medicines come to us in small stones and little temptations. We must give the glory to the Lord. When David, through a sling united the stone and the Name the Lord of Hosts, then he smashed the face of evil. The victory required was in the confrontation. The old sword of battle would not do, it had to come from a new revelation of the Name of the Lord of Hosts. When this designation was spoken, many of Israel's soldiers were wondering if God was still with them. They knew He had departed from King Saul, who was diminished into Saul, the son of Kish. There was enough here to build a thousand characters when they operated God's charter. Let this become the playground of every young believer.

Each word taken from the battle is as medicine to a hurting heart. What happened not only healed Israel, it heals us, and helps us to go further. It knocked temptation flat. The Lord steps in to heal the hurt and to help the wounded. Israel felt victorious when the Lord was leading them into battle.

The Almighty is small enough to choose a stone and large enough to defeat a giant. In that defeat was all the medicine a sick nation would ever require. He made the small feathers of the sparrow as well as the large rainbow arching the sky. He takes care of large and small, tall and short. The dust and the diamonds are His. God is not just in some ditty or chorus; He is real, as real, oh, so real as can be. When Goliath disappeared, God was still there, He remains faithful as any unbent sword. When fear and unbelief have been blown away, you will see Him dressed in the full costume of His sovereignty. His affective power was still intact, remaining the same for future battles, and for that which is just over the hill. Jehovah is no more powerful, when you face an onslaught or mention His Name, He is always powerful. It takes adversity for you to discover both adversary and Advocate. In the overwhelming flood discover the Everlasting Arms. As Noah discovered the worth of the ark during the storm, and as Moses found that 'baby ark' sufficient to convey him into the presence of Pharaoh's daughter,[6] so is the Lord of Hosts.

The most powerful Name is with you

There are so many Names for God. The best is the One you use to work out your own salvation. From that description authority is stamped onto any situation. It is as if that temptation is a large piece of grey clay and God stamps His authority upon it, establishing the principles of His kingdom. Your trial can be so shaped by your Lord into a figure of Jesus Christ with a spoon in one hand and the cross in the other. He is giving you medicine to help you bear His cross, as each difficulty is diffused. Taking the lost and the broken, He builds his throne through the Name of the Lord of Hosts. That which is broken, at the mention of His Name comes together, to be pieced as part of a plan. That plan is part of His palm. In the past what has happened might be as a bundle of sticks, but God wants to build those sticks into a fence and a gate, thereby making every temptation useful and helpful. It is the best that is required in your situation.

You must know His Lordship, every part of it, throwing its arms around you and helping you through. There is a Public House where I live that is called 'Help Me Thro.' The man needing help is only wearing a barrel. God grants you far more than this when He is Lord. Each letter in the Lord of Hosts lifts you higher, stands you under the flag raised for victory.

All these Names of God are in the Name of Jesus. In the early books of the Bible, name after name is revealed.[7] It is as if each experience has to take place in order for you to fill in the frame with the Name of Jehovah. God sketches the outline, and you have to fill the body of the text with that particular Name. God was given a Name after each great event in the lives of the patriarchs. Jacob asked the question, 'What is your name?'[8] Each designation meets a need and God is called the God of that experience. They often built an altar to the Name revealed. He was crowned here as Lord of the Battle, Lord of the Valley. He has to be the Lord of David before he is the Lord of anything else. In His Lordship He is far better than the best the Philistines had to offer.

The Romans and the Greeks had different gods for different areas of life. They had a god of war (March) in Mars; they had a god for the beginning of the year (January) in Janus, the god of hope and the opening door. He was the god with two heads, facing both ways, looking backwards and forwards. The Greeks had their god Aphrodite, who arranged life for them. The Lord of Hosts is to the right, to the left, above, below and around. God must be proclaimed God over every temptation. What was partial in the Roman and Greek gods is full in Jesus Christ. There was the god of peace and of love. They might have had different gods for each month of the year, but we have a God for every day of the year, and every year of a life, in fact a God for eternity.

The Lord was found between the whirling sling and the flying stone, right where the giant fell. The Lord carries his own crowns with Him. What He crowns becomes part of the gold and jewels, riches and glory of His Name. We know that all the Names of God, from Elohim to Jehovah are found in Jesus Christ. Throughout the gospels Jesus is discovered as the God of all circumstances. He is the One who multiplies bread, the One who is King of the sea with its shoals of fish; He is the King of the winds and waves, He is the Master of Words, for 'no man spoke like this man.' He dealt with Satan using the Name Lord, God, just as David did.[9] You do not discover a new God in a battle; He is there all the time, waiting for you to call upon Him. He is the extra resource. These are revelations that are not attributed to flesh and blood,[10] when we know with deep conviction what God wants us to do. The next marching step for the soldiers of Israel was to believe the Supreme One.

The title used by this young man was filled with history and spirituality. It belonged to the annals of war, to marching armies and conquering heroes. It was as carefully chosen as any of the stones that were hand picked from the brook. His title 'The Lord of Hosts' suggests the captain or defender of Israel. Isaiah 1:24, calls Him The Mighty One. The God of battles, the God of force, hence the God of power, who is able to deliver from any other authority. You cannot call Him the Lord of all power and then bow down to a lesser authority.

This title depicts God in all His powerful fullness, powerful enough to send dew in a gentle manner, and strong enough to send fire until Mount Sinai belches fire. There is both gentleness and strength in power. Using this Name is like a flag fluttering in the breeze and as he speaks the colours are re-introduced to the army. That sobriquet became the standard and the trumpet blast. It is far better than new equipment or refreshed soldiers. It became to Goliath what the trumpets were to the walls of Jericho. As the young shepherd utters that description the whole of heaven stands still, the hearts of the Israeli soldiers miss a beat. The Lofty One is at work. This valley is His stage, His factory and workroom, His best acts are seen here.

What is influenced in His presence will go throughout the land as a triumphant sound. God is being supplied with a throne, and onto that throne the glory of God will come. For the first time the Almighty is introduced into the battle. As the title is shouted towards Goliath, God caught hold of it and used it. He recognised what belonged to Him, both in David and the Name used. Jehovah will readily identify with that which belongs to Him in the Name and the person using it. That epithet turns a shepherd boy into a mighty warrior. It went beyond the wildest stretch of his imagination. The Eternal knew that here was somebody who believed in Him. It took faith to shout 'The Lord of Hosts.' Another soldier would have been shrieking and crying, while David used the title as a form of prayer. That designation was the safest piece of ground before, during and after the battle. It isn't the one who shouts the loudest who wins, for Goliath's voice sounded like a line of trumpets! It was the future king using the Lord of Hosts who produced the best results. It is not the length of your prayers but the language of them that produces results. It was a short prayer, given as a rallying call and a battle cry that led to the King's coronation. The Lord of hosts was as the sacred cry soldiers uttered before entering into what they felt would be their last charge at the enemy. The soldiers of Israel had a special cry, which sounded from their lips when they were facing great odds. To the young Israeli, that cry was the Lord of Hosts.

The Lord governs in every realm

It is the governmental Name of God, referring to His power in controlling the hosts of heaven. 'Angel, go there! Star, come here! Sun and moon with brothers and sisters called clouds, I command you, and you obey as readily as that clothed with obedience.' God commands, and it seems as if there is a string attached to that which is commanded, for it responds as a puppet on strings. These all obey as swiftly as the eagle swooping to take the prey. The whole world is found in the palm of His hand.

In giving David the victory, God lent a little of His power and ability to a shepherd. He uses His little finger to bowl over the opposition. This title can mean the angels or the stars; even the clouds are His weapons. The whole of creation is His, and He can use every part as He wants to, sometimes to deliver, at other times to conquer. He sends one thing in one direction, while He directs other things into the battle. The Sovereign has so much to use as a strong man with the ability to command and send.

The Eternal can call upon any part of His creation to report for duty as a soldier. It is Jehovah who can call clouds, sun and moon with their stars, along with the angels to fall into ranks ready for war.[11] It is God with every form of life at His disposal Who, when called upon, has used even rain, snow and hail. What an array of weapons, what an army is His! You call upon God, and He calls upon others. His authority is higher than the highest mountain, His compassion deeper than the deepest valley. Call Him into action by using His designation, and see Him call others into action on your behalf. There are more for us than are against us. Powers that would not obey the voice of others will readily fly to the army of God, as cherubim and seraphim, for with both wings they fly in Isaiah chapter 6:2. He commands the storms and the sea, but also the calm and the sweet small stream with its many sparkling qualities. The cedars of Lebanon and the small leaf coming from the bud are part of His army. What the young Israeli suggests is, cannot the God who controls things which are above do the same below? Why should His power be seen in other victories and battles, and not in this? Why should your God only be in the Bible, wrapped in its pages as one taking a towel after bathing? Why should the Eternal work wonders in other nations and not yours? Working in other homes but not yours?

The Lord of Hosts throws you back onto the power of God. At the mention of the Name it allows the very nature of it to be set free to do its work. When the Almighty fights He wins. There are no half-measure or partial victories; they are complete. He did not leave the man of Gath standing on one leg nor even with one word still in his mouth to be uttered as a fresh challenge in some future battle. The Almighty takes the legs from that which is opposing you. As the Lord of the land, God 'pulled the carpet' from under the giant. It will never run, shout or walk again. That which has been conquered by God is buried deep, too deep for your thoughts to reach. When you try to resurrect an old temptation, the Lord helps you so that it might be left where it was slain. Where past sins and failures are buried, do not even grow flowers on the grave!

The caring God cares for you

2 Samuel 7:26, Psalm 46:7; 48:8, the title 'Lord of Hosts' is used of God's particular care for Israel. As the mother bird covers its young with its feathers, so His care is revealed. As the deer will keep so close to its fawn, so the Eternal keeps close to us. See the partridge pretend to have an injured wing as it drags it along the floor simply as a decoy, so that its chicks can escape. There you have but shadows of the care of God. Watch the eagle teaching the eaglets to fly. Folding its wings, and letting them go into 'free fall', but then catching them before they fall too far. It is the ability of the Almighty to destroy or shelter in some peaceful cove. All His Names are care-shaped, heart-shaped, moulded into the shape of your need.

When the Almighty stands up others must sit down. David is saying 'We are Your children, not really soldiers, and we are coming back to the heart and the arms of God.' This young man sees the whole of the nation as children running to their Father's arms for protection. When the battles get too big and strong for you, go to the refuge, the Name of the Lord. Your life might have been as a broken weapon, useless, unstrung and incapable. That reputation means God had all materials at His disposal, and would use them to bring about a victory on such a large scale. He has more clouds and stars than the archer's arrows, or any army has weapons of warfare. He does not constantly command He speaks once, it stands fast, and it is accomplished. All fall in behind Him as soldiers falling in behind their leader. Every part of creation is ready to dare and die for the cause. Using His epithet lets you enter the sphere of the power of God. That power breaths new life into your small attempts, converting them into achievements.

When God is challenged, all heaven works together

It wasn't Israel that was being challenged but the God of the heavens. Goliath would have torn Him from the heavens if that had been possible. The bones of David would have been given to dogs to chew. You cannot restrict a Lord who occupies the heaven and the earth. Pride lifts us up so far that we think we are unassailable. Babel appears in our hearts, and we think we can build anything high, but the end result is confusion. God destroys Babel, our confusion, with His Pentecost, which was His arrangement.[12] The victory that was given to one, He would give to many. The realm of giants would fear and tremble because of this Name. The Eternal did not roll a mountain on Goliath, for that is not the way He accomplishes anything. He used a small stone to kill a large being. He could have used a bolt of lightening, but instead He used a small stone, a few words, and a small lad.

That which was so small brought what was so large in the eyes of men to nothing. The God who has a million soldiers and all power at His disposal is called upon. The very term 'lord' in the English language means 'the one who has the loaf', the 'bread-winner'. The one who supplies the bread and meets the need just as the Prodigal Son's father. When hunger is the need and the giant, God becomes the whole loaf and not just a crumb. Jesus is the Bread of Life and Lord of the universe. It is this 'Living Bread' that strengthens us in warfare. The Lord is the One Who has the substance for living and is able to impart strength into weakness. David didn't need the bread and cheese he was taking to his brothers, for he had 'meat to eat that you know not of.'[13] The term 'lady' in the English language refers to the one who 'serves the bread'. God doesn't throw a loaf at us and tell us to divide it among ourselves. Jesus 'took bread, brake it and blessed it.' Whatever the need, the answer to your prayer is reduced to the size that you can handle. When Jesus fed the crowd, miracles were passed on the size of a piece of broken bread. Just as the mother bird will tear the flesh of the prey until it is small enough to descend down it's chick's throat, so God arranges answers that you can handle. He is Lord at the commencement of the battle and at the conclusion. There is only one conclusion you can reach after witnessing what happened, and that is He is the Lord of Hosts. We discover that God answering a prayer does not diminish His power, rather it increases that power in your situation.

The Name of the Lord enables

When, like David we are too short to reach the giant's vulnerable part, God grants us that extra reach and power. The description of the Lord of Hosts is the bridge between any gap. It is that appellation bringing everything within your power and reach. If God doesn't lift you up to the height of the giant, He will bring the giant down to your measurements. He is your Master wanting to prove that He is Sovereign in sorrow and in joy. Wishes and desires can find their Father and their birth in the promises of God. When we cannot lift ourselves up to that great height, God does it for us. He lends us the hands, feet, eyes and arms of His Lordship. Israel was a wandering sheep and the shepherd boy responds by calling upon the Heavenly Shepherd. The flock needs to follow as a thirsty bird will follow a stream. Don't let us be as an army without a leader, lacking skill, training, discipline and direction. The stone that brought about the victory followed where He led. It only takes one person to believe. Here, David was that one. Think what havoc one believer can cause to the enemy! The God that deals with pebbles also topples giants.

God must receive all the glory whatever our accomplishments. It might be the defeating of a giant or the catching of a fish, but God must have the glory. Leslie Treacher is a Lincolnshire artist of great quality. His paintings are breathtaking, and evoke much admiration. He said, 'I hold the paintbrush, and God paints the pictures.' After signing his name on each canvas, he then adds a small fish. When he was asked why he did this he replied, 'This symbol of the fish gives God all the glory.' The same glory that David gave to God when he used a small stone to overcome a giant, used the Name of the Lord to accomplish it. Do not be foolish by looking for a small stone or some other avenue of victory without including His Lordship. When He is Lord of your life it affects all those around you, for it is as if the sun has risen after your dark night with healing in its wings. There are those you meet who eat, breathe, speak and live Lordship. Every small stone in Israel, after this battle would be treated with respect. You could hear the echoes of soldiers shouting the Name of the Lord of Hosts across every valley, as they practised for future battles. It is in accepting His authority that He grants you the power to *Dwarf Giants*.

Notes: -

1. See the Gospels and the Epistles.
2. 1 Samuel 17:45.
3. The two extreme points of the land of Israel.
4. 1 Samuel 4:21.
5. Leviticus 25.
6. Exodus 2:3-5.
7. Follow the life of Abraham, Jacob and Moses.
8. Genesis 32:29.
9. Matthew 4:1-11.
10. Matthew 16:17.
11. Exodus 9:18-34.
12. Acts 2:1-4.
13. John 4:32

Chapter

14

The Zeal Displayed in Battle

There was nothing 'slip shod' about the way David presented himself in the battle. He went into it straight and true. He had Jah's® plan, and he was Jah's man. He did not go in as the dromedary, running from side to side, like its relative the 'headless chicken'. Where David was called, there he fitted in like water flowing in a stream. The challenger and the challenged both showed great zeal. They were each committed to their cause. They had eloquence in the way they spoke, and a glory of its own revealed in their demeanour. They would have made good preachers, speaking with great passion and clarity. For both, it could have been their final words; an epitaph could have been taken from here as one might take a sentence from a book. They both spoke and acted as men with a mission. It was dare, do or die.

David didn't have a mission he was the mission. The distance between him and Goliath was a missionary journey, taken one step at a time. Many times we must acknowledge that if we have as much zest as the enemy displays with his fiery darts, then we too would be conquerors, great men and women of God. Much of the accomplishments of former generations can be attributed to their zeal. They were clad with it, as Jesus was.[1] When any problem goes on to the attack, it is fully armed, prepared to do its best to defeat you. This brings into action that faith of yours, carried not in a sheath or in pocket, but in your heart and ardency for God. There was a combination seen in the zeal of youth, and in the tenacity of the giant in his might and power, of zeal and consecration to a cause.

Temptations can seem impenetrable

Just as the giant tormenting you is large and encased in brass, standing head and shoulders above you, so temptation can appear the same. In facing tremendous odds, you are like a child trying to row your boat across the Pacific Ocean. The difficulties you encounter are as large as any bank vault door and just as impenetrable. If you ask some people to do a job, they take three weeks and four months before they make their minds up! Even then, because they lack the zeal of David, they answer in the negative. I have discovered in Church life that if you want to reveal a character, then give that person a job to do! Give some people a ladder to climb, and they will just rest on it. Their devotion, or lack of it, is seen in how they act, and the time they take to accomplish. It is amazing how many are going to enter into zeal, next week or next year! While some are putting their running shoes on, others have accomplished the task. While those around David dreamed of defeating the giant, the young lad did it with aplomb. It was noble desire that enabled him to carry out what he had felt compelled to do. He went in at the beginning, and came out at the end. It is this desire that sends us running errands for God. From this encounter we obtain a picture of the New Testament word deacon-one with dust on their feet.

The stage was set for the servant of Saul to become in public what he had been in private. If we have 'carried the bread and cheese',[2] then we can expect God to do the rest. He had journeyed from Bethlehem to the battle to help his brothers. Now he had to travel another journey between him and the giant in order to help a nation. Sheep with birds flying overhead and streams flowing quietly by his feet would not be his congregation any longer. God has something better for you, in the challenge now facing you. Instead of the quiet pastoral life, it was trained soldiers who were watching him, waiting for teaching. There was nothing 'Jim Crow'[3] about the shepherd lad. The thought of a turncoat or renegade are embodied in the term 'Jim Crow' from the words of the song 'Wheel About and Turn About'. The only 'turning' this young Israeli did was to turn to face the giant. It is only strong passion coming as a tin opener to the tin that will strip this huge temptation of its power.

You have to meet fire with fire

The need before the future king demanded intensity. It would be the real commitment that mattered as they came near to each other. David had to have as much pluck as the temptation he faced. Meet darkness with light, meet hate with love, and sorrow with a sure spirit of accomplishment. The time for dangling the hand in the stream or stroking the sheep's woolly back was gone. David not only out-ran, he out-manoeuvred the giant. If you move swiftly you can run ahead of the enemy. Run 'to' the Lord, run 'because' of the Lord, but best of all run 'with' the Lord.[4] Wearing Saul's armour he could have bravely walked into the battle, but he would not have been able to run. There must be no limitations to your desire, it must not be tied back or tied together with string. Look in the book of Hebrews chapter 12:1, 'Lay aside the 'weight' and the sin'-the surplus fat that would impede. Part of the Christian race is the space between you and a temptation. Why do you attach yourself to that which is ready to hold you back, making you less than your best? It is useless being an electric or steam engine if you have no electricity or steam. It is the need and the testing time that promotes and demands zeal. The battle is not to the faint, but to the swift. Your love for Jehovah has to be greater and stronger than any affliction. When the difficulty comes walking towards you, then run. Run to meet it, as if your child has come out of school and is running into your open arms. Accept it as first prize even before you have concluded the matter.

We must be as those small cherubim and cupid who are presented with small wings on their feet. This was a symbol of the fact that they were ready to fly into action. The seraphim that Isaiah saw in Isaiah chapter 6 had six wings, and used them all. One of them flew to bring a coal from the altar to purge the sin of the prophet in Isaiah 6:6. The Johnstone family in England used to have for their crest a spur between two feathered wings, denoting moving more swiftly than the spur could goad into, and flying further than wings could carry. David had both these qualities in his zeal for his Master. Your zeal will become your driving power. Zeal will eat away at the opposition better than a shark with its row of ugly knife like teeth cutting through everything. A modern car advert states: 'All we do is driven by you.' Apply that to your service for the Master!

David's symbol of zeal was in running feet, whirling sling, and a flying pebble. What he said left his mouth like God saying in Genesis chapter 1 'Let there be light!' David had feet that ran as if they would leave his legs and body behind. When what you believe gets into your hands and feet, then you know it is faith and not fiction, fact and not a fable.

In the New Testament, they 'ran' into wanton excess. The marathon is no challenge when we have climbed a mountain. If we have wriggled with worms, we shall not be ashamed to fly with birds. Why do we sometimes limp in obedience and run into sin? This young Israeli ran into the battle, through it and out of it. He had as much zeal at the beginning as at the end. He did not run himself 'into the ground', but to where the giant stood. Some just 'run' with no word from God. When they arrive, they don't know they are there. When they leave, they don't know they have arrived. Some run 'from' trouble but the 'Sweet Psalmist of Israel' ran 'into' it. It was this zest that carried him through. He went into battle, as that which is set free to achieve. He moved as a sword being lifted and brought down upon an object to cleave it. The same hot spirit helped him to lift the giant's sword out of its sheath. If we come with such energy against any form of destruction, when we arrive to face it, it is no longer a power or threat. Zeal in desire can eat away at any object until the loaf becomes a crumb. The substance has become a shadow, and the great rock has been turned into a particle of sand when we exhibit dedication.

When you wear God's provision temptation is already defeated. This ardent spirit is for the Christian soldier to help him to stand. It becomes a trigger that sets you going towards your target. There must be a Divine driving force. Without the power of eagerness we are just empty shells, at the mercy of the sea swell and tide.

Devotion destroys temptation

Zeal can be as running feet, but it can also be as a burning fire, that converts everything into its own nature. You see the fire as a hungry tongue, licking all before it, gorging itself with every form of material. Your accomplished victory will become the valedictory of another. They can live by the light from your fire. There must be 'heart' in you for the fray. Others can light their torch from your burning devotion. As your glow goes forward, so many follow that glow. As a fire that is hungry, when it is fed it causes everything around it to boil. There is nothing lukewarm about this sort of zest.

Other soldiers, servants and shepherds saw in David what they needed to change their lives. Zeal is the axe head to boredom. David had been in training for this hour. He had been devoted to his parents and to the sheep. If the sheep were attacked, he had been willing to lay down his life. This heartiness has not lost its ability to run and win. It treats each temptation like running a race, and is fit enough to run to win. For each generation this white-hot spirit for God remains the same. It takes on different shapes, but the end result of victory is always the same.

It is not something to be spat out of the mouth as meat gone-off, or poison. It is attractive, wholesome and pure, commanding many soldiers to fall into its ranks. It is calling you to rise up against the enemy and defeat it. Love never fails-never falls short of the target, never misses by a mile. If you really love the Lord with all your strength, display that strength as you come to the next evil suggestion.

As the feet covered the meters and moments into one step at a time, so is your victory in God. It was one step for David, but a giant leap for Israel. He ran to win, but he ran as a winner. Once the sling and stone had gone from his hand that hand was open to receive the sword of Goliath. He travelled 'light' because he walked in the 'light' of God. Nothing could ever hold him back from accomplishment, not even a giant standing as a metal door at the end of the valley. This temptation overcome didn't guarantee the next victory, but it helped. One stitch in a garment isn't the whole sewing, but it is the beginning, and as you add one to another, so the work is complete. When you see the next rung in the ladder, it does not guarantee you getting to the top, but it helps to provide a platform from which you reach higher. Here was one of God's private lessons in a public place on 'how to overcome'. Certain countries now teach music by listening and watching another play. Watch this young shepherd man, listen, learn, then love the whole story until you become a part of it, and the 'story' is turned into glory.

You need to pray as you go

The Almighty could have lifted David by the hair and planted him before Goliath. He could have killed Goliath without using the Bethlehemite. That didn't happen, because David needed to pray and trust as he ran. He was part of the plan. At the heart of intensity God must be on the throne. The large Philistine was the poker used to stir the young man's fire and love for Jehovah. It wasn't a negative prayer, 'Oh, God get me out of this!' It was the prayer and praise of thanksgiving from a man who was a winner before he even entered the race. He had to think on the goodness of God. That time spent in running was part of the training programme. It would help later when he had to run for his life, chased by his own son Absalom. [5]

The words of David's mouth were the meditations of his heart. These words were a prayer. It was prayer that made him swifter and keener than any other soldier. They ran 'from' the giant, Israel's boy ran 'to' the giant, to chase and kill him. Prayer will always make you into a giant-chaser, a winner, not a loser. As he ran towards the Philistine, in his spirit he shouted 'Hallelujah!' Meaning 'praise Jah'. The power of Jehovah was illuminated when the 'stripling' faced Goliath. It was almost as if the wind he stirred up as he ran blew the candle of the giant out. The giant could not hit David while David couldn't miss the man from Gath. Some thought David might as well throw a stone at the moon and hope to strike it as he fired a stone at the man from Gath. Zeal will always enlarge the target, but that target will never be bigger than your desire. Plenty of enthusiasm will kill a large giant. It is exuberance that takes us where we can strike a blow at the head of torment. It will get you there while your first love is still intact. The shepherd had 'chased' bears, eagles and lions, while he had 'led' sheep. This lad must have had a great hatred for Goliath, and love for his Friend, for it manifests itself in his running power. He was running to obey the call of God. Running, not walking or limping into his destiny. Prayer and meditation will always send you God's way with God's message, to a Goliath who is standing in God's way.

As the boy from the Bethlehem hillside ran, it wasn't simply to face an uncircumcised heathen. He was running the way of God's commandment, into the outstretched arms of God waiting to receive him. Behind Goliath he saw God in the skyline. If you have true love, then the journey of a thousand miles will seem but a step. The best running shoes you can wear is love for God. The Prodigal Son in Luke chapter 15, who went into the 'far country', found the journey from home to that 'far country' was such a short one because he loved the 'far country'. The way back to his father was even swifter because of the father's love. Your tempestuous temptation is reduced to a 'dead head', when you follow in David's footsteps. That love put a spring into the step of the shepherd. He had been used to walking slowly, but the moment demanded a greater obedience. Love of the Nature in Jehovah squeezes the miles into minutes and the meters into moments. He ran as that being set loose from a bowstring. Which moved the quickest, the shepherd in his spirit, or the stone from the sling?

Love will lead you back to the Father

That road back for the Prodigal Son seemed to have a carpet on it all the way making the tread lighter and the approach to an offended father easier. The carpet was the love of the father with all its yearnings and tapestries. This reminded the young profligate of the carpet on the kitchen floor at home. The Australian Aborigines always measure a journey, not by the miles, but by what is at the end of that journey. There was a throne under the feet of Goliath, and a king must sit upon that throne. This trial passed through was taking the power of God and condensing it into a pebble and sling. A foreign power was in control in the man encased in brass. God's little people are stronger than this world's giants. We need that burning glow to take us in, but we need the same swiftly moving feet to bring us out. Don't let the distance between you and the enemy, and torment of opposition slow you down for God. With zeal like this we can out-run a chariot as Elijah did before the oncoming storm.[6] Don't enter the battle as a hare and come out as a tortoise, so slow, hardly with the strength to go. Come out better than when you went in. Go in with human feet and come out with feet as polished brass, with wings on them, helping you to fly where you previously have faltered. Let 'falter' be turned into 'altar'. The torch of truth in the Bethlehemite's heart was ignited from the altar of God, fanned into a flame by the wind in the speed of his travel. Wherever David went, the whole nation followed him. It was his love for God that was demonstrated by his zeal.

Within the scope of this zeal David didn't just run, he had somewhere to run and an enemy to fight. It wasn't running to hide, being chased, but running to chase. He was not as a loose arrow flying through the air. His life had a target, and that target was the challenger of Israel. The son of Jesse became part of a race, and he runs gladly along the beaten track between himself and this man that stands in the way of the glory of God. We need such desire displayed as we come to God. David's only banner or form of recognition was a pebble and a sling. The obstacle never became the destination. This was but a part of the great plan that the Eternal had for his life. When this had been completed, there would be more to follow. The artist never makes another stroke, of paint on the canvass until he has finished his first stroke. There is 'more' in the magnitude of God.

Fear can be outrun by zeal

No excuse made such as 'he is too big, too tall, too strong. I am but a boy, and I fear the giant.' Do not let fear become your foe. True energy does not measure the opposition or think of its might, it runs to obtain. This son of Israel so ran that he outran fear and despondency. When we have strong desire and know that we are doing God's will, then send us where you will, we can do all things. Whichever way we go, it is forward, towards victory. Fear was left in the incapable hands of King Saul, left to its own doom and gloom. History and memory were left far behind. The glory of being introduced to Saul was left behind. The shepherd boy didn't stay to ponder what it all meant. There was only one thing he was now concentrating on. He would leave the past in the past, and the future in the future that had yet to come. He operated in the present, shining as the sun in all its splendour. Apples, pears and oranges have skin, so that you can unwrap one at a time, like your future a little at a time. If this was the lad's only mission in life, he accomplished it with all his might.

David didn't become part of the problem by fainting. That temptation before him might be a great hurdle, but he recorded in Psalm 18:29, 'By my God I will leap over a wall'! His feet didn't become like lead or jelly, one to hold back and another to fold under him as he went on. They gained the speed of greed as he travelled towards the need. Here is a young man hungry for battle; nothing will stand in his way as he seeks to enter into victory. The thought of defeat never entered his young heart. The victory was at the far end of the valley and he had to speedily go there to gain it. Sometimes the achievement isn't in the valley itself if it is at the end just before you come out. Where God stands He stamps and any onslaught is enslaved. Jesse's son had to run through the valley. That conquest was not at the commencement or half way through, it was at the far end. You are only there when you arrive. The more zeal, the more he ran the sooner he would overcome the Gath man. As he planted his feet firmly onto the strata David was thinking, ' I will reduce that mountain of flesh to the size of one of my shoes. No, the giant will be minimised to the size of one of my toes. He, so large will be made to fit into the shape of my foot. I will have his soul for the sole of my shoe.'

The nearer to the Eternal David came, the larger God became, whilst the giant shrivel into the size of one eye. Had not the God of Israel declared that 'wherever you place the soles of your feet, I will give the ground to you.'[7] If all the brothers of Goliath had been here this day, then David with his sheer audacity, would have defeated them all. It would have been 'sheer folly' if he had put his foot on the head of the giant, while the body remained alive. Zeal sees the end from afar and completes the task. It moves backwards, sideways, upwards, downwards and onward, until it arrives. In overcoming one giant, he overcame all the other Philistines. Desire is a marvellous commodity when it is so great. It is like a burning fire, and fear can be as water thrown onto it, but the fire is so great the water just makes it burn brighter.

While some are thinking others are doing

I asked certain building constructors to give me a quote for some new windows; different firms sent their estimates to me. We chose the one we felt was the best. On the day that the double-glazing was being fitted, the telephone rang. One of the firms I had approached three months earlier was offering me a quotation. When he heard the sound of banging, he asked me what it was. I replied, 'That is the constructors fitting the double glazing that you are giving me a quote for!'

In the Old Testament under the law of the clean and the unclean, you will find that all those slow moving things, such as the tortoise, snail, heron and kite are classed as 'unclean'.[8] This is because they are so slow and, along with other reasons, they are disqualified. When there is work to do it must be done with all our might. The pebble came from a hand accompanied by running feet, a heart beating wildly, and a single eye for the Lord. Working together they made a great team.

When I was in theological college, one of the lecturers told me that he could tell what sort of a person a young man or woman would be in life by the way they participated in sport. As he saw the sliding tackle, the strained look or the absolute commitment, he interpreted this as devotion revealed that would appear in future ministry. How right he was! While Saul was numbering the Philistine army, David had reduced that army to one-Goliath.

Israel's future king ran into battle

Three times in 1 Samuel 17, it says that David 'ran'. Verse 22, he 'ran' into the battle. The finishing line of this race was the outstretched body of the enemy. Desire that doesn't overflow the limits of the walls of the heart, and flows into hands, mouth, feet and lips is not desire, it is only a whimper of the real thing! This was as one running to embrace a loved one. Verse 48, he 'ran' towards the giant, as a child might run towards the sea when seeing it for the first time. Verse 51, he 'ran' to take

Goliath's head off once he had been slain, as a soldier taking the treasures of war to his leader. The conqueror takes the crown. Where was Goliath's power and taunts now? The boy from Bethlehem ran as if this head was buried treasure, waiting to be unearthed. He had found the place on his map where it was buried! He was like a bloodhound with a fresh scent of its quarry. He kept running during the battle. Don't walk or dawdle when the hour demands that you run to achieve. If you are going to overcome and defeat your giant, then you will not have to come to it as that which is set as meat in a snare, to distract and then to destroy. Using only one leg or only half a heart will not prevail. All our conquest demands all out zeal, zeal that is for real. You can be excited, even joyful, but true earnestness cannot be copied or pretended. Nobody ran like this youthful warrior. He ran just as his forefathers had run into Ai, and into the city of Jericho.

This zeal wasn't dry theology; it was truth in action, part of a youthful thrust. Another title used to describe the Acts of the Apostles is 'The Young Church in Action'. Here was a true 'Coventry Blue', which Depicts the blue cloth and thread made in Coventry, England, noted for keeping true to its dyed colour. A full-blooded battle demands great zeal and commitment. For all time and eternity David illustrates what we require if we are going to *Dwarf Giants*.

The zeal required to overcome is as penetrating as the edge of a sharp blade. It is not enough to resist; we have to defeat. It is not enough for Goliath to surrender; only enough to see him killed. Don't meditate upon victory, achieve it! Be as the 'Ironsides', who proved they had 'iron resolve and capabilities' during the battle on Marston Moore, England against the 'Roundheads'. The 'Iron Sides' became part of Oliver Cromwell's army of 'Roundheads'.

In giving your all you conquer

If we fight with less than our all, then we become the pygmies, and a dwarf not a giant. The young son must not give less or be less than the opposition. What the boy lacked in stature, he gained in zeal. He could have outrun the fastest thing on earth. Goliath of Gath never lacked zeal for his cause, should we have less zeal than he did for our Lord Jesus Christ? Should we have less zeal than the religion of certain people in Manchester, who insist that the toilets in new houses face the rising of the sun, in order they might pray in the right direction towards Mecca?

That same religious group had a driving instructor who gave driving lessons to twins. The father rang the Driving School to complain that during every lesson the instructor was leaving his sons outside the Mosque for ten minutes, because that was the time they were called to prayer! Another person of the same religion was prosecuted and found guilty of dangerous behaviour. He stopped his car as the sun was rising, on the 'hard shoulder' of the M62 motorway to pray! With enthusiasm, not physically but spiritually, you can out-run any form of torment, meeting the fire of it with the fire of your intensity. Zest is the best! To youthful feet and heart, and first love for Jesus Christ, no mountain is too high to scale no river is too deep or too wide to cross, no journey too long to travel.

The man who has a cause and is totally convinced of its value will carry out what he has to do with great devotion. Some are so hot for God you can put your hands on them and find true spiritual warmth. They impart the joy of service as they speak. They enter a room, and the whole room is made warmer. They enter a conversation that is dead and boring and as they speak they breathe new life into it, and you witness a resurrection from the dead before your very eyes. They add salt to the insipid.

There were no half measures with Israel's future king. As he was in this battle, so he would be in every day life. If you feel you cannot, and sometimes that means you will not resist the weakest temptation, what will you do with that which is so strong? If you can't face dwarfs, how will you face giants? If the waves of the sea frighten you, how will you walk on water?

We only tend to see great acts, but God sees what we are like in our zeal in the smaller things of life. While some are drawing out the tape measure, others have gone around the world. David didn't just have a 'religious turn' and become totally zealous at the time of battle. He ran into the battle at the beginning, towards the giant. At the start and at the finish, he had such zeal as God's that always accomplishes what it sets out to do. The radiance of his zeal was as God's, and the Almighty was gladly associating with the young man. It wasn't just 'first love' he possessed, and that possessed him, it was something that would stay with him all the days of his life. There wouldn't be any ashes or sad memories here. We can feed fire as our desire, or we can let it burn out. The flames, once so hot and burning can become cinders. The trophy Jesse's son obtained was one of giant proportions. He gave his all to receive all. What he surrendered in devotion was greater than this giant.

If you want to see the real giant, then look at the life of this young man. He grew as he grappled with a giant.

Zeal is described as a burning fire and a boiling pot

There is in the word 'zeal' the description of the boiling pot with a roaring fire under it. That fire will boil what is in the pot. It will cook all the contents of the vessel. Then it will be reduced to the size of a plate, then onto a spoon, and into a mouth as you eat. Every thing is reduced to acceptable size because of the burning fire. It is the maintenance of that zeal, that is so important to see the battle through to the end. Anyone can carry a sword and a spear, but can they carry it right through the battle? When you come to the end can you lift the armour? This was more than 'talking his way through'. The man who carried the colours of the army had to carry them right through to the end, so the colours could be paraded as a reminder of the accomplishment. The 'hop' must lead to the 'skip' and the 'skip' must lead to the 'jump'.

For Israel's future king there was no turning back. To turn back would be to turn his back on Goliath. There was Saul with the javelin in his hand at one end of the valley. The Bethlehemite's sarcastic brothers were on one side of the valley, while the Philistine army occupied the other. Goliath, that great mountain of a man was awaiting David at the other end of the same valley. God was in between and at both ends. He was everywhere. The only way out was through, through the door that God would provide.

The zeal exhibited in the initial response has to be maintained right to the end. It is seen in the word yeast which stretches all before it and causes it to rise to another fullness and new dimensions. It is the yeast that causes the dough to rise to meet the hand coming towards it. Who can tell if the bread that contains yeast shall pass into a king's mouth? Literally, this huge monster of a man made the young man's 'blood boil'. The whirling sling and the flying stone became the emblems of the House of David. Both had no restraint on them, both were used as if nothing else would be accomplished if they did not function correctly. Without desire nothing will be achieved. It is to live a life as if nothing else matters but this one thing. Paul said, 'This one thing I do.'[9] One fire, one iron in the fire, one object to be overcome. The person in such a conflict needs all these qualities. You may enter the battle as a boy, but with true zeal and grit you will come out of that battle as a crowned king.

Boldness can be the evidence of intensity

Kingston-on-Thames, England was named after the stone that the Anglo- Saxon kings used to kneel upon to receive the anointing and be crowned. The stone that came from David's sling was the platform for his crowning. There was a rich resource in that stone. It was flung into its mission, as the young boy entered his with relish. The word 'bold' used in the New Testament suggests that which is 'sticking out' like a jutting rock or piece of stone.[10] It can suggest speech without an impediment. It can describe, as you speak, the lips opening like a prison door, to uttering words with passion. The prisoners, as words held in the mouth, are thrown out and set free. You are the prison keeper. All these things were part of the thrust in the life of a young shepherd boy. The power of the giant will be within your grasp if you are full of ardency. Don't go into the battle until first love floods your heart and mind, and don't leave that same arena until deep desire has performed its perfect work. Even Noah's ark required the wind and waves to lift it up and bear it along. In the creaking of its timbers was the shout of success. Boldness can defeat a giant called shyness. You require the boldness of the Holy Spirit to set you free from the giant. Enthusiasm may wave a flag and shout, but it is the nature of zeal to bring you in and to take you through. When you have lost your boiling and then lukewarm becomes the highest degree of the temperature gauge you need another baptism in zeal. When the fires of first devotion burn low, you can re-ignite your first love from the desire that David had as he entered into battle. The wonderful thing about this ardour is that it will take whatever is stumbling and cold, and convert it. That which is forlorn and withdrawn can be taken into leadership. When the human body is hot, you can be wounded and not feel a thing. It is the heat that produces the nullifying effect. It is aptitude that shrugs off the hurts and weaves pain into praise. This zeal can be an ointment for your pain and suffering. David stood out-that is boldness!

You carry the glory of God with you into battle

As the child of Israel runs into battle, the hearts of others run with him. He is carrying with him the glory of Israel and the glory of God. He was, for the moment, the lost Ark of the Covenant. All the pride of every battle is upon this young man. That spirituality having been turned into history needs an injection of youthful endeavour. From the religion and the ceremony of the day, a new fire began to burn. David is the man to accomplish this. Glory is the way a thing is accomplished. The glory of anything is seeing it through to the end. It is a lonely race, but it is a race where the baton is passed on. Other hearts, empty hearts, yearning to see the God of Israel perform another miracle were opened wide. The influence from this battle comes into parched hearts like cold water from a spring. As he defeated the object before him, so he was giving heart to others. As he came through like a 'chariot of fire', so others would be ignited by his example. That day dispirited soldiers proclaimed 'I too, am an Israelite, and David is my brother!' Here is the true 'brother-hood of man'. There was such a zest about this young man, that every man in Israel wanted to be part of it. They wanted to share the glory of it all. It added weight (glory) to their cause.

Sometimes we have 'no stomach' for that which leaves us broken, bleeding and dying. It is then that true tenacity is called for. It is not enough to creep out of a dead religion, and think that will take us through. It is only your love, which is another word for zeal, that will take you in as a young man and bring you out with the same amount of devotion. Nothing was lost everything was gained. Only Goliath lost his head, sword, armour and standing. He even yielded the ground he stood upon. The shepherd was 'set at large' and as the French phrase suggests, he was set at liberty as a ship in the ocean, free to move and to become what God had called him. The child became a man, and the man became a king. This is the word and work of zeal. David had no sharp weapons; the sharpest thing was his heart towards God. If you serve God let love get down into your feet, as an overflow from your heart. When everything else is blunt, and the limbs feel so weary that we are unable to go on, then zeal steps in and becomes the very force we require.

We must face up to broken relationships

We must face our broken relationship and whatever thing is of gigantic proportions with such zeal as to help and heal. 'Fools go where angels fear to tread,' but what about going where angels do tread? True zeal will not stop or trip up before it has accomplished all. When we are not so clever, and cannot work it all out, it is then we need to have fervour of spirit. Fervour depicted in chariot wheels as they race along, or as a horse that has been prepared ready for battle. You can speak in a whisper, and that is what religion does. You can speak the promises of God, dressed in zeal and be stronger than any Goliath in armour. It isn't what you say but what you believe that has the desired affect. Yours can be a triumphant voice coming from a triumphant heart.

Be part of the 'bull dog breed'

We in England are known as the 'bull dog breed.' This is because we take hold and will not let go until there is an accomplishment. A South African once described the British as being as 'tough as old shoes.' You can't readily see the zeal of the artist until the picture is complete. If you have 'no heart' for the fray, then let God put something from the youthful spirit of David into you that will make you youthful and useful in His kingdom. Devotion takes on many forms. The sunshine of it all illuminates the dreary valley pathway.

Envy and jealousy are zeal for the wrong thing. Jealousy and envy is seen when we talk of one thing. It is to return constantly to the one topic. That which is provoking envy and jealousy must be converted into our battles. Have rage, but have it against evil and those things standing in your way. A fanatic has been described as 'somebody who loves Jesus more than you.' Tenacity is taller than the tallest temptation. In your glow for Jehovah you will go with David, and what he had can be yours. Be as the Greek god Mercury, meaning 'quicksilver', the god of speed and haste, merchandise and eloquence. The image of mercury was placed at the crossroads by the Greeks to show which way to go, as you journeyed along. It said 'go this way quickly.' This was the god of commerce and success, which speedily flew with wings to do whatever was bidden. This was the god that brought good news swiftly, the god with wings to fly in service.

Iris was the god of the rainbow. When there was faction or quarrels, they appealed to this god, known as the 'bridge builder.' The god Iris built bridges over chasms, and brought warring parties together. What a lovely thing to be able to do in your ardency for God, to build bridges of rainbow quality. David did this between every man and his neighbour in Israel. Love forgiveness because it is the bridge you must pass over as another forgives you. Be 'bull dog' when getting closer to others, and entering into relationships. When your business is God's business, as it was in this battle, then you trade in silver, not in rust or brass. Do your best work in rainbow qualities and colours.

Don't be poured out as that lukewarm, be red hot, having received the breath of God that turns cold water into boiling water. When and where you boil, there you will bless. When you have desire you will defeat. When desire is diminished, defeat dictates. With tenacity you will triumph as you *Dwarf Giants*.

Notes: -

1. Isaiah 58:17.
2. 1 Samuel 17:18.
3. Jim Crow, a song from Adelphi in America.
4. Solomon Song 1:4.
5. 2 Samuel 15:17.
6. 1 King 18:46.
7. Joshua 1:3.
8. Leviticus 11.
9. Philippians 3:13.
10. Acts 9:29.
® Another Name for God used in Psalm 68: 4.

Chapter

15

The Recognition of Your Authority

Authority gives us confidence, and confidence grants us ability when facing any foe. The very meaning of 'power' is 'to be able', to 'be capable'. There is a thought in the word 'king' of one who 'is able'. The authority of David wasn't simply that which has been granted by king Saul, it was of a higher nature. The young shepherd was not simply an ambassador for the king, or acting as a go-between, he was not even a Daysman or an umpire; he was a champion, a winner! He did not simply act as a mediator for the ruler of the day, if he had done so, then he would have been doomed to failure. In king Saul there was no power or authority. The word power means strength, but Saul was weak. The natural man in the king represented weakness, that which had been rejected. He had as it were, left on one side as a weapon from the hand of a wounded warrior.

There is a greater authority than that given by men

The giant-challenger had to obtain a greater authority than that given by men, he had to turn to God and receive from Him the authority to act on His behalf. His academy had been the hillsides of Bethlehem where he was schooled to walk and talk with his Lord. As he had fought with a lion and a bear, he had done so as the defender and representative of the sheep. Now he was representing the Great Shepherd of the sheep. David acted, as a priest, as a bridge builder as he faced the mountain of flesh that was in Goliath. David had to walk the first plank of the bridge alone, in his quest to build bridges between failure to success, and between God and Israel.

We face battles every day in every place

When we deal with temptation, we are not only overcoming for ourselves, we overcome in the Name of the Lord. As we do this, we bring the Kingdom of Heaven to earth in a fuller way. In the heart of this young man was the heartbeat of every soldier in Israel. The light had gone out in the nation, blown out by the giant's breath. David was to restore that light so that a nation might know where it was going and would not continue to walk in the shadow of the giant. As this young striping was Kingdom building, so are we. Wherever there is darkness and the power of evil, or is that which is savaged by sin, we must not rest. The moment you step outside your own home, no, even while you are in that abode, the battle rages from wall to wall and seat to seat. Every day, when we switch on a television or listen to a radio, we hear the challenge of the giant of Gath coming to us trumpet clear, challenging the very reason for our existence.

If we have authority it must be demonstrated at home and abroad. We must have the ability to deal with the small as ably as dealing with the large. Valleys are not just in Israel, they can be where you are. The fiercest giant can be around the next corner waiting to rob you of all that God has given to you. The Devil wants to crush the plans that the Almighty has for you, to see them go from being set in stone, to running through your fingers as rock which is crushed into sand.

Recognise your authority

The son of Jesse had not only to recognise what he was in God, he had to take that recognition further in challenging the giant of the valley. Authority is only power when it is used to accomplish something. Philip, one of the disciples in the New Testament can mean 'man of power'. You have to be as the hand at the end of the arm that has such power and strength in it. Act as the eye in the head, for in it there is power for vision and the authority to see all things around you. One blind person said 'There is a worse condition than being physically blind. That is having two healthy eyes, and not be able to see, to have eyes yet lack vision.' This is to lack authority, to deny power its ability. We have all the potential of a hundred pound bomb, yet we explode as a damp squib!

The giant represented all the power of the Philistines, but David didn't only represent the power of Israel, he recognised, received and used the power of God at his disposal. Goliath came towards the future king, dragging the flag of Israel behind him in the dust. That flag was known as their Ebenezer; on it had been written 'Before the Lord helped us.'[1] David took that flag and raised it for all to see, witnessing that God was in charge of Israel. He used Goliath's sword for his flagpole. It was this noble act that became a choirmaster in Israel. The people began to sing as if in a revival. It put new light into their eyes, new songs into their hearts. It enabled the nation to take down their harps from the willow tree, hung there in despair as they identified with the weeping the willow tree suggests, and let their soul sing again.[2]

The promises of God must mean something

The promises of God will only remain promises on paper and not power in personality until we use what is ours from God. We need to take what belongs to us from the enemy of our souls. This young challenger not only saw the potential power in God, he not only believed it, but he demonstrated that belief by laying flat the largest thing that had ever challenged a nation in the form of a man. He took what God said was his, he made his heart into a Bible, and the promises were written in it. He knew the Almighty had promised to lay giants flat, throw over great walls, and send the enemy large or small, scattering as birds disturbed in a field.

Authority is not subjective it is objective. It is not given for you, but to be used against your enemies. This young Israeli used Elohim's power to conquer and to kill. The Gifts of the Holy Spirit set out in 1 Corinthians chapters 12 and 14, are not mere toys for children, they are weapons for soldiers. Real authority is not when David is in charge, it is when he saw God dealing with the situation. There are times such as when this youth faced a man of war that we must let go and let God.

The ability to defeat opposition through authority wasn't the shepherd lad having his own way, for that would have been self-will and tyranny. David wasn't here to 'sightsee', or to spend a day picnicking by the seaside. He was no tourist on a travel expedition. He was a pioneer in the power of the Lord. He took with him, tugging at his heartstrings, every family in Israel. David's heartstrings became the tying tape on every mother's apron. In the past Israel as a nation had known the Lord in miraculous power. Now it involved an individual seeing miracles enacted. The Sovereign Lord was revealing that He operated alongside the individual as well as alongside the nation.

We only become as powerful as our submission

Real authority is when we submit to a greater power and use what is given to us. The Queen of England has no real power. She is a constitutional monarch; as such the power that she denies others is what makes her so valuable and great. Jesus has all power. It is that power, invested in others as treasure in earth vessels that adds to His lustre. His greatness is seen in the power He puts into others to act on His behalf. Jesus said, 'All power is given unto Me.'[3] Then we add, 'all power is given unto us, through Jesus Christ.' 'You shall receive power after that the Holy Ghost has come upon you.' [4] The Holy Spirit descended on the early disciples. The suggestion is that He would come as a tunic to be worn by them. The tunic is the emblem of the servant and of service. The Holy Spirit would become their badge of office. We see this tunic displaying authority in every policeman, postman, airman and seaman. Their uniform distinguishes them from others. In the Acts of the Apostles, when they showed boldness, the people knew that they had been with Jesus.[5]

This authority given from others and used is seen in the arm of the law. The policeman, the soldier, the airman has no conviction until it is given from a greater source. To be in authority is to act on another's behalf. It is having the 'power of attorney'. When we become self-willed, there is a giant of Gath within us that needs defeating. True authority is only released when that within us is defeated. David knew he was a nothing and a nobody. He was as the empty shell that the wind blows into or the sea surges through. Authority that is not controlled by love and used to defeat temptation can become rebellion. Rebellion is not authority it is anarchy. A horse is a wild thing when left to its own nature, but it can pull, work, win races and be used in many different ways once it has been tutored to use its power effectively. One of the words translated 'perfect' in the New Testament means 'to be fully trained'.[6]

Jesus illustrated the authority received when we subject ourselves to a greater authority in Philippians chapter 2. The King James' Version records 'although He was in the form of God, He did not think it was robbery to be equal with God.' What it really means is that although He was in the shape of God, He humbled Himself and became obedient unto death. In that humility, He did not become a robber, seeking to rob God of His glory. He didn't treat authority as a prize to be taken. Through abnegation He went lower than hell. Then, in exaltation, because He submitted Himself to the authority of God, He rose far above the heavens, and is seated at the right hand of the Majesty on high. 'Let this mind be in you which was in Christ Jesus.' David began this battle as a son and as a servant. He concluded the matter as a soldier warrior, as a marksman and as a swordsman. Previously he might only have squashed gnats, now he slew giants. Humility pays in the authority it confers.

When Charles 1st King of England tried to go into the Houses of Parliament he was resisted by the Speaker of the House. The King challenged the Speaker as to where he received his authority? Was he acting independently or on behalf of others? The Speaker replied, 'Your Majesty, I have no authority, only such as this House has given to me.' Here was one resisting a king because of imparted and not imported authority. He was acting on behalf of others. Even the monarch of England is subject to authority. When the Queen of England visits the Houses of Parliament, the Black Rod has to knock on the door of the House, before royalty is admitted. The ruling Monarch is only allowed into that house by the express wishes of the Members of Parliament.

Recognising authority in others gives you power

All that was in David was God given and God driven. When Princess Elizabeth, the future Queen of England was asked who she was, she replied, 'I am not important, but my daddy is the King of England.' 1 Samuel 17:34, David mentions how he dealt first with one thing then another, and what he did with Goliath was an extension of the power that he had already received and witnessed. The capability of the challenger was not fenced in by human power. What David was he released into the battle, the Almighty being the Source and the Giver. The idiosyncrasies of the youth did not make him inferior to the challenge, it was the very thing God took and used to conquer. It was Saul and Goliath who pointed out the deficiencies in David. It was God who clothed him with power, and ability. If you can be as empty as a water pot with a light within, ready to be smashed into nothing, then victory can be yours.[8] 'Not 'many' mighty or noble are called.' It does not say 'any'; it says 'many'.[9] The foolish and the unwise need to become the mighty and noble in the cause of Christ, and they accomplish this through God-given ability.

We have been delivered to deliver

When David recounts the story of success over the lion and bear, the key word in 1 Samuel 17:34,35, 37 is 'delivered'. The God, who has delivered, does deliver and will deliver. His is a deliverance ministry.

When people fall into deep pits, He places under them His everlasting arms to save them from falling further, bearing them up in case they dash their foot against a stone. The youth's heart was full of the exciting things that the Almighty had accomplished. This deliverance was written under the word 'deliverances'. God snatches us away as a brand from the burning. The Almighty delivers us from the snare of the fowler and the pestilence. If you don't believe me, ask King David. God takes us away from that which faces us by destroying it. He reaches out His hand, and catches the falling, fainting soldier. Deliverance and victory happen every time you say 'no' to the enemy and 'yes' to the Lord God Almighty. When God blows the trumpet, victory is only a few paces away. Goliath was left alive long enough for God to use him as a tool to shape a future king. What you have in Jesus Christ is great enough and powerful enough to overcome many things that will descend as dark shadows across your pathway. The giant will stand as a great rock obliterating the light, but with the power of God you will be able to dynamite it out of the way. The deliverance isn't always in the spectacular such as a helicopter swooping down to rescue you; it can be in the secret silence of your own heart and life.

Heaven's authority meets earth's needs.

If the Lord can get you to use your dominion on earth, then He can trust you to use that same authority in Heaven. What you bind on earth will be bound in Heaven.[10] What you set free on earth will be found in Heaven. The Israeli's ministry developed from caring for the sheep which was another attribute of the Eternal nature, to challenging a giant, which speaks of the part of the Lord that is fierce, like a roaring fire. Your ability in the Almighty can remain as a spark forever. This same youthful man of zeal wrote in one Psalm 'While I mused the fire burned.'[11] David knew he was going to be successful before, during and after the battle. He didn't have to look back to know that he had defeated the giant. In the Sweet Psalmist of Israel's heart, he knew the man of Gath was dead before he lifted a stone.

We take our convictions with us, and what we really believe is revealed when we face a crisis. If you squeeze a piece of fruit hard enough, the very nature of that fruit will ooze out. It is in the fire where you discover what will or what will not melt. The pressures of every day living will make or break you. Between the strain and the pull, the oarsman takes the boat through the winning line. Learn to trust, take time to love the Lord. Every workhorse should have a green field. If you lack power and authority you will be but a rocking horse! We all need space to have a time of quiet abundance. Psalm 91:1, a modern translation says: 'He that dwells in the secret place of the Most High, will be in touch with the almightiness of God.'

Authority is not ambition

Authority comes from the word 'author', one who causes things to be, and someone who creates. It is the foundation formula. Something that is useful is created out of one thought. Authority is so different from ambition. The ambitious person needs to 'catch votes' before he can be of any use.[12] The man with authority has it given to him by another. As the hammer, saw, or even a whole cabinet of tools is the extension of the man, so David was an extension of God's power in the valley. There was no extension of power in the man of Gath. When he fell, the fire went out. When Goliath was killed, all his potential died with him. If David had fallen, there was still so much for so many more in God. This Fountain doesn't dry up in the time of drought. If there is a drought He splits rocks and water cascades from them. I believe if a thousand Israelites had realised their potential in God all of them could have slain giants on that day. Authority is to receive orders and then obey them with the same zest as they were delivered to you.

Real ability does not commence with the overcoming of just one obstacle and that is the conclusion. It continues with us all the days of our life until we reach Heaven. The deliverance ministry seen in this young prince was not deliverance only for himself, it was also for a nation. It rescued his family. If you cannot be in authority or exercise any in your own home, then you are not fit to rule in the house of God.[13] In delivering yourself, you deliver others. Within the scope of David's authority was a new lease of life and boldness for every soldier on the battlefield.

Israel had become the tail and not the head. Instead of driving, they were being driven. Instead of leading, as they used to lead their sheep, they were being led as going into captivity. How you handle power will determine the future of those around you. The son of Jesse was the weapon that the Eternal decided to use. Without that which was given by God we shall be left headless, at the feet of the enemy. With the realisation of what we are and what we have, all power is given unto you,[14] we can overcome all things. You can be as the finest built boat, but without the sea you are a mere plank of wood. The audacity of the boy was in his ability to believe that Sovereignty was always at his side and on his side.

Authority is seen in words and actions, not in reactions

Many expressions of dominion were seen in the shepherd. His power was not reflected in a 'bad attitude' or simply a reaction against the challenger of Gath. David wasn't 'out to get even' with the man of the valley. The greatest expression and explosion was seen in a giant toppled. Beyond his ability to use a sling, to run and to speak, there had to be another realm to move into. There comes a moment when we decide to move from that flat, earthly plain of yourself into another dimension in God.

When Goliath's body lay flat at the feet of David, the ability of God was written all over the circumstances. The Almighty was making a statement about His sovereignty. He stamps on giants and stands on them! He uses one defeated temptation as a platform to defeat the next one. People will recognise true authority. The ass brays at the fence and wooden shed, but nothing moves; yet the leopard moves a paw and everything runs! After the lad's conquest, there weren't many living things that dared to challenge him. You could say to the stripling, what Jesus said to a woman, 'Where are all your accusers?'[15] They had gone out one by one.

People often questioned the authority of David's greater son, Jesus Christ. They wanted to know 'what made Him tick'. How did He do that? The secret of both David and Jesus was not in gimmicks or tricks, but in truth, and the truth was, that they had been recognised by God. That same Lord came to their aid with His eternal power. 'God anointed David and Jesus of Nazareth with the Holy Ghost and power.'[16]

To win means taking risks

A Jewish relative, named Esther, who adventured her life for the sake of others, had also accomplished what David did. In the Book of Esther she acted under the authority of Mordecai.[17] Because she acted bravely she saw Haman hanged on his own gallows. He was the Goliath of her day,

Queen Esther using and acting under the authority of others, undid him. She required signed letters to act in the king's name.[18] We are letters, epistles, written not by pen and ink or computer, but by the Spirit of the living God. The Almighty had signed David's life with His hand. God became his 'underwriter'.[19] David became Goliath's undertaker.

The distance between David and Goliath was filled with the authority of God. That same sovereignty was in the sling and the stone, and in this son of Israel. What the Eternal recognises, He equips for the battle, not with man-made machinery, but with Divine power. What is required in temptations is a display of Divine power. The young man felt in his heart, and was convinced in his spirit what Goliath felt in his head when the stone struck him. It was God's knock at the door telling him that the time of his eviction had come. Goliath, because of David's authority, became a 'wasted space'. A greater authority had come to take the place of Goliath, not just negative ability to destroy and cast down, but the prerogative of God to lift up, and set on high.

The power in the potter's hand is seen in many shapes as he forms a piece of clay into a cup or an ornament. That same hand can crush unyielding clay, even as it can form the most delicate pattern on that same wet piece of daub. The authority is in the hand that takes hold of it, to make it part of the poetry of the hand. The glory of this achievement came from the Lord of glory, it returned to Him on the platter of a yielded heart.

Authority is to use your own armour

In the Old and the New Testament there are a number of words that describe authority. Esther 9:29 the word 'authority' suggests 'strength'. Proverbs 29:2 it means to be 'great', 'many', 'mighty'. Mark 10:42; Matthew 20:25 it is to have a 'privilege over another'. Acts 8:27 authority suggest 'a powerful one'. The best use of the word authority is in 1 Timothy 2:12 meaning 'to use one's own armour'. Isn't this what David did when refusing to wear Saul's armour? That which has been snatched from another in a wrestle is not authority at all. There is armour that is our very own, proven in a testimony of God's grace.

Lawlessness is not authority but anarchy

That which is without law is not liberty, neither is license to do whatever you decide. It is as a stormy sea with a small sailing boat held within its grasp, without power or control. This belongs to the book of Judges, in declension 'every man did, that which was right in his own eyes.'[20] It is the removal of restraint. Remove the bars from the cage or open the door to a lion or tiger, and what happens? Lawlessness means to 'act outside of the law'. That is not grace, for grace can act within the law and still be successful. David broke no laws. He didn't set himself up as an independent king.

The Greek word for authority *exousia* means 'it is lawful'. It is the right or privilege to do it. It is to rule as a government. It is used in John 19:10 of taking care of domestic affairs. Another word *huperoche* suggests standing out like a mountain peak. Authority will distinguish you in everything.

Then there is the word *dunamis* from which we obtain our English word 'dynasty', 'dynamite' and 'dynamo'. In Luke 1:52 Revised Version it is given as 'princes'. All these words fit into what the shepherd of Israel displayed on that day. In Acts 1:8, the early disciples were commanded to tarry until they were endued with 'power' from on high. That word 'power' is *dunamis* meaning 'dynamite'. Acts 1:8 was power promised to act of behalf of Jesus Christ, just as David was acting in slaying Goliath on behalf of God. Goliath was challenging the armies of Israel.
That army should have been a reflection of God's armies in Heaven. In God we should be a bundle of dynamite as a church, and as a stick of dynamite as an individual. The word 'explosion' means to 'clap the hands'. It is describing the noise of clapping. You will not *Dwarf Giants* simply by clapping your hands! That comes later after the victory. You require the explosive power of the Almighty. Jesus came to destroy the works of the Devil through you. David had to establish the works of God, not the tyranny of Goliath. This is still the *modus operandi* through you, walking as light in the light.

Don't be as a burned cinder

Where did the young man get his dexterity from when dealing with a giant? It wasn't from Saul, he was a burned out coal that had rolled off the altar. It wasn't from the army of Israel, that was acting as a shed of headless chickens. It wasn't from the prophet of the day, because he was not there. David did not stand alone; he simply stood by the throne.

He believed what God had said, and he saw faith in power go into action. He had more thrust than any chariot pulled by ten horses careering along. The Eternal had sounded the battle cry, and the charge into battle, but only the shepherd responded as a sheep to the call of the shepherd. He became the echo of the call of God.

That authenticity in David was never out of control. It was never used for himself. Under total control the power of God makes the greatest impact. The soldier fights the when he knows a good General. One who is under authority, as the centurion was in the New Testament, commands him. That centurion said, 'Because I am under authority, the authority of Rome, I say to this soldier, do this, and he will do it. Do that, and he will do it, because he recognises that greater authority in me.'[21] The more you recognise the power of the Almighty, the more you know about His character and charter for your life, the more powerful you will be. Weakness is a sign that we do not know our power base. When Goliath stepped into the valley he had no power supporting him other than that within his own personality. His power was in himself. David took his power with him; it was before him and behind him, because it was the Lord who was his authority. Strength shown in the stripling was seen in that he first yielded to God verbally, and then went out into the valley to show to all what a great God he served. You are the shadow of your God. You are a reflection of that glory of the Almighty. Men will judge God by what you do or do not do. If you are a failure, they will think that your God is as other gods. This was the doctrinal and theological mistake that the army of the Philistines made, and Goliath of Gath to his own folly and to the losing of his head and his power base. It was the authority of Goliath that had made the ground tremble, and caused the soldiers to run. David's plan, in Jehovah, was to make the soldiers run, not from God but to Him, to be helped and set free. One authority brings into bondage and fear, while that in the Lord sets you free to be what He intended for you. Soldiers could never be soldiers while they feared the shape of this Colossus.

Never surrender God's power for something else

It did not matter how far David travelled along the valley, it did not matter how deep the shadows were, for he never lost the sense of the power of his God. There is an eternal flame that no darkness can extinguish by simply blowing on it. The Majesty that took him into battle was with him in it and brought him through into daylight once the Goliath blocking out sunlight and the way to the throne had been removed. It was the same power that helped him to overcome the giant and later helped him to overcome Saul and Absalom, and established him as a king. David ruled in this same power. He lived and moved in the authority of God. It is not the realisation of how great God is for one battle, one minute or one day, but the sublime realisation that the power that created the universe is in your heart by the Spirit of the Lord, and through that same Spirit we cry Abba, Father.[22]

At the end of the onslaught God wasn't more powerful nor was David. There was a release and realisation that the Eternal was what He had always been. He had been waiting, as a great fire for some simple shepherd to come and light his fire from God's. Weakness and defeat are the offspring of unbelief. David repainted the Lord of Israel as he defeated Goliath. The Lord appeared in the fullness of his glory. God was seen in all His war paint. Each soldier had their own conception of what God was, or at least what they thought He was like, what His limitations were. By the power of God David exploded any such myth that God was dead, and couldn't be bothered to help His people. He brought the Almighty into the position of leading a nation into warfare.

When Goliath called David a 'dog', it was because he couldn't spell 'god'! The giant saw everything back to front. The stripling put power and Pentecost back into the form of Elohim.[23] Not that He had ever ceased to be powerful, but He had been diminished by a backslidden king in Saul, commander of a fearful army, fighting against a fearful foe, yet ready to run if a leaf fell from a branch. No one expected a victory until it came from the unlikely source of someone acting in the power of God. You cannot judge the character of the Lord by an empty altar. He cannot be assessed by an empty heart. He is revealed, as a young lad convinced of His power runs towards a giant. As he ran, Israel was fanned into a flame. The power of God through a personality was revealed. The emptiness and the powerlessness of a giant were seen as God stepped into the equation. Jesus said, 'By their fruits you will know them.'[24] God would be known in Israel as the most powerful One.

Prove by your authority that Jesus is Lord

Jesus said, 'You call me Lord, Lord, and so I am.'[25] You can call the

Supreme One the Almighty, but you, in every circumstance of life have to prove that He is. The Lord doesn't go to sleep when you have said your prayers at night. He is not only the God of the belching Mount Sinai, and the wilderness, the quiet stream and the soft wind; He is Lord of the Universe and the universal God. He is in the still, small voice, as well as in the earthquake and fire. Get the whole picture of what the Almighty is. Look on Him in prayer, then, 'go in this your might, you mighty man of valour.'[26] Giants can become stepping-stones, and part of a stone stairway leading to the Lofty One. Do not just see Him as a God of love, but see Him as revealed in the Scriptures as the Lord of the universe. You have to prove for yourself that He is the God of valley and mountain, and you do it as you *Dwarf Giants*.

Elohim fits into every part of His creation even as the sun fits into the sky or the embryo chick fits into the coloured shell before hatching. David saw the Lord in action in every part of his life. Knowing Him and the full measure of grace that is brought to you, seeing you through every wild temptation is worth having. Some things in life have to be avoided, and we are less than crass if we don't avoid them, but other things must be faced and conquered. The authority of God is your shield, and for your victory you must rely on the power of the Almighty as the arrow relies on the bow, and as the pebble trusted the sling. So the authority of another is passed on.

Submitting is overcoming

You never have less power by submitting to leadership. When we feel at our lowest ebb it is then we are at our strongest. There must have been times when David was so low that he felt the bottom of his staff rather than the top of it. True reigning with Christ commences with God. As the leadership submit to Him, then you submit to them, as David submitted to Saul. In that submission the youth must wait for his manhood to develop. His young shoulders must be developed so that the king's mantle, when it was put upon him, would be measured to fit those shoulders. There is no merit in touching the Lord's anointed, in doing His prophets harm. The young man had to be fully engaged in the warfare that presented itself. He was so taken up with the giant, he forgot all about Saul as he remembered the One with authority. In leaving Saul's side, he was leaving a broken sword. Having Jah[27] on His side was weaponry indeed, and all he would need. He did not want a distracted mind. His mind must be on the great hulk of flesh. He must not come into battle thinking about Saul, Goliath and God. One was weak, one was strong, and One was above the other two, as far above as the earth is from the heavens. He shut out the first two words to concentrate on the third. It was through God that he did valiantly, and *Dwarfed Giants.*

Notes: -

1. Samuel 7:12.
2. Psalm 137:2.
3. Matthew 28:18.
4. Acts 1:8.
5. Acts 4:13.
6. Luke 6:40.
7. Philippians 2:5.
8. Judges 7:16-20.
9. 1 Corinthians 1:26.
10. Matthew 16:19.
11. Psalm 39:3.
12. Ambition means one who canvasses for votes by any means to gain influence.
13. 1 Timothy 3:5.
14. Matthew 10:1 Mark 3:15. Luke 10:19.
15. John 8:10.
16. Acts 10:38.
17. Esther chapter 4.
18. Esther 9:25.
19. People are referred to as 'Names' who underwrite insurance policies at Lloyds of London.
20. Judges 17:6.
21. Matthew 8:9.
22. Romans 8:15. Galatians 4:6.
23. Elohim, the creative name of God, used in Genesis chapter 1
24. Matthew 7:16.
25. Matthew 7:21,22. Luke 6:46.
26. Judges 6:12.
27. Jah, the shortened name of Jehovah.

Chapter

16

The Knowledge of what you are fighting

Goliath's challenge was a daily one. It wasn't something that happened every day. The daily trumpet call was supplanted by the giant's challenging voice. Temptation is like that. In 1 Samuel 17:16, he presented himself morning and evening for forty days. Just as the morning and evening sacrifice was being offered, then the challenge came. It is reasonable to expect that, if you get close to your Master temptation will come. Just as you make that supreme sacrifice of commitment the giant arrives. Jesus, just after His baptism was driven by the Spirit to be tempted for forty days and nights.[1] Within each enticement there is as much potential as a pioneer going to discover new lands. In any battle the soldier gets to know his enemy and also his weapons.

Know your enemy and the target

For the young Ephrathite it wasn't a stab in the dark when he met with his assailant. It wasn't in a corner or in some dark alley. It was seen with a great cloud of witnesses looking on from each side of the Valley of Elah. David didn't simply let a stone sail from his sling, he had a mark, and he was aiming at the giant standing before him. The shepherd had a vision and a mission to fulfil, yet it did not stop him being attacked. The lad knew the object he was aiming at, and we need to know something about our enemy. David didn't eat, sleep, think, wake and talk Goliath. He had hardly met him when the challenge was uttered. Allurements come in different shapes and sizes. They appear in different guises, but they are not of God. The years come and go, one generation following another, but temptation remains the same. They can be individual, as with David and Goliath, or they can come as a flock of birds, as described by Jesus.[2]

We don't know if the son of Jesse had met with Goliath before or seen him in action in some other battle. Stories would circulate, and the man standing about nine foot two inches would grow as the stories were repeated. What was a giant, by means of exaggeration would soon be described as a mountain with the moon on its peak. David had the firm conviction that what he didn't and couldn't know, the Lord knew for He knows all things from the end to the beginning, and the beginning to the end. The Lord has complete and competent knowledge of good and evil. He does not expect us to wear blinkers like a horse when facing a dilemma.

Concentrate on the one thing

There was no unbelief, because unbelief holds a certain amount of torment. David did not have fifty battles to fight, or fifty irons in different fires. He said, as the New Testament battler said, 'This 'one' thing I do.' 'Forgetting those things behind, I press on towards the goal'.[3] David didn't have to mathematically work out the equation of boy meets giant. The youth did what he had to do, with his entire mind and might as part of living for Jehovah. In the heart of that adolescent there was something larger than a range of mountains. To 'out-do' a difficulty you have to be more determined and consecrated than that which is attacking. David used his gifting, related to a sling and a stone. It was similar the task for rescuing wandering sheep from the paw of the bear and the lion. With the Lord on your side, as He was with David, there will be no 'calamity'- a word which describes corn that has been blown down by the wind or a storm. David was standing strong and true at the end of the battle. The giant's feet did not 'walk all over' him. We must bear the marks of Christ and the cross, followed by the etchings of grace, not evil and tragedy.

Walk and win with God

There were not many examples for David to follow. Through temptation he became a true pioneer and was able to help other warriors as he trained them for war. He could have passed on the words of Oliver Cromwell who led the Ironsides in the English Civil War. On wet days he would say 'Trust in God, and keep your powder dry.' The Ephramite simply walked in the footsteps of God, along the road the Almighty had provided for him. He went with such confidence towards the giant, as if he was going to feed sheep or was on an errand for his father. Some sheep in Goliath! Some errand as he faced the Gath one!

Do not over emphasis evil

There is very little written about Goliath of Gath. He appears to have been a descendant of Rephaim, living in the area of Ammon. They took refuge with the Philistines when they were defeated, Deuteronomy 2:

20,21. We know he had four brothers, 1 Chronicles 20:5. 2 Samuel 21:19. Elhanah slew these other brothers. Even when David had knocked Goliath from his feet to the pitiful position of having no head, there were still giants left. Trials are not single, they come in many ways and with much diversity. Jesus could have removed all temptation, but He did not. There are certain things, that we must take and use to develop in us that godliness and holiness which is the hallmark of Christianity. Even when Israel came into the Promised Land, the marauding tribes were there to keep them dependent on their Savour. Each temptation is meant to bring out the best in you. It is God allowing giants to come and, in the battles with them, so we become real soldiers. That which surrounds you can act as a mould. We must not conform to this world, but be transformed from within. There must be nothing Bacchius about us, the sacred bull in Egyptian mythology who changed colour every hour of the day. We cannot remain as raw recruits forever.

Men of war are developed through warfare

Men of war are only developed in war. That which brings victory must enter into advancement on all fronts. It is not the things we run away from that change us, but the things that challenge. If we run away then we never find the true spirit of victory. Your trumpet will not sound a victorious note. It is 'between a rock and a hard place' that we are trained.

Not much is written about Goliath, because we must not spend our time giving expositions on the enemy of Israel. If some spent as much time in prayer as they do discussing Satan and his mannerisms, more prayers would be answered and God's people would be set free. Discussion can make things larger, when they were meant to be smaller. The mouse can be turned into a mountain if you talk about it long enough! Have you seen children's eyes grow larger as you tell them a 'far fetched' story? There was no epitaph erected for that which was defeated. It is the winner, the over-comer who is remembered throughout Israel. Let that which is now happening to you become but a faded memory. Use what has been your struggle to help someone coming along the valley behind you. You may suffer thorns tearing at the substance of your soul, but leave the perfume and the roses for others. Whatever you leave behind let it be worth having. What you have been prepared to die for, let it be worth living for.

There are giants in every life

More than discussion, which was so short with David's brothers and Saul, there must be that which can be gained from real contact with a real enemy. Once the Hercules fell, the youth knew how to bring a giant to the ground. There is a giant in every life, around every corner, occupying till He comes. The brothers of Goliath were ready to take his place and continue the persecution. They wouldn't have minded using old armour, but Israel's favourite son removed it! We must not leave 'skeletons' in the cupboard, leave them at the cross. When God has dealt with the giant He puts up a sign which says 'no entry.' Another such sign reads 'no right of way.' If you leave the shoes that the giant walks in others will use them to march right up to you, and tread where it hurts the most. You must get complete victory to continue your advance to the throne. Even when you have resisted 'unto blood'[4] giving your life, there will be further conflict as other temptations line up as a Philistine army. David's victory wasn't achieved at one stroke. He gathered stones, hid them in his bag, walked through the valley, and then he took the ground the giant occupied. Eventually all the land was his. That piece of earth the large man stood on became the earnest of David's inheritance. He dealt with the strong man's history and geography (where he stood), before he was able to proceed.

It is manly to overcome

The taunt of the giant was to 'find a man, and send him to me.' The challenge is still the same in Christianity. 'If any 'man' be in Christ Jesus, he is a new creation.'[5] 'Let a 'man' come and take up his cross daily and follow me.'[6] 'Choose you out 'men' from among you.'[7] The boy was the man in the making. It was as a result of meeting with this man of Gath that the boy was to become a man. A 'pious man' to the Romans was a man who looked after his father and served him well. The term 'pious' was used of one man who rescued his father from a burning house. David was truly a 'pious man' in that he revered his heavenly Father. As a man he was on a rescue mission. His Father's house was burning with the wrong sort of fire.

We become part of all we meet. Even the brass that the giant carried with him was to become part of this youth. The bronze target, the helmet of brass, the coat of mail, the staff and his spear had to be taken and used in future conflict. All that Goliath was speaks of the very things we obtain in our experience of temptation. There is a vein of gold in every rock, but it needs extracting by hard work. Sometimes that hard work is to suffer to achieve your goal. In the shadows of the valley, places where the sun never shone, were rare flowers that were found nowhere else; these can be taken to adorn your soul with the 'sweet smell of success'.

The trial is strong when you are weak

Everything happened in the valley. At your lowest point the trial is so real and strong. You need to dig deep, in order to ensure that your foundation will be sure, before you can rise to any height. You need to know that others are involved in the same battle. Men and women of God throughout the ages recorded in history have been in the same fight for the right. David left that valley battle with far more than he took into it. There is treasure in the truth of conflict with the Adversary of your soul. When we meet with opposition it is not enough to say 'what will this do to me?', as if we will be defeated. We need to say instead 'what can I gain from this experience?' This moment is choice when we face huge difficulty. 'What can the Lord of glory teach me while I am here?' That is why Psalm 23 speaks of 'walking' through the valley of shadows.[8] Take time to lean, learn and love.

God can limit every temptation

Goliath represented a kingdom, the kingdom of the Philistines. He was one of many, and part of the whole system of evil in his day. The way in which he approached the Israeli army was one of total disdain. He was the champion of the day, 1 Samuel 17:4, the proven warrior of his day. He had many tokens of victory in broken weapons of warfare. Satan has the same tokens in broken lives and families. Every drug addict is a testimony to the evilness of Evil and the persuasive power of Satan. If he had been a Redskin, he would have worn many feathers, carried many scalps in his leather girdle. He had lain so many in the dust of defeat, and been so successful that they thought Israel would never provide a challenger for him. He was introduced as their champion.

The title 'champion' suggests a field, the place where games are played and won. Very often in olden days, they would choose two combatants, and the outcome of the war was based on the result. This man was the size of a field, but David, in God, would plough it, and sow seed in it. As a 'champion', they are describing a 'warrior of renown', just as the men of Rephaim had been in the past. The 'champion' is the 'double interval'. It describes the space between two armies. In modern warfare it is called 'No Man's Land'. God had to fill even that space, because He dwells in all things. He is everywhere, and He is here, where you are facing your foes. Foes can be woes, but the Lord seeks to take from the 'champion', and make you one through the championship of suffering and resistance. Goliath is the 'man of intervention'. A go-between who needs defeating, because there is 'One God, and one mediator between man and God, Christ Jesus.' [9] Your Man has won the battle already, but He has left one or two snipers to keep you alert!

Three times Goliath is called their champion, 1 Samuel 17:4,23,51. The first time the word is used it suggests a broad expanse of water. Those trying to swim in it will be drowned. If you go with the tide you will be swept away, and as a Jonah, you will be spued onto a beach not knowing where you are.[10] 'Champion' describes the gap between two mountains. When David defeated Goliath the giant is referred to in 1 Samuel 17:51, as their 'champion' but it is a totally different Hebrew word that is used to describe the dead man. The word 'champion' in verse 51 means 'just another man.' The young lad, in God, had reduced the mound of flesh to the size of a normal man. Reduction in temptation is not enough. That lustful enticement must die. The Old Nature is illustrated in the giant of Gath. That carnal nature must be crucified in Christ. The Lord always brings things into captivity, and shows them to you as they really are. Every imagination must be brought into the captivity of the mind of Jesus Christ.[11]

God's champions are called and chosen

In the days of William the Conqueror, England had men known as 'Champions of England'. On Coronation Day when the king was about to be crowned these soldiers would ride amongst the crowd challenging anyone who disputed the right of succession. They were dealt with without any ceremony! We must dispute the Devil's right to rule over us. David stopped Goliath being adulated and coroneted. David wanted to see the Almighty back on the throne, loved and obeyed by His subjects. Among the crowd that day was a man named Goliath who was questioning the right of Israel to be in the land, questioning the sovereignty of the Lord. With the title of 'champion' as used in the English language, a castle and estate was given. This would come later for the youth. Heaven is the land, and a mansion in John 14:1-3 has been promised to you.

Do not be ignorant of Satan's devices

We must not be ignorant of the devices of the Devil.[12] We must know, not simply through study but also because of experience what the Devil's stratagem for war is. As Goliath challenged daily, so we must face the 'wiles' of the Devil in the daily round. We cannot, dare not, be ignorant of his devices. In the form of the giant was the map of evil. The bad word, the argument, have a satanic source, and we must see it for what it is. There must be an ability to discern between good and evil. When you are challenged, God changes you, but you need to recognise within the challenge and where it came from. Wrapped up in the great figure lumbering towards the youth of Israel, there was a nest of evil waiting to be hatched. If the man after God's own heart killed it now the history and geography of evil would cease. Let the cross of Christ become the full stop for every lust and temptation.

Temptation can be like a fiery dart

Each giant can be a fiery dart that is sent to wound and hurt. When the flaming arrows strike,[13] as words spoken by this Hercules, we must make sure that there is nothing tinder dry which will encourage it to burn without remorse. We must not spread the flame from the arrow by causing a wind as we panic. Within the hurt is the salve for healing. At that moment, the arm and hand of the Lord becomes your shield. His wings are for your protection.[14] David stood before the giant as defenceless as a chicken before a field of foxes. In the battle, you get to know the protection and power of the Sovereign Lord, and are able to assess the position and personality of the evil assailing. In the recognition of your enemy is the recognition of your Friend. It takes an attack for you to discover the true worth of your protection. As the armies gathered together, you number those on your side, and look at those in the opposing army. As you realise all that are for you, it makes you stronger. There are so many soldiers in your army righteousness, the blood of Christ, wholeness, peace, joy, trust, there is no end of the list that are fighting under the flag of the faithful.

There are enough promises in the word of God to kit out an army. Each promise is a soldier. This stripling only needed one shot, one stone, one sling and one promise from God. Enemies and friends belong in different encampments. Fighting against your enemies teaches you to trust your friends. With a common enemy, friends move closer. 'Two are better than one.'[15] Even David's brothers stopped eating the soldier's rations of corn, bread and cheese and, instead of criticising their younger brother, began to cheer him. Nothing feeds the spirit in men like success.

The enemy seeks to restrict you

The enemy you fight against is what David found in Goliath. It is the same enemy that Jesus encountered. To have knowledge of your attacker is part of the victory. During World War II Field Marshall Montgomery of Alamien had a picture of Field Marshall Rommel, posted in his tent. The best knowledge of the enemy who attacks you is gained when you spend time in the valley, at war. Life will take you where the giants are. Seeing, understanding and assessing all that he does, as you meet in close combat will enrich your skills. In the Word of God we have the short Roman sword that enables us to fight and win at close quarters. Spend time in prayer, for in prayer you have the longest weapon in the universe, reaching up to heaven. Prayer travels the length, breath, depth and height of the world rescuing men and woman from horrible situations.

What Goliath sought to do with David, so the enemy of your soul seeks to do with you. He wanted to make the future king part of the brute creation by taking his flesh and feeding it to the beasts of the field and the fowls of the air. The attacker wanted to turn the future ruler into manure, but the Lord wanted him to mature. Sin and Satan will always make you less than what you are. Goliath would ruin God's creation. Gath's man wanted to bury the son of Jesse, to let his bones be picked over by vultures, so there would be no memory in Israel of their champion.

Satan might appear larger than anything else, but time and time again in the New Testament he was subject to the power of God.[16] God has a stone for you; something to 'say' and 'do' that will 'down' the evil that pursues. As Goliath had brothers, so Satan has many demons to fight against the believer in Christ. All the Philistines were ready to walk in

Goliath's shoes. Your enemy is already defeated! Satan has only as much power as you grant. David couldn't lose, Goliath couldn't win. He was a defeated foe even before he fell.

Beware of the wiles of the Devil

His ways are called 'wiles' in Ephesians 6:11. 'Wiles' means 'craft', 'deceit', that which is twisted as any snake. The word 'wiles' points to one waiting in a ditch ready to spring. The small snare was set for the large man, and it was only a stone in size! The son of Israel didn't get entangled. He was no fly in the spider's web. You must not live in the shadow of temptations, live in the shadow of the Almighty. Ephesians 6:11, the word 'wiles' is in the plural, proving that there are as many as could be numbered in the Philistine army. Apollyon only leaves you, as he left Jesus for a season. He will return to what he feels he has a claim on if you submit to him.

Only once in the Old Testament of the King James Version of the Bible is the word 'wiles' used, Numbers 25:18. It means to 'defraud' or act 'deceitfully'. It is the giving of less weight in the package than should be. When Goliath spoke of David, he was giving 'under weight'; it wasn't what the boy was like at all. Israel's choice was heavier by a 'stone'! He was heavier than he appeared in the scales of the giant's mind. It was a malicious description of that which was good and wholesome. The label the giant read did not describe the true contents of the child of Israel's character. He is not called the Accuser of the Brethren without good reason.[17] The tempter, as Goliath, was out to steal from the babes of Israel.

'Wiles' can mean 'slight of hand'. Belial sees life as a card game and he had double-sided cards to cheat with. Guess who the Joker is? When you deal with God, He is the king of the pack of cards that are dealt out to you in life. In the term 'wiles' there is the thought of 'travelling another way', a devious and round about way when it should be straight as a stone flying from a sling to its target. This 'way' is in the form of darkness, it is the 'way' of Cain[18] and the 'way' of Balaam.[19] There is no other Way like the Christian Way.

The New Testament speaks of those who have come in 'unawares' [20] i.e. 'sideways'. Not front first because they might be discovered. They have to make themselves smaller, more acceptable, and then they become what they really are. Once you yield, then the nature of that which has been yielded will become apparent. It is like a few seeds of ivy planted into an aperture in a wall at the side of a house. It takes over, and it demands attention everywhere.

Some make shipwreck of their faith

There are those who do not overcome Goliath, and they make 'shipwreck' of the faith, 1 Timothy 1:19. We have all seen parts of a vessel sticking out of the water as a warning to other shipping to stay away from that area. Their precious cargo becomes the haunt of birds and barnacles, fish and fossils. Goliath sounded out his warnings and cursing, but the youth wasn't ready to listen to any suggestion such as Eve and Adam listened to in the Garden of Eden.

What Satan does in confronting us with temptation is called 'devices' and 'stratagem'. He uses dirty methods, knowing no 'Queensbury Rules'[21] when fighting. He breaks time and time again that which is already broken. He does not add injury to insult he is insult and injury. Assault and battery is in his right hand. The word 'devices' is translated 'thought' and 'mind'. In Matthew 12:25, when Jesus was dealing with Darkness, He referred to their 'thoughts', where the 'device' began in the temptation coming from the Pharisees. The mind becomes a battlefield, and a minefield. Paul the apostle wanted to help the early Church so that Satan would not corrupt their minds or destroy the simplicity they had in Christ. That they might know nothing of double-talk or double standards.

Many weapons are formed against you

The weaponry and strategy of the Adversary is in a mood, a frown, something that is said or done, and something that is taken hold of and used against each one. He wants to bring offenses to your heart. Each time you yield, what should have been a promise in stone become a stumbling block and a hurdle in the Race of Life. The Archfiend wants to see you fenced in, limited in every way. The Evil One desires every church become a 'limited company', going so far and no further. The word 'weapons' in the New Testament is always found in the plural.[22] We have weapons given to us by God. There are many that the Old Serpent uses, and they belong to one evil hand. The carnal nature is a sure stockpile of weapons for the Powers of Darkness. For the Adversary you have the Advocate. Carnal Nature is a Goliath. Every lust is a weapon formed against you.

Be realistic about temptation

There was more to Goliath than mere armour encasing flesh and blood. Behind him was the power that has sought to defeat God throughout the ages, an enemy who would crush every child of God. Behind every dark temptation learn to look further than Goliath or any other form of trial. Be realistic see the enemy, and know what and with whom you are fighting. See beyond all that is arrayed against you. If God be for you, He is more than all those against you.[23] Elijah had to pray that the eyes of the young man might be opened to see the valley full of horses and chariots.[24] There are more trying to help you to stand than there are trying to push you down. The valley was only until Goliath of Gath met his match. He only remained until he was put under the feet of David. God wants to witness you putting all things under your feet, laying aside as a weight the sin that so easily besets us.[25] If you have knowledge of what you are fighting, you will *Dwarf Giants*.

Notes: -

1. Matthew 4:1,2.
2. Matthew 13:4.
3. Philippians 3:13.
4. Hebrews 12:4.
5. 2 Corinthians 5:17.
6. Luke 9:23.
7. Exodus 17:9.
8. See the author's book *Paths of Righteousness in Psalm 23.*
9. 1 Timothy 2:5.
10. Jonah 2:10.
11. 2 Corinthians 10:5.
12. 2 Corinthians 2:11.
13. Ephesians 6:16.
14. Psalm 91:1.
15. Ecclesiastes 4:9.
16. Luke 10:17.
17. Revelation 12:10.
18. Jude 11.
19. Numbers 22.
20. Jude 4.
21. The rules governing boxing, first introduced by Lord Queensbury.
22. 2 Corinthians 10:4.
23. Romans 8:31.
24. 2 Kings 6:17.
25. Hebrews 12:1.

Chapter

17

The Fresh Evidence of Victory

The desert sands soon blow over the footprints that have been left by the traveller. When the winds of change blow it is impossible to tell anyone has ever travelled that way. The same thing happens in our memories when we think of past achievements in God. Time and tide not only wait for no man, they sweep all before them as if they had never existed. You can see big rocks, shaped and wasted by winter weather along the Pennine Way in England.[1] It brings to mind that nothing lasts forever. There needs to be constant renewal if we are to remain relevant in the Battle of the Ages. The only evidence of what has happened in the battle between David and Goliath was seen in broken weapons and discarded uniforms.

We don't see things as they are

Broken promises can litter the ground around us, what was so real diminishes with the passing of time. It would seem as if time turns the lamp low, leaving us to see through a glass darkly.[2] Time draws a veil over most things, and nothing appears to be what it was. This is why we need new experiences with God, just as King David did. This moving of the Holy One of Israel must be contained in more than the five stones taken from the valley. They must be so numerous and enormous that they cannot be counted or measured. David's life is so rich with the many happenings that moulded his destiny. It seems as if he never stops long in one place, because God has more and more for him. We can stay with the one thing, and it can become a breeding ground for staleness and boredom. The human heart craves the cherry red manifestation of mighty power.

New frontiers beckon us to join them

To keep things fresh they need to be watered or filled. Even for David to re-visit the valley and pick up a few stones would not keep the memory of his victory fresh every day. There had to be a visitation from Jehovah. There has to be many knocks on the door of the heart before we respond. New frontiers need to beckon us to join them. The throwing of the stone from the sling was different to removing the head from the giant. The best way to keep the *Fresh Evidence of Victory* is to enter into another battle, and be just as victorious. Most measurements are made up of inches, feet, centimetres and meters, and it is little by little before we grasp the whole. That which is stale reigns when we come to a stop. We must be ahead of time. When we come to a standstill, even the refreshing waters from the well at Bethlehem dry up or became stagnant.[3] Waters have to be stirred in order for them to retain their potency. All we have accomplished can become as a well without water, counting the stones, nothing coming out of an empty sling.

The rock that water poured from for Israel can become just a rock.[4] The Red Sea that parted can see the tide coming in and going out as if nothing has ever happened.[5] The bread and fish that Jesus divided among so many becomes just a few loaves and a few fish again.[6] That miracle can be reversed by time, and we are left holding just a tradition.

The conqueror would have none of this as he held in his hand a fresh decapitated head. It was so crisp that David's words were still ringing in the ears of the severed head. Death had hardly time to mark it with its own authenticity as David displayed it throughout the villages of Judah. It was so inspiring the women took up their tambourines and began to dance. This dead brain was better than a harp or a psalm. Was it from this that David received the inspiration to write 'my cup is full and running over'? That so recent triumph brings music to the soul. Songs, signs and wonders go together. That which has never happened before brings in a new creation, a new and exciting vision from the head of the defeated.

Don't let time rob you of your essentials

The son of Israel didn't let time or decay sit on the throne of the day, as this new thing happened in battle. He wanted to hold onto the moment, and the thing that had happened for as long as he could. There are not many Generals in the history of war who have been able to walk from the battle carrying a flesh and blood photograph of their victory. Each time, as David travelled towards Jerusalem and someone enquired about the battle, he showed them the fresh head. It overcame more in death than in life. Let that invigorating become part of your handiwork.

He was not prepared to let go what God had given to him. His memories of the day, and his encounter with the best of Gath would not be allowed to go with a sword, and be hidden in a tent. Anything fresh must be displayed. So real, so new that the blood was still dripping from it.

To counter any staleness and formality, Jesse's son took hold of the head of the giant and brought it, eyes not yet closed, the wound fresh from the battle. Bring out your best moments of zeal and passion, and put them on display. The zeal of accomplishment needs to be with us after the battle. You need to maintain the 'spiritual glow'.[7]

You can lose your freshness in your work for God. Tiredness worn and folded up can become your nature. The wrestling and the struggle as you encounter opposition can rob you of your vitality. When we are tired of being defeated we become worn and stale. We repeat the same old words and stories. What might have been renewal can become ritual. The outcome of the battle presented David with a new story, a new light in his young eyes. The testimony of a new convert is like a piece of fresh bread from the miracle hand of Jesus. It is not the stale crusts of a crisis that we require, but a spur and a star to goad us on, to guide us into something real. We don't want to count stones, or examine slings; we want to see stones as promises taken and used that fell the foulest. It is useless going into battle as a fire and coming out as cold ash.

New every morning are His mercies, and we need to see them at work. The young man came from the battle with a trophy that had not been handed down from generation to generation. It was mint at this moment. No other hand had taken hold of the giant's head. It was exclusive to Israel's son.

Go back to the cross for reassurance and refreshment

Many times in spirit we must visit Calvary, and see afresh all that Jesus accomplished in be-heading Satan at the cross as He spoiled his thought-pattern, and his ability to make free decisions without God allowing it. 'His heel shall bruise your head.'[8] To see any battle or work of grace from different angles does not retain freshness in our spirits. It has to happen to us, and be part of the plan for a life, even as it happened to the one fighting in the valley. He might have gone into the area of battle with weary feet and aching arms, but when he came out he had wings on his feet like a cherub. David came resplendent, as being set free after years of imprisonment. He felt as the scientist when he makes a new discovery. Jesse's son had slain 'the troubler of Israel.' He wanted to stop and tell every body he met! The young man who falls in love is so dynamic in his expressions of love, he almost overwhelms you.

We must always carry the hope that is within us, as the youth carried the wet head of the most recent testimony. It cannot live in the valley forever. It must be made to count on the path of life, among the family, and in the neighbourhood. You don't have to make it up as you go along, but in zeal repeat to others what God has said and done for you. Be like the writer in the New Testament at the end of the Book of Hebrews who says, 'time would fail me to tell'.[9] We require that which is virgin from the Lord that it has not been touched by history, or thrown into the past by memory. It needs to be as fresh as the plant that grew in your garden this morning. That came up with the sun to share the sunshine. The victory could never be copied or repeated. Some could hold in their hand the head of a lamb, a fish or a chicken, but not the head of Goliath.

Remain fresh in the blessing

1 Samuel 17:54, the head was as fresh when it was severed from the body, as it was when the champion brought it to Jerusalem. The ability has to be developed in you to allow the carrying of the head of every temptation to Jerusalem, just as fresh as when it happened. We are journeying to the New Jerusalem.[10] There must be no diminishing of what has been wrought by God as you travel. David wanted to have that fresh inspiration to offer to the King of Israel. Your testimony of deliverance, the work of grace in your heart, God acting on your behalf has to be maintained. Holy fire must remain holy. The fire on the altar of Israel must never go out.[11] That which has been wrought by Jireh must not be pulled apart or found to be fraying at the edges. It must be 'wholesome', just as it was on the first day it happened. It must be as long lasting as the grass is green, the river flows and the mountains stand. Some people have a good testimony of triumph on a Sunday, but by Monday, mildew has gathered on that testimony. Time will take your accomplishments from you. It will, through suffering squeeze your hand open until you let that which was new from God fall to the ground to be buried into obscurity.

Do not become as Lazarus

The testimony and its freshness can become as Lazarus, who had been in the grave a few days and 'by now he stinks.' [12] Many times we have to be as our father Abraham, who had to beat off the birds that came to take the pieces of meat that were part of God's covenant with him.[13] The Book of Hebrews was written to those who were letting things 'slip' as oil running from a leaking vessel.[14] Flies and the heat of the desert would soon make short work of that head. As David had fought off the wild beasts that came to take away the sheep he was caring for, so he would ensure that nothing stole that fresh head from his hand. You have to ask the Sovereign Lord to tighten your grip. Some things are given to us forever. In the passing of time it is good to have that which cannot be shaken. We must strive to keep what we have alive and fresh in God.

Experiences in God can become stale, we need is to ask the Bread of Life to 'give us this day our daily bread.' Each bite and taste stimulates us. Each new step the child takes strengthens its legs to run, walk and jump. Yesterday's blessings hold no merit for today's challenge. You require that which will keep you fresh, unopened. David held in his hands what he needed to use in the present and in the future. It could not be used in the past. You can only drink the full measure a little at a time. The whole loaf disappears slice by slice. What God grants to us has to be taken little at a time. This keeps us sparkling and trusting.

Do not jettison the old because of the new

David appears as one perfectly balanced the shield in one hand and the head of the giant in the other. It takes victory to bring us into perfect balance, to take us on to our destiny. He didn't have to get rid of the old to promote the new. The vivid head promoted the sling, the stone, and every other weapon that he carried. We have a fresh experience with the Lord and the first thing we want to do is to jettison those of past generations. New wineskins are required for new wine, but until that new wine ferments keep drinking the old.

God cannot trust us with the head of a giant because we think what happened to day is all there is in Him. There is more, much more, as much as can be found in the Eternal nature, He is Jehovah Jireh. The Lord only grants us in our zeal what we can ably carry with us from the battle into the main areas of life. David wasn't called or challenged to carry the dead body of the giant through the streets of Jerusalem, only the 'brain box'. The apostle to giants carried an old harp but it still played the songs of Zion. Now he had a new song the battle and triumph provided for him. We can have perfect balance in a combination of the old and the new. He had in his hands something that had never happened to him before. Into his soul the Lord Jehovah was taking all the strands of life and weaving them into a beautiful design. When he was old, cold and grey headed, he could wear what the Lord of the Universe had weaved over his shoulders. It would bring comfort and warmth on cold, dark, dreary days.

Victory puts a new 'face' on the old

When Israel's boy returned from the battle with a giant's head, he had something as fresh as that which had been produced in the night, revealed in the morning light. It was carried as a token of grace and the help of the Master he served. He had not entered the war with a head hanging from his fingers it had been given to fill his hand. This needs to be in our hearts fountain fresh. He came out of the battle with a fresh face, in the face of the dead Goliath. *The Fresh Evidence of Victory* was put where everyone could see it.

The soldiers saw the Philistines in a new light. The whole army of aliens was within their grasp. It spoke volumes, for it said to them 'you can do great things. Every one of them is as a dead man. Go seek a new experience in your Lord.' Those with empty hands get something *de novo* into them. Every time we battle for the right and are called upon to take a stand against a giant, that enrichment grants us a new face, a new idea. Here was the boy's new plan from God, let us go and win. What we take from any altercation what is as fresh as a daisy in a meadow. It is very difficult to find something new and alive in a valley, which speaks of death, gloom and doom, but David found it, but it would only remain part of him as long as it was fresh.

Let the new break the monotony of the old

The army had stood the taunts of the giant for forty days and forty nights, and it was getting a little bit stale. As David slew the giant, for the first time something was put into the battle scene, rather like a master painting where a figure is added, which completes the artist's intentions.

The giant while he remained alive was a huge smell awash with the stench of battle. From that stagnation the youth found something fresh to carry around with him, to take on his journey. This was more glorious than a packed lunch!

When the people saw *The Fresh Evidence of Victory*, they knew where David had been, and they knew who he was. They knew where he was going, and what he was going to be. We are going to rule as kings unto our God, and first time experiences will help us on our way. There is nothing quite like fresh paint to brighten an old 'master'. Freshness, and another happening in the Holy Spirit will add another head to you. It will increase you fourfold, making you larger than life, and deeper than love. This is why the Bible speaks of the 'new' birth, 'new' tongues, 'New' Testament. Sometimes when the word 'new' is used as depicting that which is 'fresh' it doesn't mean an entirely 'new' thing, but something old that has been reinvented. It can be new in time or nature. It also can be so new as to be unique. That which has been freshly slain by the future king was new in time and nature, it had never happened before. Matthew 9:17, the word 'new' is translated 'fresh' in the Revised Version of the Bible. The Greek word *prosphatos*, Hebrews 10:20 originally signified 'freshly slain'. When we realise that Jesus is the 'new' and living way, it means that anything that comes to us such as a different temptation or some 'new' trial that we don't understand, in Jesus Christ we have that which is 'new' with which to meet it. We are not left to our own devices. Those things wrought by God need to be balanced, not only on our hands but also in our hearts. The experience of defeating giants will make us heavier, even as that which was carried by the Ephramite made him larger and heavier.

New victories will add to your stature

The Fresh Evidence of Victory was because Bethlehem's son had fought a battle and won. Freshness and depth do not come without cost being involved. If you are going to purchase, you must be prepared to spend. You have to have an open heart if that sparkling stream is going to run into your heart. Battles and new victories will add something, like a new flower appearing or new oil being poured into your life. Where you have limped, you will run. This vital happening didn't stop David fulfiling the will of God. He didn't get taken up with this one new thing, he moved on into something even more stimulating.

It was fresh because he had been with the Lord of hosts. He had called upon the Name of the Lord. The son of Bethlehem had been in fellowship with the Sovereign, and have received something new. That which lies within a creative Elohim will be passed on as we seek deeper experiences with Him. He is fresher than the green grass, the fruit coming into season or a new moon. The head was only the earnest of what was to follow. Israel's warrior commenced with one giant, but there was much more to come. The size of that face was but a shelf on which to store new experiences. In the past his conversation had been about sheep, or domestic things, but now a new vocabulary was born as he spoke, because of his encounter. The mouth in the head usually does the speaking. The son of Jesse was not short of something fresh to talk about. I is so lovely how when that comes part of you, even the birth of your first child, it gives you so much more to say, and it takes you into areas that you would never have entered.

The child of Israel had to be warned not to make too much ceremony of the fact that he brought something fresh out of battle. He would only travelled this way once. He didn't keep travelling from the valley to Jerusalem. He wasn't called to do this continually, if he had done so, he would be like a ticking clock, doing the same old thing time after time. It was just the once. In the future God would add new things to his life, just as the seasons replenish trees, flowers, grass and waters.

David didn't need to shout about what had happened. The head, fresh from the battlefield, provided the evidence to show to all who would look. That fresh head was so eloquent; it spoke peace and hope into every listening ear. It grabbed men's attention, and they stood as soldiers under command as this soldier passed by. It was like a scene from past history suddenly resurrected. The Lord was alive, and through their God they could do valiantly. All could come to this scene, and take from it whatever they required. It would freshen their faith. This was better than the morning dew of Mount Hermon.

Come fresh from the 'fields of success'

Fresh from the 'fields of success' has an aroma and a glow of glory about it. No pen can describe such a spectacle, as a shepherd boy ran towards Jerusalem carrying the head of a giant, not as a monument but as something as fresh as a fish just taken from the river. In every 'stale' situation there is something fresh for the eyes which are anointed with 'fresh' oil. It is not testimonies of the past that people are interested in, they want to know what has happened to you today. Are you carrying the severed head of temptation in your heart and life? The palm of your hand is where your fortune is. It tells of your destiny, as this event told of the future of the child of Israel. Is there the skip of the lamb in your soul? Are you so fresh with your testimony that it could be used as a face wipe? Some personalities, as they touch the Lord, are a fresh Pentecostal wind as they breeze in.

The only natural way of winning a war was left with Saul and his soldiers. Those who followed the son of Jesse would be expected to defeat giants, even as those who follow Jesus Christ are called and commanded to do the same. From this time on the house of David grew greater, whilst the house of Saul diminished into just a brick. This event heralded the beginning of a new order.

Foes have to be faced in order to be defeated

David didn't have to quote the words of a prophet, the sayings of the sages or even the Scriptures. He was Scripture in the making as he faced the large man and removed his head. We never live for ourselves we live for others and for future generations. Influence is a fresh wind. The Almighty does so much for some people that their heart is a diary of days when these things happened. So many new things are in the 'new' every morning is His love the pages are full. As the scribe in the Kingdom of Heaven they bring out things 'new' and old.[15]

No one can fully explain what it feels like to have a fresh anointing. It gives you such an abundance of inspiration you feel that nothing can stand in your way. The world becomes your oyster. Every turn of the way, you are like a child making new discoveries. What you discover must benefit mankind, as David's fresh experience did.

Do not live in constant defeat

The new stone that God gives must not only take us into battle with a youthful spirit but also bring us out with the fresh evidence of what has been accomplished. You cannot go on forever proclaiming that the Lord of Heaven is yours yet live in defeat, listening to every whisper of the enemy and bowing down to the latest 'fad'. Whatever troubles you put into the hands of Jesus, as the giant's head was in the hands of the conqueror. It is easy to crown Christ the Lord of the Universe, to crown Him the king of apostles and prophets, placing their crown onto His head, but it is your crown He requires. Without a victory that head would have been another heavy burden for the lad to carry. In the spirit of success, everything we are called upon to endure becomes as light as a feather and as soft as a pillow.

We need 'times of refreshing' from the presence of the Lord.[16] That means it is Heaven fresh in order to meet the stale situations of life. It speaks of renewal, and *The Fresh Evidence of Victory* became the new doctrine of the day. If you are tired of the old life then ask the Lord to give you something fresh. Whether old or new, He is able to breath into it the 'breath of lives'.[17] This fresh evidence came because David had been in the presence of the Lord. Unlike Cain, he didn't go out from the presence of the Lord.[18] David went with the presence of the Lord into battle to smash an evil presence in the Gath person. Within his soul, and in the evidence of the giant's head, the youth felt what Moses displayed when his face shone with the glory as he came down Mount Sinai.[19] Can you imagine the look of glee on his face? It was better than the shine on a child's face when it receives a toffee. It made him both happier than counting sheep, happier even than finding a lost sheep and bringing it home. There is nothing like taking a new stand, or conquering an enemy to bring freshness into your soul as a mighty river flowing in full flood.

This sparkle will keep you from 'fainting fits' where you feel like leaving the battlefield. It would be nice if every time we came to the Communion Service we could treat it as if it was the first time. That experience of the new birth can come again, where 'heaven above is softer blue, and earth beneath is deeper green, something lives in every hue, that Christ less' eyes have never seen.'[20]

Do something that will last forever

David the Bethlehemite put a 'new face on things'. It wasn't the 'face' of the hypocrite, where a mask is put over the real face. He didn't make things different just for a moment, he wanted something that would last forever. That which was required needed keeping as crisp each day as long as memory would last. We need victories that will last more than a mere day or the measure of a thought. The young lad displayed the 'face' of sincerity, of hope and joy. There had been no hope of defeating the challenger until he came onto the scene, and he altered the whole demeanour of the battle. In that which was now dead was their life. David now held the future of Israel within his hands. The boy from Bethlehem came out from the battle, his face shining as the rising sun in its splendour. What had been a frown and a challenge in the giant was changed by the hand of Jesse's son. Those who were looking down began to look up and to thank God. The flourishing help of Heaven had arrived, to make a difference where there had been indifference.

Know the glory of your accomplishment

Goliath's head and face were in the hands of the victorious. All that you do should represent the face and form of Jesus Christ. There is glory as a shining sun in that which has been accomplished by a youth against a full-grown man. Yours is not a head severed from the body, it is the unified Head of Jesus Christ, the Head of the Church. Some can 'wear their heart on their sleeve', but David carried a head on his hand. This was the first of many happenings that would enter his grasp. It was bigger than the offshoots he fed to the sheep or the bread and corn he had recently carried. His was a hand filled with freshness, as new as flowers plucked from the grassy meadow. It was better than good news from afar; it was news as near as a hand. When the youth of Israel wanted assurance, he simply looked at what was in his hand. God wants you to look at what He has put within your power to assure you that He is with you always. In what David had accomplished was his medal from the battle. Now, he had to maintain it all with victory after victory. There had to be such activity and trust that not one of his escapades would be allowed to wilt and die, but become as everlasting flames or the flowers that do not fade. Some things are only renewed by tears.

If what Jehovah has accomplished in your life is wilting and needs a fresh burst of new life, then let God baptise it afresh in the Holy Ghost. Your joy, hope, peace and expectation can lose its glow. It needs to be re-established by the Master Builder. Fresh flowers, come with a small package to put into the water, which help blooms retain their freshness. There will always be that freshness in the Word of God to bring long lost ardency to life. Keep it as new as ever by doing what the warrior did, he carried it with him. He kept it where it could be seen and appreciated. Enjoy what you have while it is young. First love is true love, it has no rivals, it never stands in second place, and it is second to none. There is such zeal attached to it, it can run forever.

Victory will change the way you act

With the rosy head in his hand, the giant-slayer was proclaiming that the battle stopped here. He carried as the initial evidence of conquest throughout the land and on to Jerusalem. This was as good, if not better than the grapes of Eschol that the spies brought back from the Promised Land as evidence of more to follow. It says that as they entered the Promised Land, 'they ate of the corn the same day.'[21]

There were 'rich pickings' in this valley, more than vultures or scavengers could take. It was like pure gold for an impoverished people. Goliath's head became their springboard into a new revival of the activity of God. The Hebrew nation had something new to talk about. Instead of being challenged, fearful and defeated, a new vocabulary entered into their conversation. What passed from mouth to mouth was more exciting than the fresh honey they gathered each day.

Your destiny is in your own hands

Let your monuments of grace be in your hands in all that you seek to do, as you serve the Master. Your destiny is in your own hands. It wasn't just an outward show; it had inner ramifications. That which sparkled in David's heart came into his hand, as he held the giant's acme in his palm. Some gain a triumph but do not know how to use that answer to prayer to help others. Greater acts, such as slaying giants, can be reduced to a shadow in your life. David didn't, as far as we know, wrap the head in a blanket, or secret it in some unknown place. He opened his hand, and took hold of that testimony of triumph for all to see. The scene was an open book for all to read 'between the lines' of how the Lord had helped His servant.

When Jah gives, He grants us a full hand. What is given is not a few sheep or crumbs it is substantial, and real. We must keep it real! Shake off the birds of prey, the flies and the maggots, so that what God has done will remain as His nature unfading and undying. They wanted it to last forever, that is why they composed songs, and sang as David moved along the paths of Israel. As with the principle of the giant, the testimony and trial that God has brought you from may seem as messy as a head dripping with blood, but take it and use it for His glory. Some testimonies are unclean and almost drip with the blood that surrounds them. Those in the Corinthian Church had been immoral, sensual and evil and were as a giant's head in the hand of Christ.[22]

Our achievements, based on our witness, must be used as a weapon against evil and the Kingdom of Darkness. Act as a torch, to send a light across your own path, and across the path of others, to help them when things become very dark. Take each testimony of triumph, and use it as a beacon of light. A fresh stone was added as the fresh crown of the giant was displayed, but part of the building bricks that the Lord was using to establish a new reign. If you can keep your initial thrill of knowing the Lord, having it in your heart as if it has just been born, keeping it fresh as day by day you see it baptised in the love of the Lord, then, you too, will *Dwarf Giants*.

Notes: -

1. 'Pennine Range' is a hilly range in the North of England.
2. 1 Corinthians 13:12.
3. 2 Samuel 23:15,16.
4. Numbers 20.
5. Exodus 14:21.
6. Luke 9:13.
7. Moffatt's translation of Romans 12:11. 'Fervent in spirit'.
8. Genesis 3:15.
9. Hebrews 11:32.
10. Revelation 3:12; 21:2,10.
11. Leviticus 6:9,13.
12. John 11:39.
13. Genesis 15:11.
14. Hebrews 2:1.
15. Matthew 13:52.
16. Acts 3:19.
17. Genesis 2:7. 'Life' is plural.
18. Genesis 4:16.
19. Exodus 34:29.
20. Part of an old hymn, written by G. Wade Robinson.
21. Joshua 5:11.
22. 1 Corinthians 6:9-11.

Chapter

18

The Sword of Goliath

There are many precious things in life that mean so much to people. Memory closes over them as the folds of a blanket, and as the years pass by the folds are opened, and we take from them those fond and hurtful things. Time seems to add value to all things. There is, sometimes, just one event in life that we want to embalm, because it is so rare and full. Rare blooms that have been hand picked are placed between the pages of a well-read book, and as we read it we are able to meander again down memory lane. Memories of great achievements can be as rare as life in a cemetery.

Who can forget first time your child adventured up the steps of a slide, to stand at the top as if it had conquered the world. Looking down at you as if he was the king and you his subject. This was his Everest summit, and he stood in all the glory of his achievement, looking for the next great escape. That first step he took led to another, and another until he was able to climb by himself. One faltering step after another until he can run, hop, skip and jump. There are fond moments of achievements that cause us to glow as we remember them. Spiritual life, and the life of David are like that.

Rare things are beautiful

The Sword of Goliath was rare to the young champion, and he wanted to keep it forever. He wrapped it in a cloth, and placed it behind the ephod.[1] There was in the blade that which cut deep into his faculty for recall. Yet, at the time of need, he seemed to have forgotten the unforgettable. He had to ask if there were any weapons that could be used in his battle with Saul. One battle won, one moment of prevailing gives to you the instrument that will help in the desperate moments in life. In that dark happening there are a thousand swords to help you in the future.

The station where soldiers kept their weapons became known as the 'Tower of David'.[2] You must take from all the trials and triumphs all that you require. Do not come forth tired and weak from anything that tempts you. Come forth as Israel came out of Egypt, fully armed.[3] The God who calls you will arm you. At this moment in the history of an uncrowned king, David was unarmed and vulnerable.

To keep the weapon safe, and free from rust and time that would have surely robbed him of it, he placed it before the God who had given him the victory. It became a weapon fresh from the glory of God. As with every life that is going to defeat the enemy, it had to be hidden before it could be revealed, to be forgotten before it would be remembered. David returned the rapier to the Lord who had given it to him. It was not unknown to take a weapon from a victory, and present it to the Chief. When the flat steel was offered, any achievement, glory, or anything of praise or virtue was given to God. David took it to the tabernacle as a child might take a broken toy to be fixed by its father. At this moment, he never realised the full significance of the steel rod. He took it as if the Lord of hosts had only lent it to him. The borrower had become the servant of the lender. In the surrendering of a metal with two sharp edges were the surrender and the commitment of a person. When you have committed your favourite weapon, you stand helpless, seeking mercy, pleading to be taken and used. The safest place for your greatest talent and moment is with the Eternal.

Do not keep your achievements to yourself

This abode of the Eternal was at Nob, the religious centre of Israel where the tabernacle was, 1 Samuel 17:54; 21:9, Psalm 144, 151. David didn't want to keep his achievements to himself; he wanted to share them with the Lord. The flat metal with sharp edges became the platter on which the future king offered his body, soul and spirit to the One who had granted him victory. It was taken to Jerusalem, then on to Nob. As with every triumph it travelled with the king until he found a space where he could lay it to rest until God provided another victory.

Edward the Confessor, King of England, had a sword that was called *curtana-*'the cutter'. Goliath's sword was a token of mercy. David came to the priest seeking mercy, and found it in a war instrument given, so that he might achieve. David's sword of Goliath is as your Sword that cuts both ways, a *Delphic sword*, a blade that accommodates itself to any task or subject. That sword of Goliath gave David great confidence, as great as that given to the believer by the Word of God.

Your gift will make room for you

The sword became an apostle to a Jerusalem that was occupied by the Jebusites. It was taken there to make way for the future that the Lord had for a young boy. The gift made way for the giver. It was David's way of saying 'I claim this city by taking my sword and leaving it there.' That blade became the first part of the throne of David. He immediately laid down his instrument of battle as if surrendering to a greater Leader. The sword has always been the emblem of power and authority. It represents the will of a man, given to God, neither bent, broken or rusted. While it was gleaming fresh, still stained with recent victory, it was surrendered. The child of Jesse had discovered all that is in the Name of Jehovah, and he wanted the sword to be a memorial of what the Lord had been to a young man. The Philistines took the Ark of the Covenant as a spoil of war, taken from battle to present to their god Dagon.[4] The Israelite took the sword of Goliath, and presented it to the Lord. As he surrendered that steel he was granting it far more power and ability. What we offer is never lost. It might be withdrawn for a time. Giving to the Almighty completes and compliments the gift. The crowning glory of the youth was this falchion. It was the evidence and emblem of a dynasty defeated by destiny.

In giving his weapon, he gave his all. What might have been his natural means of support was given. David lived, conquered and reigned because of a sword, while Saul fell on one as he died. When a sword is presented to a Leader, it is turned flat, in order to show there is no cutting edge, no malice meant. It is a token and act of surrender. Ceremonial swords of state are usually flat and without a cutting edge. This sabre was laid flat so that its cutting edge was held in reserve for future use. David surrendered that which every soldier needed. The Lord would be his weapon of war, without Him he had no skill or power of his own. It was given back to the Giver with greater glory attached to it.

Offer the first fruits of conquest to God

The sword of Goliath, so precious to the youth, was offered as the first offering of harvest to the Lord. It had been brought from the battle with Goliath. That implement of war was the first fruit of the activity of the Almighty in the valley, and had to be offered to Him. This was virgin, true as steel and as real as it was strong. That sword with a cutting edge and a piercing point must be put into the right hands. If Saul had taken it he would have received the glory for himself. It had cost the youth a great deal, not in money, but in adventure, faith and devotion, it was the best thing he had. At the point of every sword there is a crown. David was giving as a sacrifice all that he had.

It represented what the young man wanted to be in God with a piercing point and cutting edge. It was better than the sword that Merlin gave to King Arthur of the Knights of the Round Table, who conquered the Picts, Scots and the Irish with it. Merlin's sword had magic qualities, but the sword that David used had God for its ability and destiny. He knew once it was accepted, it would be clothed in majesty and immortality. Flat metal stained with the sweat of a young body and hand that the warrior took from the hand of the priest. It spoke to him of youthful zeal and first love to the Lord. The giving of the tool of steel to the future king cost Ahimelech his life.[5] It helped the warrior to extend his life and kingdom. He had more than something worth fighting for; he had something to fight with, even as you have in the Word of the living Lord.

The surrender of the best is deeper than beauty

That which had been taken from the giant was the equivalent of the woman with the alabaster box of ointment breaking it open at Jesus' feet, letting the aroma which had been encased in alabaster fill the whole house.[6] Each particle broken was as sharp as the point of a sword, yet bathed in perfume. The surrender of the best is the most beautiful thing in the world. It is part of a new creation, brought about by a soul in love with the Lord. What the youth of Israel did filled the whole nation with pride.

What he gave to the Almighty did not make him less of a man. What Bethlehem's best achieved, what you accomplish in resisting and overcoming is worth more than the weapons of any army. The memorial of that which has been seen in the valley was set in steel, not in stone. It was an act that said to all 'the Mighty is first in my life.' 'I give to You what might, in my hands become an idol.' The greatest treasure greater than anything else was offered to the Lord as a memorial of thanksgiving. It wasn't enough to utter words, give a heartbeat, or take a sheep and sacrifice it. He gave that taken in battle as part of the spoils, as when Israel took Ai.[7] In giving the sword David was giving the victory and part of Goliath's defence. The spoils had to be dedicated to God. Once you have given what you have, then the Eternal can give you something else to replace what has been given. That which was given back couldn't be measured in what was received. It was more than a piece of steel; it represented the blessing of God in a life.

Give the best you have to the Lord

The tool of war, and the power of it were surrendered. It was given so that it might be left in the presence of the Lord. You can leave your best things with the Almighty He will not lose what you have given. In giving it, the son of Jesse was preserving it. He could not carry another burden in the shape of a sword. His tool was the power of Goliath, the power of battle was in it. That power was surrendered to a greater Power, the One Who had granted the victory. It belonged to the One who brought success and must be returned to Him.

Don't wait until you die before you surrender your best moments to the Lord. Give while they mean something. The flat steel, the cutting and piercing received in the soul needs presenting to the Lord Jehovah. It was the only thing Jesse's son returned from the battle with, but he willingly gave it while the zeal of battle was still in his heart.

How much blood was on that cutting edge we shall never know. The blood of both man and beast was on that blade, staining it with the evidence of battles fought and won. Every victory that Goliath had ever gained stained the metal. The history of murder and death was surrendered. Whatever was part of it was submitted and left in the tabernacle, to be cleansed by the presence of the Almighty. In the yielding is the surrender, not of many, but of all things. That sabre, fallen from a hand, was taken and offered to another Hand, the Hand of Jehovah. It suggests, as it was offered, that the victor was saying 'all power belongs to You. I am taking this falchion, and I am giving it to the Winner.' Your accomplishments in grace need giving to the God of all grace. This was the challenger's trophy. The rod of steel became his yardstick, for this weapon of war in future attacks would measure all other battles. There had to be the recognition of triumph, Who it was, that gave the victory. The boy warrior, on going to the tabernacle, meant he was going back to where it all commenced. He was ready, after surrendering, to commence his calling again.

To surrender is to surmount

What the young man from Bethlehem did when he offered this steel was give all the glory to God. 'Here is my sword won in battle I am not waiting years before I surrender it, for it is but a type of my will.' David was no fool, he wanted God to assist him in future battles. The person is no fool who gives what he cannot keep, to gain what he cannot lose. David gave to the Lord of Hosts what had never really been his. What he did not do was take that moment of triumph and use it against others. He stood without a weapon to his name. That which had been taken from the dead hand of the giant had to be abandoned. What Goliath ceded in death, David yielded in life. The choice moment, the greatest victory is His. The youth was saying 'I am now as defenceless as I was before the battle commenced. I will still trust in the living Lord to meet my need.' He would return to this sword much later, but in the meanwhile did not expect God to give him victories by constantly using a sling and stone. The youth entered into a time where he would not chase others, but others would chase him. He had to flee before Saul, as a partridge on the mountains.[8] There was the possibility of being shot with arrows, as he moved along.

Your victory cannot be copied

There was nothing in his life that he would make a shrine of, or turn into a religion. Hidden, it could not be copied or mimicked. No one else could take and use it. It represented a revival in Israel, for now they prayed and sought the Lord, as they hadn't done for many years. There were many swords, but only one sword of Goliath. The sword could be moved from place to place and used in different wars. There was no danger of it becoming a static part of the religion of the day, which could have happened if it had been left where it was. In the blade was the heart of the man of Gath, and that was offered to the Almighty. The giver would say 'all that I am and hope to be is offered on the flat of the blade.'

The apostle Paul felt the same when he said, 'If I be offered upon the sacrifice and service of your faith, I joy and rejoice with you all.'[9] He saw his life as a drink offering, poured out upon the sacrifice as it was laid on the altar to be consumed by fire. The best of the apostle was offered to God as a token of true worship. His life as the best wine was ready to be poured out before the Lord.

Later, in the life of David, when he is weapon-less and in great need, he visited the high priest at Nob and asked for help. That help was in the shape of a sword, reminding David of a former conquest. There was something of steel quality that he could use. It was as good as any grape that the spies brought back from the Promised Land on their first visit.[10] That sword long forgotten, was wrapped in a cloth, left behind the ephod. In the moment of darkness and greatest need, he returned to the cutting edge and said, 'Give it to me; for there is none like that!'[11] All his greatest moments had been wrapped in a cloth, hidden in darkness in that piece of steel. The time it was not in his hand was not wasted. He had a need for encouragement and when he took hold of the sword every Goliath in his way bent low in worship, knowing what could be accomplished. As he gazed at the steel, as the sun reflected onto it he would see pictures of himself in the battle with the man of Gath. This instrument of war was the Standard. The giant-slayer came and stood where it was, and from this moment the shepherd boy became a warrior. A 'true soldier' was defined as a 'man of the sword'.

Experience is real, touching every part of life

Every battle after the events in 1 Samuel 21:9, was fought with the sword of Goliath. Experience is deep and real and must be used in the future. Anything that has given you a cutting edge, a penetrating point must be taken and used. It must not only be seen as that which is offered in worship, it must have a practical application.

Your spiritual ability must not be left wrapped up in a cloth, no matter how religious or near the altar it is. It must not be left in the church; service must not degenerate into ceremony. Go into the presence of God but don't stay there. Be more than a blade of cold steel, standing as a statue. Come out, and let the world see what you are made of. You were made for blessing and battles. Let those around witness the metal of your mission. The blade spoke of what God had done in the past and also what He could and would do in the future. He took that from one success, and made it even greater by fully using it. He simply put it to the use that it was created for. That is the story of every life, being used as we were intended for the Lord God Almighty.

From each giant faced we must take a sword as experience helping us to overcome in the future. There are times when it will be laid in the folds of memory, but it has to be brought back to life if we are going to go forward to conquer. Spirituality is best seen and tested in the 'hurly burly' of life. You are a greater witness on the high street than within the cloisters of some hidden place. Let the naked eye see your flashing metal as the sun strikes it.

Your cutting edge must be used

The cutting edge of a victory must be claimed. It must not be left in history or in the memory. It is not enough to make any experience just 'religious' by leaving it in the church. The true nature of the blade meant it should be taken into battle, where troops fought and died. We must get into the real world, where the cut and the thrust of battle is. It must take its stand among the greatest men of the day. It must become a rallying point for the men who came to the cave of Adullam.[12] What you accomplished in the past is good for today. Get it out of the religious jargon and ceremony, and use it to gain many other victories. Remember, you are not yet seated on the throne? That is sharper than any two-edged sword, because it happened in your life.

Make sure that what you have is individual to you. If you do, there will be 'nothing like it'. Whatever you give to the Lord as an offering will be given back you. The sabre had been in the presence of God it retained its cutting edge. It came out from that presence ready to be used, even as the apostles did in the New Testament after Jesus had commissioned them. It was as fresh as a new blade. It had been held in the darkness like some flower, until it was brought out into the light. Wrapped in a cloth, it became a 'disciple of the cloth'. We do not surrender our swords, our talents in order to keep them out of the war; we give them so they can be returned as this blade was sharpened by the darkness and the presence of the Almighty. That scimitar (that with a fine edge) had not seen daylight for many months. When David asked for it, this reminds us of the time Jesus went to the small family in Bethany, and the sisters said to the other, 'The Master has come, and He is calling for you.'[13] The sword, like you, had to be a willing servant. Now, the battles of the past didn't mean anything. The stick of steel had a point, pointed as a finger towards the future.

Surrender will determine usefulness

The power of our lives is determined by what we surrender. The measure of your greatness will be the measure of your surrender. God only gave back to the youth what he had earlier given to the Master. That which had been won as a trophy had been put away. Others had forgotten about it, yet it was presented as so useful after it had spent time in the Lord's presence. It was as Moses and the apostles Paul, or John on Patmos who spent time in the Lord's presence. Yet who were unnoticed until they stepped forward to do their greatest work. From the shadows and the shade of previous encounters the sword was taken to be used again.

As the priest gave the sword to David, so your great High Priest Jesus Christ is ready to give to you that which will help in the battles of life. Help was received in 'the time of need'. Ephesians 4:8 says 'He has taken 'captivity' captive. 'Captivity' is to 'take by the spear'. He has gifts for men that are concealed in the hem of His garment as this sword was laid up in a cloth. From 'manifold' grace, from its 'many folds' comes the sword of help.

His promises are a Sword in the Word of God.[14] We all require that with the hot breath of Jehovah upon it. After He had examined it, and it had been re-polished, it was taken again to triumph. That which goes forth from His mouth is a sword with sharp edges. We have what He has said wrapped up in our own thinking. When we are desperate and hungry, without any form of weapon, there is that waiting for us to take and conquer with. Use what is offered and you will win. God will give to you that which will identify you with success.

The ability to succeed is where you left it

From the day it was laid behind the ephod, the weapon was always there, where the future king of Israel had placed it. The ability to be great is where you left it. The promises of God, those assurances are still there, waiting for a heart to take them and believe all that has been promised. It was there for the asking and for the taking. The shape of the weapon, like the Lord it represented, never altered. Only the circumstances changed. There comes a moment in every life when the right thing must be done, not simply the easy option.

Without the sword of Goliath the warrior was undressed. He could never function at his best. He was less than he could have been. He was a king in waiting. He went into the tabernacle as an ordinary man, but when he came out he was fully armed and ready for conflict. It is not what we are but what we shall be that wins the war of the soul. That which is in our hearts will help us to be the complete Christian in Christ. We must be fully armed with all that was taken at Calvary. There is in the Word of God that which makes us into warriors, fully armed and dressed. The sword, as the man, was rescued from perishing. The battle with Goliath of Gath, the great victory, meant nothing to David at this moment. It was a sword, not fond memories that he required. He probably went to the tabernacle to ask the Lord for direction, and in seeking the will of God, came out holding a sword. This was the Word of the Lord, to go and fight with all his might.

The presence of God will equip you

The youth came from Nob, where the presence of the Lord was revealed, an equipped person. Without God we are poor, ill clad, needing so much that we are at the mercy of every temptation. There is no cut and slash about our living. Once we have waited on God, then we are someone to be reckoned with. We become fully equipped, ready to go into battle. If we can take from the many things the Eternal and the Word has to offer, reserved with our name on it, then we will *Dwarf Giants*.

Notes: -

1. Ephod: the garment worn by the priest over his shoulders.
2. Song of Solomon 4:4.
3. Exodus 13:18. 'Harnessed' is to be 'able bodied', and it suggests being 'armed as a soldier'.
4. 1 Samuel 5:2-7.
5. 1 Samuel 22:16.
6. Mark 14.
7. Joshua 6:19.
8. 1 Samuel 26:20.
9. Philippians 2:17.
10. Numbers 13:20,23.
11. 1 Samuel 21:9.
12. 1 Samuel 22:1.
13. John 11:28.
14. Hebrews 4:12.

Chapter

19

The Drawn Sword

Many have wondered why the future king of Israel did not keep the sword of Goliath with him during his many battles between taking it to Nob and returning to collect it in a time of need. How could he ever forget that instrument of warfare, taken from the heat of the battle? The chapters between 1 Samuel 17 to 21 cover that period. Those chapt-ers are part of David's schooling. If you would see, learn and unders-tand God's dealings with the human spirit then read those chapters, see through windows into the soul of a man destined to be a king.

There are some experiences in God that have to be laid aside until the time is right. The sword was made for a man, now God had to make His own man, and bring the man and the falchion together to triumph. Not every victory over temptation yields peaceable fruits there and then. The wine must ferment in the casket or the bottle, before it can be poured into the cup as a mature substance. The ground that the Tree of Righteousness is to be planted in needs to be left until all the stones are removed. Even a lion or wild beasts will take the leftovers from their kill, and secrete them in a hole or up a tree until returning to it in the future. That sword was treasure left to be collected when the time was right.[1] God brought the man and the means together at the precise moment. The giant-slayer was reduced to poverty, and in that state of body and mind he revisited his glory days.[2] True revival was in the soldier without a stick of steel. Although he didn't posses the rations of a serving man, Jehovah was constantly feeding his hungry spirit with eternal realities.

David left the sword of Goliath in a folded garment in the tabernacle at Nob. He came to the place of 'fruitfulness' (Nob) to receive the fruits of his early endeavours. There comes a time when we harvest what we have sown. It is when we grow that we begin to reach for old promises that have not been fulfiled. What we have long forgotten suddenly seems important. There is a garden of quietness we need to come to and take from it fresh breathings for our soul. David was being hounded, and he needed a place of refuge. In that refuge he found just what was required to take him further.

There has to be a time of germination before the beauty of the flower can be appreciated. We lose our appreciation of so many things in the dash and dare of life. We do not seem to have time to stand and stare. There are moments when we must stop to take spiritual stock of where we are in God, and what has been accomplished in life. This is what David did at Nob. He had to be pieced together again. In Sheffield, England they have an area called 'The Peace Garden' reserved for those who want to come and collect their thoughts, and allow the soul to catch up with the body.

The sword had been folded into the priest's tunic called the ephod. On every page of the Bible, there is that hidden from view, reserved for your eyes only, speaking of a sword to help you in the day of battle. Sometimes in our weariness we turn to the Scriptures to find the rest we require. Time spent with the Word of God is restful, helpful and healing. We feel as the son of Jesse when he went from Nob fully armed and ready to chase rather than being chased. From the fabric of that around us we are able to take our sword and use it. Within the folds of every trial there is that sharp, gleaming, steely and waiting to be taken. The receiving of that taken from a giant gave David a new cutting edge. Life had blunted him turning that which had been so sharp into that so dull and ordinary. It was gleaming bright as that minted. As he took hold of the sword, he filled his hand with victory. This implement of battle was like an extra musical instrument, because it sent music into his soul.

Without the sword he could have been ignored, with the sword in his hand every giant took a backward step. Those held captive by foreign kings began to rattle their chains as if they anticipated freedom was on its way.

Relationships are important

When David took hold of that sword it was like two old friends being acquainted again. Proverb 27:17 says 'Iron sharpens iron; so a man sharpens the countenance of his friend.' Both of these had some steely qualities in them. The sword was a reflection of the character of God, steel and unbending, but able to help in the time of need. These two were as hilt in the hand, as the sword and the man came together. It was like the taking of the hand of a firm friend and favourite weapon. Whenever David saw another sword it brought strong memories to him. In the swords of battle, he saw the smaller picture of himself battling with a giant. In the sword of Goliath he saw the bigger picture and the larger vision of what Jehovah can do. As the stick of steel is no use without the hand of the soldier, so David was quite useless, as that wrapped in an ephod without the Lord taking hold of him. Without the Lord, the weapon of war becomes a tool laid on oneside as if the workman has finished the task. Every soldier knows that long before the trumpet sounds for the attack, the weapons must be in place, and the soldier 'fully kitted'. This belonging to Goliath meant that David was ready for whatever the Almighty had prepared for him.

There had to be much development in the life of the youth. A relationship had to be encouraged between David and Jonathan, a deepening of love one for the other. There had to be more than a sling and stone or armour in the life of Jesse's son. He had to be shaped for his destiny in the Lord, and much superficiality had to be dealt with. Circumstances had to do their perfect work, developing a soul to become even more sure of God. The Almighty had to be proved, not just in one battle but also in the constant battles of life.

The taunt of foreign powers was that their Lord was a God of the mountains but not of the valleys. How would the shepherd boy respond to natural relationships with other people? The cup of Psalm 23 needed to be filled until it was full and running over. The harp in the hand of David had to minister to troubled Saul. There were new melodies in different keys to be heard coming from the harp. With King Saul looking on David menacingly, David had to blend those moods and threats into his musical score. The sounds and the sights of the palace must not turn the young heart or head in the wrong direction. There must be nothing in any place to turn his feet into another way.

Saul sought to slay David by smiting him to the wall.[3] Taking that dull sound of the spear striking the wall the youthful musician used it to develop further musical strains- music in the minor key! He had to escape by night, helped by Michal. In the darkness of the escape he discovered a God of light and opportunity. He found it was better to flee than to take a stand when there was no hope of being victorious. He could always return with polished shield and sharpened staff of steel. God had to be seen in all the vicissitudes of life. Was He only the Master on the battlefield? Was this Lord of Hosts as real when dealing with social issues? The answer is yes, every time.

We can always start again

All these things prepared the youth to return and take up the sword of victory. The instrument of war suggested both a calling and a challenge. It had to be taken and used, its worth being fully realised only when it was used in the purpose it was designed for. That weapon of metal became the starting line as the young man began to think again of battling for right. It is always the Sword as found in the Word of God that establishes the Kingdom within our hearts. The direction the sword is pointing in that is the direction we must go.

Soldiers usually spend time in training. The One training the future king was a perfect swordsman, well accomplished, having fought and won many battles. The variety of life had to enter David's soul. He is not only the Lord of the quiet stream and blue sky; He remains the same in do or die. Sometimes the Lord has to take us back, in order to take us forward. It is as the shuttle flies backwards and forwards, and from side to side that the multi-coloured pattern of gold emerges. Such a fine pattern, designed for people to walk on! The finest work of art is produced as the brush is moved through many degrees in the hands of the artist. A picture is a multiplicity of colour and brush strokes. We have to penetrate the darkness in order to receive the light.

Lessons learned need to last

There are many things in the history of happiness and dullness that have been buried, even as the talent was, waiting for you to grow a little more, so that what you need in the present can be brought back from the past. A 'blast from the past' can be a challenging call into the future. Not all that has happened is bad. That forgotten remains the same. What the Almighty wanted you to accomplish last year, if it has not been fulfiled, it remains as this sword which kept its shape.

There are many good things that you have forgotten about. Spiritual lessons you thought would never be forgotten have gone from you between leaving the front door and arriving at the garden gate. They escape as a bird through the open door of a steel cage. We may not witness all that the Eternal has promised but wait a while and see him take us back to where we left the sword, speaking of dedication, adventure and overcoming.

The teachings of the Spirit are greater than those of the sword, and must have more relevance and impact than a flake of snow or a bead of sweat. These teachings of David had been reserved for such a day as this, to ensure that his hand was strong enough to handle the large implement of war. When he came to collect the instrument of war, he found it at the heart of worship. It is when we bow low and offer ourselves as an open hand that we find what we are looking for, and what we really require to be successful. When we worship at Nob, those things required are added, not only to the hand but also to the heart.

There had to be an interlude, when physical and spiritual growth took place in the future king. As small children, we stand on tiptoe in order to gain more height! We want to see over the fence or wall, to take a peep into what is before us. In the wisdom of the Almighty, this child of God was given time to grow, so that the hand would be large enough for a heavy sword to fit into it. If he had continued with that same flat steel, it might have fallen from his hand after only a few strokes. The word 'tired' might have supplanted the word 'triumph'. He might have been as the man in the New Testament who went to build a city, but could not complete it because he didn't count the cost.[4] The disciplines of the intervening years did their work.

David didn't go to seek a new sling or more stones that would have given him a monotonous God Who did everything predictably as water flowing down hill. The stone and sling had served their generation well. The sword was about to have a coronation that came out of a crisis as the hand of the wielder crowned it with his fingers.

Growing is more important than defeating

There was a time for war, a time for peace, a time for worship and a time for growth. The growth principle was just as important as defeating the giant. What is developed in us is far more important than what we do with that which surrounds us. In fact, we capably handle that which surrounds us because of the word and work of grace within. We defeat those things around us, as we allow what is inside us to develop. The man was going to be king, God's man and representative. The complete character was not simply a man with a length of steel in his hand. Anybody can lift a meter of steel, but it has to be used to good purpose. It is useless having a plan that does not work.

The swordsman needed maturity to handle it well. Jehovah trains us through truth to receive and retain His gifts. Without maturing, the young soldier might have run amok with the sword. Maturity granted him targets at which to strike. He had to be convinced that this was the right time to receive the blade with a cutting future. He had to have steel in his hand, after it was placed in his heart. This weapon was no flag post. It was not a small flag to be held by a child waving it in a fresh breeze. It was a gift from God to be used as a means of accomplishment.

Clay jars that are precious and very costly take a lot of making. They are moulded according to the gallons they are to contain. The brim, not the bottom, is their destiny. They, as you, were created for fullness, not ceremony. The Eternal will make the soldier, taking him through certain battles and through the vicissitudes of life until he is fully matured to handle the instruments of war.

Most of us in the in-between stage are taken there time and time again after failing. We never seem to enter into the conquest of the sword, but have remained in the wilderness until eventually there comes a moment when we must take the sword to enable us to stand in the Promised Land. We do not know the Word of God or handle the Sword of the Spirit, as we should. There are promises that we have never received. The Lord wants to take us back and forth until we are made strong in the power of His might. We need space until we discover the mind of the Lord. David went into the presence of the Lord with no weapon or cutting edge, but he came out from that presence so different. Oh, to come from His presence like a sword with two sharp cutting edges!

Times of inactivity as we wait on God are not wasted

It might have seemed as if the sword had grown into a spear or a lance, but it was not the sword that had changed. The steel weapon seemed to have a sharper point and cutting edge, as if in the darkness and seclusion it had been sharpened. Something had happened to this youth of Israel. It was Mark Twain who said he was surprised how much his father had grown when he moved through the years from seventeen to twenty one. Was it his father who had really grown?

Israel had a command that every seventh year the land must be left fallow,[5] for a year, so that the soil might be enriched, in order that a fuller crop is developed in succeeding years. The time the field spent simply as soil was not wasted. New structure for the soil and vital ingredients were being put back into it by the rain and sunshine. As seed claws its way through the darkness reaching for the light, it is not abandoned, but used as it grows into a magnificent crop. The times of inactivity are never wasted if they prepare us for activity and glory.

When the man and the weapon came together, they became partners as thunder and lightening. The man was larger by the measurement of the sword. There was some new penetration, dare, dash, cut and slash about him. He would go into future battles with a stick of steel, but also as a drawn sword thirsting for blood.

Let the promises of God excite you

Spend much time borrowing grace from 1 Samuel 17 to 21. Find things in these chapters that will be a Balm of Gilead to your soul. We all need to grow each day by at least three chapters, that is why we read the Word of God. To grow by one Word will make us into sword handlers going on to greater escapades. We begin to know how to skillfully handle the Word of God even as Israel's best handled the sling, stone and sword. We must know the Word of God as the champion knew the value of his weapon. Be as excited about the promises of God, as David was about Goliaths sword. 'Give it to me; for there is none like that!' The Bible is like that, and it should inspire us. This is why in the Acts of the Apostles they gave themselves to the Word of God and prayer.[6] If you do the same you will follow apostolic succession of truth and will lack nothing. Those who don't cannot see afar off and will always be between the two banks of the stream. They will never return to their moments of conquest to use them in future battles. It is not where you are, what you think, or what you say the importance of the hour is how you grow in God.

When the Prodigal Son was in the far country he never fed from the father's table. He drank from no love cup. He never took a crumb from his father's hand or received the training of a son. Be big enough to go back and collect those important things you have left. Find again those things you have lost. It is repentance for wrong that puts a new shining sword into your hand, a glitter into your soul. There is the kiln where the brick is formed, and this was the kiln to the man in the making. When he was chased by Saul there were certain aspects of David's character that needed further growth. Where there is a lack, the opportunity for it to be met will be ushered into a life. Before he commenced warring with this sword, how would he deal with his fellow man? We can all be so spiritual after downing a giant, but the real test is when the glitter of the sword is hidden away. How are we in private when all the shouting and clapping has subsided? It is not bad to return to former glories. A man is far more useful when he returns to the Holy One. It is awful when we return to that which is rusted, bent and irrelevant.

The sword of Goliath was worth having and worth using. It was always there, reminding the shepherd of Bethlehem of his finest hour, but it had to be collected to make him into the complete soldier. Without a weapon such as this no warrior is complete. 'Put on the 'whole', 'full' armour of God.[7]

Many lessons from the past will help in the future

1 Samuel 17:51 says, 'He took his sword and drew it out of the sheath, slew him, and cut off his head with it.' That sword didn't remain in his hand. These hands had other tasks to complete. The stick of steel had to be left on one side; no promise or weapon must take the place of the Holy One of Israel. The hand that grasped the metal had to be empty in order to be raised in worship. David never mistook that steel rod for the finishing line of a race; it was the starter's pistol. During and after every battle he must remain faithful to the Lord of Hosts. The work for the sword and the man was complete for the moment.

Get to know in God when to lay aside your work. Understand that, before you come to a conclusion. Don't wait until the Almighty has to break the sword or defeat you with a sling and a stone. The sword chopped off the head of the giant; that is all it had to do. It had to be laid aside so that it would be even more useful in the future. A fresh hand would take hold of it with renewed vigour. What it learned at the moment could be used later. Putting it away doesn't mean it will be lost forever. The silver coin in the pocket does not lose the image on it or its value.

Losing your position doesn't mean you are all 'washed up'. It means that you can return to that very place sometime in the future, to complete what has been commenced in you. 'He that has begun a good work in you will perform it until the day of Jesus Christ.'[8] The past has no need to govern the future. If you have handled a situation well in a small way, you will not be as vulnerable next time you come to it. The person who has climbed mountains will laugh at trees and walls.

You need a little sword practice before going onto greater things. David practised his skill of swordsmanship on a dead head before he ever used it in a battle.[9] It matters how we deal with that defeated in the giant's head. In the corner of the valley, almost without a word being spoken, he chopped off the head of the giant. At that moment it didn't matter if he made a mistake because of his inexperience, but next time he would not be able to make any mistake. The thing he faced would be alive and aggressive. He had to prove the worth of faith and God without a sword in his hand. Success must be in one thing, but many things through the Lord of variety.

Life is a discovery of the nature of God

In a limited way, Jesus has left for us the dead body of a giant, and we have to chop the head off every temptation. Ephesians declares that Christ has put Satan under His feet, defeating him openly, never to retain power over us, Ephesians 1:22. As we grow we face real situations, that we have to overcome. The Lord will not do it all for us, we have to 'work out our own salvation'. The very thing we need to overcome in one temptation will not necessarily be used the next time. Life is a discovery of the variety of Jehovah, getting to know the many aspects of His Divine nature, just as the fighter will get to know his weapon.

That Divine nature and power is witnessed in Genesis chapter 1 in sun, moon, stars, river, flowers, birds and streams. All these are acts of His nature, but there is a deeper inner work that has to be discovered. When you get to know His nature, you will say 'Give it to me; for there is none like that!' We don't say that of every pain and hurt, but we can when the rainbow surrounds us after a storm. When, like Noah in Genesis chapter 7 and 8 we have been through a storm, it will lead to an open door, as God opened the door of the ark. We will understand how others feel when we have been where they are. Be as sword to them helping them to fight through great opposition. Don't cut them with that steel measure, instead lead into battle.

There would be another day of grace. He took the steel weapon and left it somewhere else. There were many reasons why he left the sword. He didn't throw it away; it was reserved like the crown he would wear for a future day. The sword and the crown have always been the first two steps to the throne. There had to be a development in the young life that was rare and more useful than killing a giant. It is good to overcome a temptation, especially one as large as a giant. The demonstration in slaying the giant was public, but John the Baptist appeared with his teachings in the wilderness of Judea.[10] Maybe, physically David could not handle the sword of Goliath. There are times when we seem to have only the strength to make one effort against evil. We are so limited in our success that we have to move for more training in the business of life and work. Some things are too greater a burden for us to bear while we are young and feeble. They are left so that we might return when we have been made stronger. It is then that we can manage them. Even when it rains from the sky in measures, it doesn't all come at once. The sun releases its power little by little. The secret is to match your skills to the opportunities presented to you. From where you are go to where the Sovereign Lord wants you, there you will unearth treasure hidden under a cross in the shape of a sword.

Grace is measured to the need

The Lord God will only allow you to have what you can manage at any time. It is the power of love that will lift. Life in the Lord is one step at a time. Thank God that you have only two feet! If we had more, we would run further away from God, probably to the end of the universe! What you require is not given you all at once, if it were you would sink and not swim. The heart that loves you measures temptation and grace in equal proportions. One act, one burden at a time is enough. Some things are better left on one side for future days. In any experience there has to be a time of waiting, until the Almighty sees that we are ready to handle greater things. Life is like a book; we need God to turn the pages.

Could there be anything greater than slaying a giant? Yes, in the every-day happenings of life, holiness has to be seen. To be 'sincere' meaning 'without wax' is more important than the great show and all the plaudits. Life in Elohim is not just a stone and a sling or even a flashing blade. It is a song and a sigh. If we don't lay the sword on one side for a time, then we shall find ourselves weak and defeated, as defeated as Goliath of Gath. When a trial takes place God allows us to leave it on one side, to return to it when we have grown into full manhood. There are some 'teachings' that we cannot receive. The Universal Lord lets us move away from them, before facing them for a second time. Note that some things are better left where they are until, in the workings of God, we are led back to them. If you are afraid and too weak to master that which would overcome you, then let the Universal Lord lead you to a place of sanctuary and rest awhile. 'Come ye apart' so that you might not fall apart.

We must continue making progress

It is one thing to draw the sword, it is another to continue with it drawn. That drawn sword was a challenge to any to do battle with the man holding it. No one serving king and country has a drawn weapon all the time. He is every ready but not in a permanent state of action. Miracles are marvellous, but character is of greater grace and growth. The man must be made to handle the experience. There were many gems in the handle of this sword, experience maturity, victory, obedience, faith, endurance and hope.

The last time the son of Jesse used it was in the zeal of youth, the next time it would be in the zenith of his manhood and power. Some things are too great for us to bear, even after a famous victory. David, only being used to a stone and sling might have found a great sword too difficult to handle. It was taken and left with the Lord until he was man enough and strong enough to handle it. It was taken to the place of worship as an offering, to the place where the people worshipped and where God spoke as glory appeared. The Almighty did not have to work on the sword, but He had to do many things with the soldier.

The battles of life will always be there; we must not be weighed in the balances and found wanting when we are assessed according to our value. To lay aside such a distinguished thing was no sin, it was salvation, the salvation of this son of God. The great Potter of Life had more work to do on this creation. When we lay down what we have, He gives us what He has, and we receive what we really need for the coming crises.

Experience is worth more than gold

Nothing is wasted in God, even the earth gathers up the leaves fallen from the trees and uses them for further growth. The skies call up water from a dirty pool, and transform it into raindrops. Everything that happened to you is stored up as the squirrel will store nuts for the coming winter months and icy conditions. Once you have overcome any temptation you have experience that is worth more than gold and many swords.

The sword didn't need changing or polishing; it was the man who needed refining. It is not what we enter but what we go through that makes the man. You can use the finished work of Christ on the cross, but there is still far more work to do in you. When the blade of the plough cuts the first furrow in a field, that field has not been sown or completed. There has to be much more work until the harvest appears. The same applies to human character. The blade must be used time and time again and sometimes in suffering. When the time is right the Lord will so arrange circumstances that the sword and the man are again brought together. Don't travel along a known path in suffering, go where no one has been before and leave an example for others to follow.

If the Lord God allowed you to have everything at once, the burden of it might crush you into further misery. The loving Lord arranges small training sessions, such as cutting off one head, yet we do not recognise what is taking place. We think it just 'happened' when it was part of a Master Plan. You have to be trained to take power and use it properly. Power, opportunity and responsibility go together as foot and shoe. A runaway train may show great speed, yet although it is very powerful, it delvers its passengers no safety. It has to be controlled in order to arrive at its destiny.

Divine arrangements are the best

The sword was drawn but was not constantly used. It was left until the youth was ready to handle it against others. Even new wine has to be left to ferment. Your spiritual history is full of incidents that have had to be laid on one side. The corn and the chaff have to be separated. The day will come, after the seed has been planted, that the flower will grow. There has to be a time delay before we are allowed to continue along that pathway. In your life there is a 'time lock', such as those on the doors of a safe which allow the safe to be opened at the right time. In the meanwhile, God takes you to fulfil plans that seem lesser to you, but to the Almighty, they are as great as handling the sword of Goliath. The small moments lead us to the hour of our greatest achievement, unnoticed moments will lead to prominence.

In the soldier without a sword you have limitation. Put a stick of steel into his hands, and you have the beginnings of conquest and Lordship. Involved in Divine arrangement you are sometimes left alone, even as the sword was.

When Christopher Columbus set out to discover new worlds including America, he records that there was a moment when he put the maps on one side, because he had gone as far as man had ever been. He was prepared to go further without a map of reference. David's life was virgin at this time, as he slew a giant with a sling and a stone. None one had ever accomplished what he had done. We all need to go boldly where no man has gone if we are going to fit in with what has been arranged for our lives.

There are gifts that have to be buried until there is a resurrection in you. It would be folly if you were allowed to drag the sword of Goliath along behind you. Lots of wisdom has to be poured into you. Just as sleep will refresh the body, so the space that the Eternal grants refreshes us, making us into able soldiers of Jesus Christ. This is how David, and we, are made into kings who will rule well. The experience does not grow, but you do, and if it is brought to you at the right time then it can be used as a sword for the glory of God. The sword of Goliath became the sword of David, not by inheritance, but through battle and victory.

Notes: -

1. 1 Samuel 17:51; 21:8-10.
2. 1 Samuel 21:8-10.
3. 1 Samuel 18:11.
4. Luke 14:28.
5. Leviticus 25:3.
6. Acts 6:4.
7. Ephesians 6:13.
8. Philippians 1:6.
9. 1 Samuel 17:51.
10. Mark 1:1-7.

Chapter

20

The Armour in the Tent

When we face any giant, it is not just winning that brings real success. Nor is it the way we enter into battle, although that is important because without faith and the zeal of youth we shall be defeated. It is seeing God defeat the enemy in unusual ways. In all that David accomplished, the hand of the Lord was at work. He was not shoved into the battle by Saul and then left to the mercy of the blowing winds. Saul had said, 'The Lord be with you.' That was an empty phrase until God filled it with His presence and purpose. God stood with him, entering into the fray to bring him out as victor. The testimonies of people confirmed the mysterious ways in which God works. Fellowship with the Almighty in the day of battle will put iron into your soul, as it did with Joseph.[1]

We must move onward and forward

There is more to take from any battle than just the flag of victory. We do not fight or resist simply by maintaining the 'status quo'. We battle with the enemy of the soul in order to overcome and go forward. This was not the only valley in the life of the son of Bethlehem. The lad went into the battle with nothing, but came out with great spoil that would help him in the future.

Once Goliath was dead, there were the spoils of battle to be taken. What would David take and make his own? The giant had no possession or great riches, no lands or fields. He didn't even wear a crown, and was only a representative of the Philistines. Yet there were vital pieces of equipment that could be taken and used by David in the amour of the defeated. The soldier's equipment cast in bronze had been as well prepared as any vessel for service. The content of the armour had been defeated, now he turned to that which kept the giant intact. When Goliath advanced, it was one great show of pomp and strength. He was made to look even larger than he really was. Satan is given more power and equipment than he ever possessed.

Take your strength from every attack

In any attack and the darkness that would enfold us, there are many precious things. In a present distress we can find the shape of things to come. Even the broken pieces can make sense when they find their wholeness in the Hand of Jehovah. We must take the spoil when we overcome the difficulty. We not only have to realise what is happening to the enemy, but also the ministry it is developing in us. To take from an enemy gives credence to the soldier in the great assurance of further victories. We obtain our 'convictions' from our battles. The word 'conviction' comes from two words 'complete' and 'conquer'. I can take from any experience, as a fisherman will take fish from a stream flowing at his feet. It is vital that we retain the evidences of our victories. That is why the New Testament was written; that we might know the 'certainty' of those things believed among us.[2] The word 'certainty' was used of evidence produced in a court of law to convict a felon. It can describe medical notes taken from a patient, set down in order. There has to be much evidence within our hearts of those things that we have triumphed in. Everything that crumbles before us leaves the evidence of its presence. Sometimes, what we require to give us strength and stability is not found in facing a giant, but in the quiet corner of the heart, in every day happenings. In some things that take place in our lives we are unconscious of the fact that metal is being placed within the soul. Your heart is the mould, and the metal taken from any affront is poured into it.

They will know when you have been with Jesus

In the New Testament, they knew they had been with Jesus because they were as 'bold as brass'.[3] If all we do is come through a battle gloriously, then we have failed to capture the real spoils of war. The sunshine of the day must be found in our hearts. The song of the dawn chorus must be in you for it to be another 'red letter day'. What is with the enemy needs to become ours as we struggle in life against the odds. Every temptation can be used to the glory of God. The sensual desire can become hunger for the spiritual. Hatred can become a passion for seeing souls won to the Lord. Much speaking can become much praying. The ability to cheat and swear might be as 'sounding brass or tinkling cymbal'[4] but it can become pure gold.

Learn your skills from your mistakes

Man learns skills by making mistakes. The very mistakes become our teachers, but not our masters. Some would have seen nothing in a dead giant, but the quick eye and mind of the youth saw potential in the armour. That metal equipment was taken, and put where the youth needed it, in his tent. He slept with it, ate with it, arose with it by his side as a reminder. Living memory is better than dead history. These pieces of bronze were the winner's cup. His name was now written on the armour. The armour was taken as a prize contended for.

One house is as safe as another until an earthquake comes to test its foundations. Once it has stood the test, then we do not fear another shaking or rattling. What happens to that house tests the wisdom of the builder, and the character of the building. Was the building 'thrown up' to be 'thrown down', because it lacked depth and expense? If it is going to last then much planning must go into it. Things of an eternal nature will always be tested to the limit. David would be tested again and again until it was discovered who his God really was. Was his allegiance, the duty of the soldier to his liege or sovereign, to God or to Israel? The man that shook the ground did not shake the future king. If there is nothing 'stuck on' nothing will 'drop off' when we are challenged.

At the end of the road, just around the next corner is the very steel that the character requires. Be as the soldier whose command was to gather the weapons from the fallen enemy. Sometimes this metal defence is taken from the 'scraps' of life. Just a small amount added will result in strength that leads to strong acts in the Acts of the Apostles. That armour acquired ascribed David as being among the heroic of his day. It marked him out a man of God. It distinguished between the 'wimp' and the winner. Many talk of Robin Hood who have never shot with his bow.[5] They brag of deeds and battles they took no part in. David was much heavier now that he had the armour, and everything he said and did was made to count. That armour was not his only anchor in life, before he ever obtained Goliath's armour the Lord was holding on to David. No wind or temptation would blow him away or off course in the outworking of his destiny.

Strength is found on the floor of the valley

David was just another Israeli until he was tested, then it was discovered what he was really like. All the metal he took to the tent was found in the valley, not in the palace, or with the sheep and the soft pastoral grass, or where the people sang and danced. It was found in a severe test of character. The harness of war didn't come from David, because at this time he had no armour. It came from that which David had overcome, the wrestle against flesh and blood as represented in Goliath of Gath, and against all the wiles of the Devil that makes a person into a true champion. What you overcome gives you more power and authority. In each battle there is the potential for recognition of bravery, decoration, promotion, and medals of distinction.

The giant challenged Israel daily, fully harnessed for war. The metal David took from him was a mountain of steel. Goliath had a bronze helmet. He wore a coat of scale armour made of bronze weighing five thousand shekel (125 pounds or 57 kilograms). His legs were covered with bronze greaves a bronze javelin was slung over his back. His spear shaft was like a weaver's beam. The point of the spear weighed six hundred shekels (7 kilograms). Goliath of Gath carried with him a sword, a spear and a javelin, 1 Samuel 17:45.[6] This was the armour that the youth took into his tent. There was armour for defence and weapons for offense. He did not return an empty hero. The only thing of worth that Goliath left when he was defeated was his armour which represented his achievements in life. His challenge and voice has long since disappeared. He no longer shakes the ground. In Jesus Christ, David lives on forever. There is that in the Lord worth wining and keeping.

Take from life's battles what will help you through

After any battle there must be taken from it that which will help us. The Bible says of the youth of Israel 'He put his armour in his tent.' We must come out with more than we took in. As with the sword left in Jerusalem, there had to be a time of growth in the young man's life, before he could use this armour. Some would take captive men women and riches with cattle. The enterprising youth decided to take hold of the armour of Goliath. The very metal that encased him would be used to protect against others. If we can use the very heart of an experience, it will help us to overcome. In overcoming temptations we shall not only be an example, but a book of reference, a living epistle of the teachings of warfare.

The armour in the tent would serve many purposes. The youth of Israel visited it, looked upon it and dreamed dreams. Every carpenter sees a tree and dreams of beams and boats, chairs and tables. The potter feels the same as he gazes on a lump of unwrought clay. There was metal in cloth when the harness went into the tent. Should the tent blow away, the metal of the man would remain. The armour acted as an anchor, binding him to the Almighty. There are solid achievements in every battle for the right.

We can lose so much in life, but what remains is eternal and valuable. Long after Satan and temptation have gone, what will be left are the substantial spoils taken from each attack of the enemy? It is good to have those things from any attack that are solid, true and real; that the winds of change or false doctrine cannot take from us. No emotion or wind can blow away what has been won in war. The anchors for soul and spirit will be forged and found in the fiery trials that come upon us. When the storm is approaching, the captain of the ship orders the anchors to be lowered into the sea. Those anchors have been through many storms, and they have been proven, they will steady the ship. Temptation has no need to take anything from us, yet it can add to us those things that make us greater and far more difficult to contend with. Your reward will be in attitude and achievements.

Be made part of the metal army

There are a number of men in the Scriptures whose very names contain the suggestion of metal, such as this armour. John Mark, who wrote one of the gospels, means a 'hammer'. In the Old Testament there is a man who became a servant of David named Barzillai, who would not be persuaded by this same David to dine at his table when he became the King. The name of Barzillai means 'the iron man'. It suggests 'the iron-hearted man'. The happenings of life had put metal into human clay. When we use the term to be put on 'your metal', it means 'the metal on the edge of a sword', to gain the most in battle. This term on 'your metal' suggests that you are at your most keen and watchful. There is no pride or show here! You have been brought to the base things of life, the things that really count. Jubal, another name from the Old Testament means 'a trumpet', Genesis 4:21. He became the man who made musical instruments, instruments that could be blown as they entered into a war, and then sounded again as a victory song to Jehovah. All these received metal from their experiences.

Put on the whole armour of God

David put the armour in his tent. It would warn any intruder what to expect if they entered into that tent. Part of his daily wardrobe was taken from battle, that is why we are exhorted to 'put on the whole armour of God.'[7] The bronze stood as one of those Roman soldiers, keeping watch over the doorway, so that none could enter in or leave without meeting the soldier, and being challenged. It wasn't left to rust and be forgotten, it was put where all, including the giant-slayer would see it. Mary, the mother of Jesus 'pondered' 'treasured up' all these things in her heart that she saw and heard.[8] That which was taken as booty was there as a challenge and a reminder. These pieces of armour were David's medals. We only have what we have taken; we have lost what has been taken from us in life. Circumstances are difficult, but we need to accept them as part of future providers. There are bands of steel in the circumstances surrounding us.

The armour of Goliath would confront anyone entering into that tent for an audience with the future king. Being dead it yet was speaking. The pedigree of the king was in the armour. The same suggestion is with us when we enter into the presence of God to pray. We have to be reminded of all the victories of our God. The promises are laid before us as reminders that God is able to give us 'more than the victory'. That metal became part of the personality of the shepherd boy. He didn't just handle it; he let some of it become part of the strengthening process. This metal was in the home, where it would be required among the domestic happenings of the day. It is required, this strength from every conflict where the baby cries, and the stress of life has its own throne. In the home where particular demands are put upon us, testing us to the limit of our existence.

In despair find that God is near

There was a certain glory about the instruments of war, a certain light that shined through them every time anyone entered the tent. Victory and the light it brings into the soul can be better than a lamp or torch. Those in dark despair found new light from this armour. Without wearing it or it being moved, it did something to the heart of anyone who saw it. It was there as a memorial to the goodness of God, and as an evidence of what the Lord could accomplish in helping each one in the day of battle.

If any young soldier was nervous or fearful, he was sent to take a look at the armour of Goliath. It may only be metal, yet it spoke volumes to those preparing to enter into battle. It put new heart into the heartless, a new spirit into the dispirited. Some had never witnessed a victory, or knew about success until they looked at the military pieces in the tent. It became more than part of a museum, it became part of a man.

A place had to be given, room had to be made, for the spoils of battle. It would have been quite useless to leave the armour with the dead man on the battlefield. Take your success with you share it with others. Make room for all that God does by jettisoning things that do not really matter. If the tent, if the life, is to be filled with anything let it be the prowess of success, not the rust of defeat. There was no dejection or rejection in this tent. Room was made for hope and glory. There are those who would bring roses from the field of battle. Others would have brought the dust of the valley in their sandals, as the only evidence of the onslaught. That which is tangible was brought and laid in the tent. Being metal it did not hold the young soldier back, but spurred him on into his future. Long after the stone and the sling had been forgotten, Israel's youth had the tangible evidence of winning a battle. That is one reason why the stone was rolled away at the resurrection of Jesus Christ, God wanted to write it in stone, so that it would not fall from Peter's memory, or the sands of time erase it.

Take your victories and use them

The 'armour' went into the tent. That which was personal to the opposition and temptation became part of the victor. The Romans carried their spoils of war up the Apian Way, for all to see. Inside the entrance to the tent, became the Apian Way for Jesse's son. His victory was paraded, not among the soldiers or in the valley, but where it would count the most within the walls of the tent. In the private life of David, was seen that which had taken place in public. We must be as strong in private as we are in public. That taken from the battlefield must be used in our own back garden. Within the folds of the human heart there must be that of substantial means, to be taken and used when we need to resist. The mail was reserved for another day.

We all require an inner strength that only comes from overcoming and treading on that which seeks to tread on us. The result of having the armour was a strong mind, strong legs, a protected back, and a strong heart to serve the Holy One all the days of his life. As he rose into battle with these pieces of bronze, so he would make a greater impact. The human fleshly young man went out to meet Goliath, but now the metal man went into future battles. He was arrayed in something greater.

This armour wasn't left in the valley where the winds of the desert would have buried it in sand, entombed forever. It was taken and used where it would mean something in the day-to-day life of the young soldier.

Don't let your accomplishments fail or fade

A reference to the behaviour of every soldier is written, used for further assessment as to the capabilities of that soldier. Men would record in pen and ink, but this was written in bronze, so that it never fades. What life has made you, so you remain, until new life in the Lord makes you into something else. You become a person with tenacity who will win through your battles. What you overcome must be relevant, and made to count where it will count. It must become part of your living.

When the armour is in the tent, you will not be easily hurt or turned on one side. There will be that in you which speaks of resolve, and your commitment will be of steel quality. There will be nothing 'chocolate' or 'jelly' about your determination to fully follow the Lord. When tin was mined in Cornwall, England, they found the deeper they went the more there was. The greater the battle the stronger the soldier becomes. Every combat you enter means there is an opportunity to receive true qualities of soul and spirit, and to be matured. That battle becomes your arsenal. You were not made for defeat. The first thing any leader wants to know of a man is 'can he carry his weapons?' This is referred to in Galatians 6:5 translated 'burden' meaning the soldier's pack and weapons. Have you enough metal in your soul to turn the other cheek when assailed by attacks? Can you accept what any contest will call you to do? 'If your enemy hunger feed him.'[9] 'Love your enemies, and pray for them that despitefully use you.'[10] This is the armour that we are trying to claim from the battle, and then take and use it to help in daily living. Let every wrong bring forth the right as a crown and make you into a king. Be something and someone that you would never have been without facing attack after attack.

When feeling faint know that God will help

What tremendous inspiration this brought to a young heart. When David went into action, and was feeling quite faint, wondering if God would help him this time, he had to go past the armour. This would give him great encouragement, because that victory of the enemy of Israel was encased in the steel of the armour. It would not trip him up, it would spur him in as entered remembered. The miracles of Jesus Christ are there to inspire us to believe that they can happen in our living.

The first act in any conquest was to take the armour from the opposition, force him to render up his sword and javelin. We must take weapons from the assailant and use them for the glory of God. Steel defenses must be taken up and used to help in future days. Let days of sorrow and night, fear and trembling become days of victory and assurance, as the finished work of Christ enters into the human spirit.

Every word The Lord Jesus Christ uttered after the resurrection is a piece of armour. Lo, I am with you always.'[11] 'All power is given unto Me in heaven and on earth.'[12] 'I send the promise of the Father upon you.'[13] Go ye into all the world and preach the gospel.'[14] These words are as good as any armour. They grant hope and comfort; they give to you a steely will to serve Him to your utmost. If you had to remove all the words of Jesus from the Bible there would be an empty crater from an extinct volcano.

This son of Israel put the 'armour' in his tent. That which is as prepared as any vessel was deposited in the tabernacle of David. This armour became the emblem of his household. Four things were used to evoke the fond memories, the stone, the sling, the sword and the steel. Two remained with the child-warrior, the sword and the armour, the sword, to attack, the iron for defence.

Let your failures be written in the sand

Saul lost his armour, while David victorious took his from the battle. He would never take that which had been stained by another man, he had to take and use what was personal to him. Our failures should be written in the sand and in the wind, while our victories should be in steel plating to remind us of the triumph of light against darkness, good over evil.

In the New Testament, John 1:14, the word 'dwelt' meaning 'tabernacled' is used of the human body. The apostle Paul, who was a tentmaker in his writings, also uses the word 'tent,' 2 Corinthians 5:1,4. He speaks of our earthly 'house' being dissolved. Peter says he must soon put off this 'tabernacle', meaning 'tent,' 2 Peter 1:13,14. The 'tent' is the place where we live. As that armour went into David's tent, so into our lives, to the very core of our being, we need to let the metal, the hard and substantial things we take from any battle enter into us. The fiery trial may melt many things, but let it turn the resistance of the enemy into metal that can enter the soul and spirit. Let it find a position within the heart. It can be there as a well to draw from when we are needy and thirsty, or as a metal jug filled to the brim with inspiration. There is capacity in your heart for more, as there was room in the dwelling of David for that he had taken in war. Let the Lord enlarge each heart, and let your experiences embrace solid achievements.

Time must not be spent polishing the armour, but using it to the glory of God. If you lack steel qualities in conviction and resolve, then go into the next affront and take what you require. Every Christian soldier must have armour on the outside, and a steely character within. Bronze used by the enemy was taken and used by the servant of Jehovah.

Let it be heart and not head experience

The only real worth or use of this armour is to have it in the heart, in order to stand against all the wiles of the Devil. If it is not used then it might as well stand as a metal post. It has to be worn, not outwardly, but in the heart. In every temptation, every fiery trial, there is metal in it all that has to be extracted as the fires lick around the soul. Many a warrior has gone into battle clad only in the shepherd's dress, but he has returned with the accoutrements of war. We take from the fighting, and not feelings that which will free our souls and bind up the enemy. That which is worth having in the heart is not found in the dead head of a giant. It is not found in the sand of the desert or even in the songs of the women, but in the heart. This is not 'steel will', where nothing touches you. It is being strong against the enemy, but gentle towards friends and your Master. Be as a brick wall and a steel door to the opposition, but as soft as a feather or a child's hand when helping others. Be resolute when standing for what you believe, but in compassion be ready to run as a tear on the face of the grieving. It is having added to your life that which will make you strong enough to be brave. You cannot have steel within, speaking of your character, until you enter battle, but once in the 'firing line' take some of the fire into your own spirit.

The best defenses are in the heart

Armour tells the history of a battle won or lost. What is in your heart tells its own story. There are so many bits and pieces there as fragmented memories that need uniting in order to mean anything. When God brings everything together it stays together as wrought armour. It became panoply for the heart. You can either be as that which is worth having, or be rejected as something cast away. Keep from every experience the things that are worth keeping.

There are precious moments belonging to you, that act as steel bars and fences for the soul. The first soul you witnessed to, telling them publicly of the Saviour. The first prayer you offered. The first time you were asked to speak. On all those occasions you drew metal from your reserves. You were as England, dealing in sterling. Retain only the important things in your memory. Memories of victory, not defeat, memories of good not bad. These memories can be nails in a sure place. Long after the wood of human thinking and endeavour has rotted, these victories can remain as nails in a sure place. Don't hold on to your precious moments of overcoming, let them hold on to you as they are placed in your tent, let them become part of your steely testimony to the work of grace in your heart. Have in your heart, those things that have been added to you as you have resisted evil.

Fulfil the proverb 'as iron sharpens iron, so a man sharpens the face of a friend,' Proverbs 27:17. Iron has to be in you, even as there has to be a reaction when friends meet. One inspires the other, and when the friend has become blunt and dull, he is sharpened again.

'He put his armour in his tent' gives the suggestion that we need armour in our hearts not simply on the floor of a tent or in the pew of a church. The best songs are in your heart. Victories run up and down your spirit, as musical scales. The best testimony is yours. The greatest miracle you will ever witness is you. What the Lord begins, you continue on into eternity. The nearest thing to the king's heart was his tent. That is where the metal taken in battle was displayed as an iron gate to keep in and to keep out. Let what was accomplished on the cross sink deep into your spirit. Let that which has happened to you, that good part, become part of your life, as this armour went into the tent. In some homes there are metal cups placed strategically for all to see of races won, achievements in sport. The son of Jesse had his achievements in metal, not in the shape of the latest sport's car, limousine, but in his heart. If you want to see the real metal in his life, study the way he lived.

Notes: -

1. Psalm 105:18 'He was laid in iron.' The margin says 'Iron came into his soul.'
2. Luke 1:1.
3. Acts 4:13.
4. 1 Corinthians 13:1.
5. An old proverb that means we talk about things we have never experienced.
6. 1 Samuel 17:4-7, the New International Version of the Bible.
7. Ephesians 6:11,13.
8. Luke 2:19.
9. Romans 12:20.
10. Matthew 5:44.
11. Matthew 28:20.
12. Matthew 28:18.
13. Luke 24:49.
14. Mark 16:15.

Chapter

21

The Distinguished Warrior

If King David had remained with the sheep on the Bethlehem hillside, he might have continued to be an excellent shepherd or even a great harp player. His shepherd's pipes, made of reeds from along the river-bank, which produced the best music, would have sold plentifully. Men would have sung his praises for raising sheep, and composing songs. Hardly anything is known about the brother of David Livingstone, the world famous missionary who went into the heart of Africa to preach Jesus Christ. His parents felt the same way as the parents of Florence Nightingale, the 'Lady with the Lamp' did when they said, 'We are two ducks, and we had a swan.'

True greatness that will distinguish our ability and personality stops where we stop. Each step forward is into new territory. It is not new ideas we require, but people who will challenge the accepted 'norm'. Those being called to God's side who will challenge the conditions, not only in the valley, but also throughout the world. David was where he could hear the Eternal speak into his soul. He went into the valley as an echo of the Voice he had heard.

God grooms the ordinary person

Even when we stop to take a breath God can work something more into our lives, if that time is given to him. He does not work by a twenty-four hour clock He does things independent of others. While we are waiting and watching, He is working. When we are thinking, He is doing. It has been completed even before we contemplate doing it.

The place of attack and the ensuing battle that would make the son of Israel famous was not conjured up in his mind. Eternity for him, and for you, had been using the years as tools. The man was in the making, and the years added new things until he was ready for service of the highest order, 'My utmost for His highest.' He knew how to add strings to his harp, to put new holes into a reed pipe, so that the music would be even more enthralling. Just as the stable in Bethlehem was prepared for the birth of Jesus, David's life was prepared for the birth of new things. Even as a youth, many years were spent preparing him for the few moments of sheer delight in routing a giant.

Long before David strolled onto the battlefield and challenged the giant, there was being worked out that in his life that which would mark him out as distinctive. This lad who seemed so ordinary was being groomed for his eternal destiny, and part of it was in the slaying of a Philistine. We only read the story after the event, yet God had written the story before David as a baby, had drawn his first breath, or sent out his first cry from quivering lips.

The valley of Elah was the mould for the man. It did not make David what he was, but provided a platform to display what God had already accomplished in him. Your battles are not your strengths; your maturity is in what has happened before you meet with the giant. What had taken place over the youthful years was poured out there for all to witness the spectacle. The shepherd entered, but the soldier emerged as one under authority, using that authority to authenticate every action. The youth, known only to his friends and family went into the fight, but a man who knew God and who could use that knowledge for exploits came from it. He was carrying with him more than bows and arrows when he came from defeating a giant. A life of achievement must commence with one victory.

The possibilities in any life are achieved through difficulty

The possibilities in any life are not limited by grace; they are advanced through every difficulty. The help of God, the 'God of Jacob' in time of trouble takes the shape of stone and sling, and sometimes a ladder of escape, not to run away from the trial, but to advance towards it knowing he was going to win. God put the tape at the finishing line in his heart long before he commenced. These probabilities become possibilities and then realities, as we trust. Trusting keeps from rusting. Testing leads to resting.

Make gentleness your goal, and you can know and write as David did 'Your gentleness has made me great,' 2 Samuel 22:36. The word 'great' is a paradox, for it means to be 'humble'. If you are going to eat 'humble pie', then there will be a giant inside it! In another tense, the word 'great' is translated 'gentleness', 2 Samuel 22:36. David is saying, 'Your gentle dealings with me have made me gentle.' Not weak or soft. We are only limited in our attitudes to what the Lord requires from us. The true gentleness of the Lord makes gentlemen. 'Lady' is feminine of the word 'lord'. This greatness is found in people who have all power, but use that power in a gentle way, as yielding as sunlight and working as the touch of a sunbeam. The root Hebrew word that 'gentleness' comes from is a word that means 'to increase'.

David bent down low to pick up a stone before he rose higher than a giant. Deutcronomy 30:6 it is translated 'multiply' and in Genesis 21:20 the Hebrew word for 'greatness' and 'gentleness' is translated 'to grow up'. Ezekiel 19:3 is given as 'bring up'. This is what *Dwarfing Giants* is trying to convey. This is the whole truth, and nothing but the truth with the help of God.

The man after God's own heart must find that heart

If he was going to be a giant-slayer, greater than a shepherd or songster, then he needed to obey the call of God, to go into battle and win. The youth would never have become the 'man after God's own heart'[1] if he had simply flicked small pieces of rock into the passing stream. He had to find God's heart before he could follow it and copy it, then be as that heart in the nation. There was no merit gained by throwing broken twigs into the stream, watching them idly glide by as they moved on into oblivion. Soldiers are not trained in idleness, men of distinction are not found in shallow waters, but in deep seas as explorers, and the challengers of a challenge.

A mountaineer explorer was asked why he wanted to climb Mount Everest, and he replied, 'Because it is there!' When you come to any difficulty, throw yourself and all you have into it, and you will emerge from it as something more than ordinary. What was in the young man was set free in a battle. He was not made for the shadows but for the full radiance of light. Everything fought for and taken should be an adventure. The life of David is an adventure story.

Prove the Almighty in extremes

Prove the Almighty in extremes, you will find Him just as faithful as in the normal. When you do exploits for the Lord, go deep and high, but don't have any rope tied to your waist in case anything goes wrong.

Once David entered into the valley to face the giant, the only refuge he had was the Lord God Almighty. There was no turning back, only a going forward. No one had been into this valley before to leave foot-prints as an example for him to follow. He had to go beyond where others had gone so that he might receive distinction.

He didn't go into the battle to be there, he went to win. The youth never looked over his shoulder, because there was no help there. Let all the failings of 'yester-years' remain there. Take a fresh breath of air, and in that freshness move forward. The zealot never went back because all that awaited him was failure and laughter. He did not even look forward, because there was the huge form of the challenger. He looked up to his Lord and Creator. In doing so, he looked beyond the problem, not at it. This is what makes him so different to others. While Saul was counting the number of soldiers, David was gazing at the greatness of the Lord of hosts. It is always good to look forward. If you look forward to the victory, you will trample underfoot failure as you march forward.

When King Arthur's Knights of the Round Table returned from battle the first question they were asked was 'where are your scars!' If they didn't have any, they were sent back a second time into the battle. Go into that which is 'difficult', but don't make a 'cult' of it. Learn to leave the shell behind after you have taken the pearl. Go into the battle as if you cannot win, and come out as if you could not lose. David would have treated triumph or defeat with the same smile on his face.

The pain suffered can be a remedy

Bleeding and scarring, hurt, deeply wounded in spirit and in heart does something to us. Those very wounds can be bandages for others. In every pain, there is extra grace, enough for you and for another. Jesus said to Peter when he had caught the fish, 'Give it to them for Me and for you.' [2] 'In My Father's house there is bread enough and to spare.'[3] The giant-slayer is saying, 'You who are scared and feeling low, come and hide under my sword!' Sacred trust remains sacred in triumph and defeat.

David didn't wait for some special anointing or feeling, he had to go and do what a man has to do. The man of Israel went forward, and found that wherever he went the Almighty was there. Go into that which is so difficult and hurtful, and discover grace right there. Fear will never birth faith, but faith will destroy fear. David reveals what the F.B.I. in America really means, not simply the Federal Bureau of Investigation, but Fidelity, Bravery and Integrity.

The man with a large heart needs great challengers. There is no development in joining a church, singing a few ditties; these will never help us to become distinguished. Promises quoted do no good if they are not believed; it is the promises of God believed that turns them into bread, wine, seed and ready cash.

In the story of David of Bethlehem and Goliath of Gath those promises were turned into armour and a sword. The man of Israel did not face Goliath of Gath in order to receive plaudits; he faced the foe as a servant of God doing his duty. He took the motto of the Prince of Wales, 'I serve,' and caused it to mean something. That service was like the taste of new wine. The God who neither slumbers nor sleeps is never off duty, and the same applies to His servants.

Duty and the will of the Eternal are to do the next thing, as if it was the only thing to be done. Beatrix Potter, the English writer who wrote 'Peter Rabbit', also wrote a book called 'The Fairy Caravan', and in that story there is a dog called 'Metal'. This illustrates the attitude of the young man who killed a giant.

Don't become static like a statue

It was only by moving from one realm into another that David became known as a *distinguished warrior*. You must not stay where you are, because activity will become inactivity, and the breeding ground of inertia. Life facing a giant will be forever at rest, unable to move you, and you will become as static as a statue. Stationary targets are easy to hit. You can remain forever as you are, comfortable, easy, at peace with your surroundings, and that will be the end of your spirituality or you can break out of the cotton wool syndrome, reach upward and outward to be what the Lord wants you to be.

You can be a distinguished person, even as Rumpelstilzchen who used to spin gold out of straw.[4] Being a *distinguished warrior* is having the ability to take hold of straws blowing in the wind, and see them converted into substantial testimonies of the grace of the Lord. When you touch that happening to you it can appear as mere straw but remember there is gold in every piece of flimsy straw! All you have to do is to work at that seeming to be ordinary, and as you take hold of it, what was light and flimsy blowing in the wind will turn into gold. In each straw or flimsy experience there is gold of Ophir quality. The word 'chrysalis' that we associate with a form of new life as seen in the butterfly, comes from a word meaning 'gold'. It is taking the adverse, and making it work together for your good. Take the adverse and make it work to better you as a person. Let every discordant sound be tuned into the instrument as David often tuned his harp.

The future leader didn't wait for opportunity to come to him; he went to the opportunity and took it by the horns. Coming through a trial is taking the bad and the ugly, witnessing the 'Ugly Ducking' emerge as a beautiful swan. Merit marks only come through merits. 'Merit' means to be a merchant, to trade with what you have until you prosper. We must not be slothful in business, but serve the Lord with all our might. When you have done your best-let God do the rest. Be as the farmer who sows the seed, let nature activate it. David was given just a sling and a stone, yet look at the distinctive thing he did with those small toys. The soldier distinguishes himself on the battlefield long before he is mentioned in dispatches or receives medals as recognition for bravery. Being distinguished from the rest is using fully whatever talents you have.[5] For the shepherd boy, life became like the 'Inch of the candle' that was used at auction sales. Only while it burns can activity take place. Once the candle has burned beyond the inch, the final bidder takes the article. However long or short life is then live in that light, and do your greatest work within the 'inch of the candle'. Live in light while the light is with you, the 'night comes when no man can work.' That which was taking place in the life of Jesse's son might never happen again. Some Christians put more into a day than other people put into a lifetime! If you see a bird flying fast and often in the evening, it is because it knows that the light is fading, and it must accomplish before the darkness falls.

Do not mistake the armchair for the throne

The lazy people who sit and watch a perishing world go by can easily mistake the armchair for the throne. These lines taken from the 'Ancient Mariner' should shake us into action. 'As idle as a painted ship on a painted sea.' It never goes anywhere and it never arrives at its destination. It meets with no waves and enters no storms. David had truth, trust and vision, and they needed to be used. He needed the giant more than the giant needed him. Opposition is required to reveal your qualities and not your quirks. You can be a rose, but it will have to be among the thorns that prick and hurt. The very hillsides that Bethlehem's son wandered on as a boy must become part of his nature if he is going to serve the Almighty in a greater way. There was iron and brass in those hills and they needed to enter into the pliable youth.

The person who is happy with a few sheep will never tame wild horses. Some spend time flicking gnats from their skin but they never find enough commitment to face and defeat giants. If the stream that runs by your feet is your contentment, you will never go into great waters to see the wonders of your God and King. King David was willing to exchange the bleating of the sheep for the shouting of the giant. It was not enough for him to continue to beat off the attacks on the sheep, or to make melody with his harp to the surroundings.

David had to be the echo of his calling from God. There was another dimension that he entered into as he went into battle. There was more of God in the valley. Every metre he moved added a mile to his stature. He went one step forward, ten steps into his destiny. In the swirling of the sling, the roundness of his character was being produced. The motto of the Isle of Man is: 'Whichever way it is thrown, it will stand.' speaking of the figure with three legs. To be *distinguished* you will stand whichever way life knocks or throws you.

It was a lonely walk. The space between David and the giant seemed so small but he used it to call upon the Name of the Lord. Was a more desperate prayer offered as David quoted what God was going to do to the giant? The Lord you know will be presented to others. Although quite young, there was nothing childish about his theology of God.

There are many things that David became *distinguished* in through this one act of slaying Goliath of Gath. There were many facets; meaning 'faces' to his faith. There was the face of the fearless and the face of full commitment. What was in him shone through the clouds that had gathered in the soldiers. When you look at the youth, you see a pioneer of new things. The best way to get anything started is to start. He was the first of many who would follow his example, who would be strong enough to carry out God's will. He pioneered how to use the sling and the stone in order to overcome. In a living illustration, the 'upstart' showed how to cut off the head of a giant. He fully displayed the use of armour, and how to handle the sword. He proved the Lincolnshire proverb 'Can he carry corn?' David did not only carry corn, he reaped a harvest in the form of a giant.

All these things came out of the battle, and they made him distinctive. He became what he did. David did not have to wait for medals and ribbons to be placed upon his chest; they entered into his heart as he overcame. If you are going to enter into your finest hour, use the minutes and go forward into the valley, let the Lord God do what He has to do. Be sunshine and not shadow in every second. A small girl, three years of age, said to her daddy, 'Oh, daddy, I am boring!' There was nothing boring about the young shepherd lad. This was the most interesting and exciting battle every fought on the hills of Israel. It was far better than pantomime because it was real.

Be made a person of distinction

There was something quite magnanimous about the future leader of his nation. It was a fight against a giant that revealed his true qualities of character. That became a charter for all who would slay giants and overcome temptation. As he advanced, the grain in the wood was made bare. What drew him on to serve in such a way? There is a sign on the side of the road in Athol, Scotland that says, 'If you are hungry, I can help.' It was hunger for the glory of God that took him into battle. It brought him through and it took him into victory. That deep desire for holiness would only be met in the slaying of the tempter.

There was distinction through difference, the difference between believing the Lord and just accepting what was happening. Doing what you believe in will result in victory. You may never build great castles, you may never be totally assured of what you believe, but giants can be toppled. If you have the conviction, crushing temptation will become your calling. This was no slide on the ice for the young prince. He became distinguished on the battlefield, and he carried that demeanour with him.

In Liverpool, England, there is a plaque erected to the memory of those who fought in the 'Battle of the Atlantic', during the Second World War. On it are written these words 'They held to their course.' In spite of the odds they did not waver as the ridges in a ploughed field. Something happened to Bethlehem's son in that valley that granted him the same distinction as Joseph with his coat of many colours.[6] It takes a storm for all the real hues of the rainbow to appear. It took Goliath of Gath to bring the best out of the young shepherd. It takes difficulties to bring out what is sometimes so deep and latent.

David was crowned in his soul long before the crown of gold went onto his head. Our distinctions are not in our prayers or even our tears, we become marked out as we battle through to win the day. It is useless crying about what we should be doing. A crisis will bring to your tongue the words you should have uttered in easier times. That which is in your heart will echo in the valley. What we forget is that each word spoken against the giant was a stone. The words spoken by David were missionaries before the real thing arrived. The motto of British Airways is 'We serve, we fly.' David was not only the best; he did his best in the only way he knew which was trusting the Almighty. Trust Him with the pebbles and he will trust you with the pearls.

There were many seeds sown that day in the dust of the valley, but the one that took root and grew was the seed of greatness that was planted within the spirit of a youth. Each step, thought, moment of trust brought sunshine and soft showers to that which had been sown. What we enter distinguishes our ability, and it comes through our achievements. David, as a youth was marked out as being above the ordinary. He was not 'first among equals'; there were no equals, because no one would accept the challenge. It took more to develop the youth than being changed in a moment, in the twinkling of an eye. There were a lot of 'plod' and 'plough' involved. It is when you attempt the extra-ordinary that you leave the flock of sheep which looks so mediocre.

The Elah valley must be left before he came to Mount Zion. Boyhood became manhood, the youth became 'yesteryear', the shepherd, the sage expressed in songs. Tomorrow can become today. Monday's child becomes Tuesday's teenager; Wednesday's warrior will soon appear. Thursday's thirst will soon develop, to be followed by Friday's fulcrum. Move through the week until you come to Saturday as a sage.

You can get lost in your surroundings until nothing marks you out as being a prime mover or example. The true meaning of 'Bishop' is 'servant'. He was described by others as being 'worth ten thousand of us,'

2 Samuel 18:3. That is more worth than can be counted, measured or weighed. David was uniquely the Lord's, and this made him different. He was not chalk or cheese he was solid rock. The man of Israel was not one in a crowd, but the crowd in him was revealed as all his desires for the Almighty came forward in battle. The man of God did not turn his head to look; his was the head that they turned to see. If only we could be baptised in the spirit of David! If only for our daily walk we could take his shoes! Wear what he had in his heart as a garment, and you will be filled with the zeal of the turning wheel without a brake.

You might not be able to walk and stand where he was, but you can walk and talk with his God. Let your 'daily reading' be the reading of the heart of God. Here was a pattern than could be followed. If you follow it you will be guaranteed success in the battles of life. Every other ark built after Noah was a copy of what he had made. The British Navy has a training ship the 'Sir Winston Churchill'. Its name reminds every recruit what England expects from them.

God makes a loser into a winner

When the Israeli became distinguished, it means that he was made different in the battle with the giant. The word 'distinguished' means to be 'marked or fenced off', to draw a ring, and stand in it, making a statement as to where you will stand. There was something splendid and unique about this growing young man. The victory marked him out as a winner. The winner's enclosure was in his heart. He had to get beyond the finishing line, and that was as he drew the giant's sword from its sheath.

The Eternal does not choose a winner, if He did there would be no glory of the Lord in that winner. He takes a loser and makes that one into a winner. He who sought no plaudits or admiration became the winner. The emblem of Kent, England is the white hare. Underneath it in Latin, are the words 'We are victorious'. That is before the hounds have chased the hare! They are suggesting that they are always ahead of the field. 'You can chase us but you will not catch us!'

The word 'distinguished' suggests to be 'pricked', as cloth is marked for sewing, held together by pins. We obtain the word 'sting' from the same word. Battling puts sting into our sayings and doings. There is a cutting edge added to our lives that was not there before we were embattled.

Embattled that we might not be embalmed! David was the first among un-equals. There might never have been another time. The sea might dry up before the tide came in again and, like ships of old, they had to go while the tide was in, or they would miss their destiny. It is now or never, yesterday will not do for tomorrow, and today is only partially left with us. He must use the day before the curtains of night are drawn across it. He had to 'seize the day!'

The negative side of being distinguished is to be marked as a slave. Slaves were branded, declaring to whom they belong. Within the slavery of sonship there is glory, the freedom to go and to achieve. At the bottom of every hill and mountain is a sign that says 'Achievers, this way!' When you see a child take its first step, you see the potential of climbing mountains. The first step on a ladder means there is the beginning of greater heights. To be marked meant to be branded a felon. What is bad can become good. The positive side is that we can be marked out by holiness.

The apostle Paul bore in his body the marks of Jesus Christ.[7] He was a 'love slave' of Jesus Christ, and this marked him out among men. Those same marks of our making, our authentication can be in our spirits. What entered into David were the essential attributes of God, making him a person after God's own heart. In adversity he acted like Adonai. The giant became a giant opportunity for the miracle power of God to be revealed. He became the platform for the glory of God that settled on the tabernacle in the wilderness.[8]

The Lord never leaves broken strands of silk

The youth first became distinguished as a warrior, then in weaponry, music, relationship, in his ability to write psalms, and on to ruling as a king. All that came later, at this moment he was a man in the mould. God does not leave broken strands of silk and work unfinished. The Lord does not tie knots He blends every broken strand until it becomes the whole pattern. 'He will not rest until He has finished the thing this day', Ruth 3:18.

The Lord God Almighty is fashioning lives, and there are no 'half measures' or 'half pints' when He is in action, He is complete in Himself, and all He does is brought to completion. He was distinguished rather than extinguished. His breeding ground, the breeding ground of true nobility was in the valley facing a giant. To the discerning eye all the weapons of the Lord were on display in David. He found greatness in the dust of the floor, in that dust was pure gold.

Every thing that happened to him was like entering into the darkness of a mineshaft and finding gold instead of coal! Get from your trial what you go into it for. Do not obtain just a handful of air or a rope of sand when you face any contest. You can take from one battle at a time as you move from victory to victory. While in the forest of Hareth, the son of Jesse didn't come out clutching bluebells, daisies or buttercups, 1 Samuel 22:5. The man who lives among trees learns to climb! Where there was no place, he made a place for himself.

What the enterprising son of Israel accomplished was a 'feather in his cap'. When the American Indians killed a warrior, such as David had done, then they appeared with another feather in their headdress. Feathers later adorned caps in order to distinguish the person who had won. If the prize was a wild fowl or a hen, then a feather was taken from the bird and put in the hat of the winner. Do not put a feather in the cap, put the Dove of God a type of the Holy Spirit into the heart.[9] The fan from His wings, will keep us cool when everyone else is hot and angry. This feather was not in David's garments worn outwardly, it was in his heart, and would distinguish him from others. God's badges are not worn on lapels; they are witnessed in love and a life being fully lived. Worcester, England is known as the 'Faithful City', because of its historical allegiance to the King of England. You can be known as the 'Faithful Person' as you are you will be a person of distinction.

Only Goliath or David could ever leave the valley

To overcome an enemy which would destroy means that you become distinguished. Always remember, only one could return from the valley. David stepped from the shadow of Goliath never to be tormented or challenged by him again. Do not die in the wrestling of life. Do not be a silly Saul, who died on his own sword, his own self-will. Do not commit spiritual suicide. While contending for truth, use that truth to sustain you. The keeper of cows, the farmer is sustained by the milk and cheese the cows produce. You are sustained by His love, and your life of faith. Being marked out for greatness, and accepting that greatness are two different things. During the battle David grew by the size of a giant. That battle became the measure used to measure all others. Each child and man would walk in the footsteps of David, as we are called to walk in the footsteps of Jesus Christ.[10] When the Greek child was tutored, he was given an example of writing in clay, and in copying it learned to write. David became that ensample and example for all who would overcome giants, and rid the nation of a tyrant. Each morning put his sandals and outfit on. Be dressed in what he did. Let his accomplishments be as water to the fainting heart. In the Jewish ceremony of the 'Feast of the Tabernacles', the candle that lights all the others is called the 'servant'. You can light your candle from the life of David. A holy glow can enter into your darkness, so that you do not stumble around but know where you are going, and Who you are following.

Resisting births new things in your spirit

Many of the children born to the King were given names that would remind him of the battles he had gone through. This fight with Goliath birthed new things into his soul. From each experience he wanted a living epitaph in a child, that is why he named his children with such care. His experience lived on n his children. He named one Beeliada, 1 Chronicles 14:7 meaning 'the Lord knows'. 'The Lord has known, does know and will know', is the Hebrew tense. There was Elishama meaning 'God has heard, God does hear and will hear', 2 Samuel 5: 16. Elishua 'God is rich', God has been rich, and will be rich', 2 Samuel 5:15. Eliphelet 'God is escape', 1 Chronicles 3:6. He had found a way of escape, not by running away, but by going through. The ship that Scot of the Antarctic abandoned was called 'Endurance'. God arranges for your escape through grace. Eliada means 'God has known, He does know and He will know', 1 Chronicles 3:8. David wanted to put his experiences into the children who were born to him. These experiences were born out of his relationship with Jehovah. He would allow them to be erased from his memory or his sight, so he called his children by his deliverances through God. The Puritans of England also did this. Whatever their experience was, as a child was conceived, they called the baby by that name. In each name there is the fact suggested, not only of what God has done, but what He is doing, and what he is going to do. The son of Bethlehem had an ongoing revelation of the Lord.

Restriction can make us resolute

David was distinguished in his writings, in what he had to say about the Lord. There are depths deeper than any well, higher than any mountain in what he wrote. In times of trouble and deep grief, we turn to the Psalms, and they become palms to us. We read our destiny in them. It is just like the finest theology written by Paul in the New Testament while he was engaged in a struggle, and put into prison. After his affront with the giant, David not only had something to say and write, he said something worth listening to. Before the battle, people only listened to what he said. After the battle they stood to attention when he spoke. The music from his harp seemed so mellow after his encounter. In Psalm 22:20; 35:17 he uses the word 'darling' to describe God. It means 'my only'. It is the word that was used for Abraham's 'only ' son, Genesis 22:2. In Psalm 22:20, it is a poetic statement meaning 'my soul' 'my life'. There is such depth in these words revealing how distinctive this man of God was. The Hebrew Lexicon translates the phrase 'darling', 'the unique and priceless possession that can never be replaced.'

Battling with every day giants will turn gnats and grasshoppers that we seem to be into giants. It is this sheer devotion that will help you to overcome anything that rises up against you. As you love the Lord with all your heart, soul and strength, then you too will be found actively *Dwarfing Giants*. That which is dwarfing you will be dwarfed, and the abdicated king within you will rise up and claim your kingdom, power, glory, majesty and dominion, until you have within you a kingdom that has no end. Your world will be without end. The rule of God will be brought into lives. It is a kingdom that has many dawns, some of them false, but the real dawn will turn into a day of light after the darkness has cleared.

When the new dawn appears, the Sons of the Morning will sing over your life. The angels will rejoice when the Prodigal returns to his father's house. All will be well when *Giants* are *Dwarfed*, not only in Elah, but also in lives. History and spirituality salute the shepherd boy who became a king. Men from each generation have risen up and called him blessed, because he set the example for others to follow. He fulfiled the Welsh proverb, 'He who would be a leader must be a bridge.' He went where others had never been, did what no others had ever done. We never need fear for the glory of God while each succeeding generation produces men and women like David, the defeater of giants and the King of Israel. When Royalty dies in England, the route taken by the cortege goes by all the royal palaces in London, reminding us of their lives, splendour and achievements. Bethlehem's son is so distinguished, that when God wanted to send His Son into the world, He chose that human side of David to provide that Son.[11] It is well worth *Dwarfing Giants* to reveal to a valley filled with soldiers resting on their weapons that there is a God in Heaven Who is actively engaged on earth. The Holy Spirit helping as a Comforter-one who makes strong and brave. The Australian Aborigines have a word they use which is 'kipper', meaning the 'boy has become a man'. This fully completes the story of David the young man who grew by the size of a giant as he battled in life to bring glory to God. The youth who *Dwarfed Giants*, that giants might not dwarf him.

Notes: -

1. Acts 13:22.
2. Matthew 17:27.
3. Luke 15:17.
4. Taken from the German story.
5. See author's book *Buried Talents*.
6. Genesis 37:3.
7. Galatians 6:17. *'Marks' is 'stigma'.*
8. Exodus 16:10; 40:34.
9. Matthew 3:16.
10. 1 Peter 2:21.
11. Matthew 1:6. Acts 2:25,29, 34. Romans 1:3.

Other books by the same author:-

Paths of Righteousness in Psalm 23
In Sickness and in Health
The Growing Pains of Peter
Dying is Living
Buried Talents
More Than Conquerors

All obtainable from the publishers at:-

New Living Publishers
164, Radcliffe New Road
Whitefield, Manchester
M45 7TU.

Website:-www.newlivingpublishers.co.uk
E-mail:-theway@newlivingpublishers.co.uk